DATE DUE

GAYLORD #3522PI Printed in USA

JOE MEEK

The Merry Mountain Man

A BIOGRAPHY

BY

STANLEY VESTAL

UNIVERSITY OF NEBRASKA PRESS · LINCOLN

Copyright © 1952 by the Caxton Printers, Ltd.
Library of Congress catalog card number: 52-5211
International Standard Book Number: 8-8032-5206-4
Manufactured in the United States of America

First Bison Book printing March, 1963
Most recent printing shown by first digit below:

4   5   6   7   8   9   10

Bison Book edition reprinted by arrangement with the Caxton Printers, Ltd.

To
ELINORE ZARUBA
BECAUSE
SHE FIRST SUGGESTED
THAT I WRITE THIS
BOOK.

Acknowledgments

EVERYONE who writes of Joseph L. Meek must first of all gratefully acknowledge his debt to Mrs. Frances Fuller Victor and her book *The River of the West* in which she imbedded his racy memoirs. Since her day, however, much fresh and vital information has been unearthed and published. In particular I am indebted to the research of Mr. H. E. Tobie and his series of articles in the *Oregon Historical Quarterly*, Vols. XXXIX and XL, entitled "Joe Meek, A Conspicuous Personality." Other principal sources will be found in the bibliography of this book.

In addition I gladly acknowledge use of the collections of the historical societies of Oregon, Washington, California, Wyoming, and the Northwestern Canadian provinces.

I wish also to express my hearty thanks to the following individuals: Commissioner of Indian Affairs, Department of the Interior; Superintendent, Crow Agency, Montana; Mr. Carl W. Beck, Superintendent, Fort Hall Agency, Fort Hall, Idaho; Mr. J. M. Cooper, Superintendent, Wind River Agency, Fort Washakie, Wyoming; Mr. Archie Phinney, Superintendent, Northern Idaho Agency, Lapwai, Idaho; Mr. Henry Roe Cloud, Superintendent, Umatilla Indian Agency, Pendleton, Oregon;

Mr. Frank H. H. Roberts, Jr., Acting Chief, Bureau of American Ethnology, Smithsonian Institution; Dr. John P. Harrington, linguist on the staff of the Bureau of American Ethnology, Smithsonian Institution; Miss Elizabeth B. Drewry, War Records Office, National Archives; Dr. Clark Wissler, American Museum of Natural History; Mr. M. W. Stirling, Chief, Bureau of American Ethnology, Smithsonian Institution; Miss Alice Lee Parker, Acting Chief, Prints & Photographs Division, Library of Congress; Mr. James C. Olson, Superintendent, Nebraska State Historical Society; Mr. Vernon Kinietz; Mr. Fred Woodard; Mr. Merrill J. Mattes; Mrs. Alice S. Acheson; Mr. George F. Brimlow; Mrs. Frances Franks; Mrs. Elinore Zaruba; Mr. Lancaster Pollard, Superintendent, Oregon Historical Society; Mr. Howard M. Corning, Reference Librarian, Oregon Historical Society; Mr. John Mackenzie Cory, Associate Librarian, University of California, Berkeley, California; Mr. J. L. Rader, Librarian, University of Oklahoma, Norman, Oklahoma; and Mrs. Margaret Roberts, my secretary.

I am also happy to express my gratitude to the publishers listed below for their kind permission to reprint passages from their books as follows: Syms-York Company, Inc., Boise, Idaho for passages quoted from *Journal of a Trapper; or, Nine Years in the Rocky Mountains, 1834-1843* by Osborne Russell; to the Houghton Mifflin Company for quotations from my *Mountain Men, Kit Carson,* and *Fandango.*

Contents

PART I

GREENHORN

PART II

TRAPPER

PART III

PATRIOT

PART I
GREENHORN

The Mountain Men

JOE MEEK was a mountain man—and proud of it. No wonder. For the mountain men were no ordinary frontiersmen, but picked adventurers who challenged the wilderness and mastered it. Those were the boys who trapped the beaver, lived on bear and buffalo, fought Indians, and caroused away their hard-earned wages. Later, when, a hundred years ago, our American frontier swept swiftly westward from the Mississippi to the Pacific, the mountain men still led the van, serving as guides, scouts, soldiers, peace officers, and statesmen. They were the commandos of our Westward Movement.

In North America the fur trade has always been Big Business. Until the silk hat became the fashion, all the finest hats were made of the fur of beaver, and the pelts of these animals were always in demand abroad. In Canada the Hudson's Bay Company and the other firms which it absorbed pushed westward, established permanent forts and factories all the way to the Pacific. They bartered with the Indians for their peltry.

Such an organization required for its success a monopoly of the business, governmental powers over the Indians and *engagés,* large capital, a network of expensive establishments, and costly staffs of traders, clerks, hunters, mechanics, and *voyageurs.* In order to maintain these, the British had to conserve the fur-bearing animals and this—though profitable in the long run—naturally reduced the yearly dividends. The Hudson's Bay Company, therefore, opposed all immigration into their territory and had authority to exclude settlers. Without such authority it must have failed.

Meanwhile, south of the British possessions, the Americans had not been idle. When in 1804, President Jefferson sent Captain Meriwether Lewis and Lieutenant William Clark up the Missouri River and down the Columbia to explore the Louisiana Purchase and the debatable land of Oregon, traders were already in Indian country. And soon after, John Jacob Astor, intent upon monopolizing the American trade, sent his Astorians overland to meet his ship, the ill-fated *Tonquin,* at the mouth of the Columbia. But Astor met strong competition; the Missouri Fur Company, organized by St. Louis merchants and led by that indefatigable Spaniard, Manuel Lisa, sent their expeditions into the mountains and even beyond into Oregon.

The Indians of the Canadian woods had always been trappers and fell readily enough into the British pattern of fur-culture. Fixed prices, British law and order let the Indian know exactly what to expect, and, if not always happy, he was in the main content. If he made trouble, the Hudson's Bay Company knew how to stop it. The Indian was under their control.

On the American side of the line conditions were very different. The Indians of the Great Plains and the Rockies were horsemen and buffalo hunters, and had no heart at all for paddling about in icy beaver streams for the sake of a few skins. On their fleet ponies they could kill enough buffalo in a day to keep them supplied with food and shelter for months on end. Moreover, they were warriors, raiders, and thought war better business than barter, since glory was thrown in. No man who knew them well could expect them to turn trappers just to oblige the whites.

Moreover, monopoly was abhorrent to liberty-loving Americans trained up in the ways of free enterprise and cutthroat competition. Any man with courage and capital might enter the fur trade in the West, as many did. Government regulation of industry and trade was in those days unthinkable in American territory. Even laws regulating trade with Indians (like those forbidding the introduction of liquor into Indian country) could never be enforced.

Thus, prior to the War of 1812 all was confusion and strife in the fur trade. Treacherous Indians boarded Astor's ship, the *Tonquin*, massacred the crew, and Astoria had to be abandoned; the brigades of the Missouri Fur Company were attacked, decimated, and driven from the Indian country. In Canada the Northwesters fought the Hudson's Bay Company, wreaking vengeance on colonists attempting to settle in their preserves. There was heavy loss everywhere. And it was all Manuel Lisa could manage to keep the Indians of the upper Missouri from joining forces with the British in the war.

But these disasters could not discourage men who had viewed that promised land so rich in fur. In 1822 at St. Louis Major Andrew Henry and General William II. Ashley formed a partnership which in time came to be known as the Rocky Mountain Fur Company, and led their first expedition up the Missouri River, establishing a temporary post at the mouth of the Yellowstone. The next summer treacherous Rees delayed their keelboats at the mouth of Grand River and ambushed their men with heavy loss. Colonel Henry Leavenworth's punitive expedition failed miserably to subdue the Rees, who abandoned their palisaded village only to scatter over the Plains and so become more dangerous than ever. These fresh disasters convinced the partners that the British system of fixed trading posts would never pay on our side of the line. They reorganized their brigades on a plan of their own.

They employed no traders, built no permanent forts, hired no Indian trappers. Instead they employed daring young white men who kn · the rifle and the steel trap as well as they knew their own hands, men who could ride and shoot, self-reliant, lusty fellows, who would harvest the fur wherever and whenever it could be found in spite of hell or high water, in spite of rival trappers, hostile Indians, or the Devil himself. Instead of permanent forts, Ashley and Henry held an annual rendezvous or fur fair in some convenient, previously appointed valley in the mountains.

Thus, every summer their trappers brought the furs they had taken, took their year's wages in goods, and obtained a new outfit for the coming year. Their trappers were kept busy catching beaver in fall and spring, spent the winter hunting and trading with the Indians, and passed the summer exploring, looking for new beaver streams to conquer. Supplies were brought to rendezvous by pack trains, which also carried the furs back to market in St. Louis.

Under this system the beaver trappers had no occasion to return to the settlements or sleep under a roof until the beaver trade played out, and few of them believed that possible.

Most of them were men from Virginia, Kentucky, Tennessee, Pennsylvania, New York, and Ohio with a long tradition of Indian fighting and pioneering behind them. But in the Rockies everything—the savages, the animals, the climate, the country itself—was bigger, wilder, and fiercer than anything their fathers had known. The hardships and constant danger faced by American trappers toughened those who survived to a high degree of courage, address, skill, and physical fitness. And the discipline maintained by their employers (both military men) was strict.

Thus overnight Ashley and Henry created a new career, a new way of life—in fact a new breed of men, that hardy race of explorers, daring fighters, skilled hunters and trappers, known then and thereafter, because they lived the year 'round in the Rockies, as the "Mountain Men."

Among these were such paladins as Christopher ("Kit") Carson, Jim ("Old Gabe") Bridger, Tom ("Broken Hand" or "White Head") Fitzpatrick, William ("Cut-face") Sublette and his brother Milton, Jedediah ("Diah") Smith, David ("Davey") Jackson, Moses ("Black") Harris, Jim Beckwourth, the mulatto, Henry ("Old Frapp") Fraeb, Robert ("Doc") Newell, Etienne Provost, and last but by no means least, Joseph L. Meek.

Of all these mountain men, none was more typically American than Joe Meek—and none so completely engaging.

He was the Davy Crockett of our Great Northwest, bold, adventurous, humorous, a first-class trapper, pioneer, peace officer, and frontier politician. More, he was the wittiest, saltiest, most shameless wag and jester that ever wore moccasins in the Rockies—a tall, happy-go-lucky Virginian, lover of practical jokes, tall tales, Jacksonian democracy, and Indian women. And certainly no other mountain man has left us half so rich and full a record of his brave deeds, witty sayings, and winning motives.

Joe ranged the mountains of the Old West until the beaver trade played out, then helped drive the first wagons to Oregon, which he helped to win and to defend. He had no small part in founding and carrying on the Provisional Government in that raw, lawless land, and at the time of the Whitman massacre made an heroic winter march to the national capital, seeking military aid. Returning to Oregon, he finally ended his days in the new Territory, after some lively times as Sheriff, Legislator, and U.S. Marshal.

Yet his character and wild adventures are only half of the man's importance. For, as historians are forever reminding us, it was our frontier which made these states a nation. To understand him is to understand the westward drive and destiny of America, the courage, enterprise, patience, and good humor of the men who made it. And these are virtues that Americans must understand, love, and practice now, if free societies are to survive.

Meek's story is a thrilling one, and the man himself mighty good company.

The Runaway

JOSEPH L. MEEK was born in 1810 among the mountains of the Old Dominion, into the middle of a large family. Folks thought it a wonder that their pappy could keep track of all of them singlehanded. When his fifteen children and their numerous cousins poured out of the house after supper, passing strangers concluded that school surely had kept late that day. If the older boys had not drifted West, one after another, the place would hardly have held them.

But the family lands lay in the far southwest corner of the state, in Washington County, within a few miles of the Cumberland Gap, the gateway to the West. And in those days the Far West was calling all enterprising young men.

Like any other husky man-child, Joe first greeted the world with a squall, but soon changed that for the laugh with which he faced most things during the rest of his life. Good-natured towards little folks, Joe carried a chip on his shoulder and sturdily took his own part against bigger boys. Tall and strong for his years, fun-loving, daring, and apt to show off, Joe managed to hold his own and get along with pretty nigh everybody in Washington County—except the teacher and the preacher.

Some of the boys took out their spite on the teacher

by putting dead varmints in his desk, stealing the clapper
from his bell, or—in cold weather—covering the chimney-
top to smoke him out. What tricks Joe may have been
up to is unknown, but certainly at school his humorous
independence was not appreciated. Having run wild all
his days, he was too big and headstrong to be disciplined.
One day, when the teacher threatened him with the
wooden paddle on which his ABC's were pasted, Joe
grabbed it and cracked the baldhead with his own alpha-
bet. Then Joe skedaddled. That ended his schooling.
When he left, Joe did not know B from bullfoot.

From the start, the Virginia mountaineers had divided
their time, Indian-fashion, between the valley and the
hills, the corn patch and the game trail, the hoe and the
rifle; they aimed to kill wild meat to eat with their corn
pone, salt sowbelly, and long sweetening. This division
of labor required a divided mind.

But Joe's mind was all of a piece. He had no heart at
all for the plow or the smokehouse. To him, the mountains looked a heap bigger than the fields. Anyhow,
Pappy had plenty of land and enough slaves to work it;
why should Joe bother? Far from sharing the labors of
the slaves, Joe often lured the younger Negroes away from
the fields to join him in his manly outdoor sports.

For who could stay indoors or labor when turkeys
called from the hills, and wide-eyed deer came quietly
down to drink? Who could remain at home of an evening
while the dogs were out to tree a coon, or hunters sat
around their cheery fire hearkening to the baying of the
hounds on the trail of a fox? Joe aimed to be the most
shootin'est man in all those mountains. He couldn't see
how book l'arnin' or farming would help him do it. If
ever he picked up a hoe, he found it had somehow turned
into his squirrel rifle. So he went his heedless, happy-go-
lucky way, learning the mountaincraft that was to make
him famous.

Nobody interfered, until Pappy brought home a new wife to care for the family.

Joe couldn't seem to hit it off with his stepmother. She was, he admitted, a good woman—but a leetle too pious, according to his idee. She was forever driving the young-uns up to the church-house, and long sermons made Joe restless. The fellow in the pulpit had no gumption, but kept on talking by the hour. And every Sunday, nearly, Joe had to wait for second table while some traipsin' preacher was saying a long grace and putting away all the white meat from the chickens Pappy's wife served him. Week after week one or another of them showed up, regular as a clock, in his long-tailed coat and high hat, slick as a blacksnake, till the squawking chickens took to the brush at the mere sight of them. They all seemed to be certain there was mighty little chance for Joe in this world, let alone the next. By the time he was sixteen he had acquired a strong distaste for sanctimonious moralists.

Well, shucks, you couldn't kick a preacher in the pants, or sass a woman, no matter how she kept on tonguein'. In those days boys left home early, and Joe felt his time to go was not far off. Summer after summer he had watched covered wagons streaming by, heading for Cumberland Gap, for Kentucky, for Missouri. His elder brothers, Stephen and Hiram, were somewhere West, doing well enough anyhow not to come running home again. Joe was already tall as a man—six feet two, barefoot. He was free, white, and twenty-one—pretty nigh. And he was sick of civilization, preachers, stepmothers.

When, one day, news came that Stephen was enlisting with the fur company at St. Louis, heading for the Rocky Mountains, to pass all his time hunting, riding, fightin' Injuns and shootin' ba'r, Joe's heart thumped with definite purpose.

Out thar amongst the wild varmints, a man would be on his own hook, with nary a preacher to threaten him with hell-fire, nary a house or a fence or a stepmother, nary a thing to pester him but a parcel of screechin' redskins.

Next day Joe learned that a neighbor was driving to Louisville, Kentucky. When the man's wagon passed the Meek place, Joe walked out with his plunder under his arm, climbed in, and was on his way. He reckoned they wouldn't grieve for him at home. If Pappy ever did miss him, the old woman would know well enough how to cheer him up.

The wagon rumbled on, flanked Walker Mountain, cut through Moccasin Gap on the old trail of Dan'l Boone, followed Clinch River through the gorge, passed Stickleyville and Jonesville to the place where Dan'l Boone's eldest son was scalped by Injuns, and so by a narrow valley to Cumberland Gap.

By that time Joe was in strange country. They passed through Kentucky, the Pennyroyal and the Bluegrass, on to Louisville. For a while he must have wandered about, as he himself declares he saw the smoke of Pittsburgh the following winter, but in due time he showed up at brother Hiram's sawmill near Lexington, Missouri. Hiram told him that their brother Stephen had already hired out to William Sublette to hunt for the Rocky Mountain Fur Company. Hunting and trapping looked better to Joe than sawing logs or keeping store for Hiram. In the fall of 1828 he went down the Missouri River to St. Louis.

That old French town had suddenly come to life after Americans began to swarm westward, settling the country, exploring up the Missouri River, the Platte and the Arkansas to the Rocky Mountains, looking for free land or trade with Indians or Mexicans—but most of all for furs. Though a town of hardly more than two thousand permanent residents, built along muddy lanes and facing a muddy river, St. Louis was the western emporium of the fur trade. No emigrant wagons rolled up the Platte to Oregon as yet. Almost the whole trade of that booming town was the fur trade.

The old French quarter, Carondelet, derisively nick-named *Vide Pôche* from its empty pockets, still went its easy-going way. But the Americans in St. Louis were showing their typical energy, enterprise, and willingness to take a chance.

There Joe Meek heard much talk of explorations: of how John Colter had discovered the Teton Mountains, had seen wonderful spouting geysers and big boiling springs—Colter's Hell—had tasted the headwaters of the Columbia, the Missouri, the Colorado, and the Yellowstone: Joe heard tell how Major Stephen H. Long's expedition of 1820 had marched up the Platte, climbed Pike's Peak, and marched back again along the Arkansas and the Canadian. There were stories of a great salt lake Jim Bridger had discovered only four years before and of the mysterious island in it believed to be inhabited by giants; and tales of how Tom Fitzpatrick and Bridger found South Pass—a pass so low and easy a man hardly knew he was crossing the Continental Divide into Oregon. Joe was glad to hear that General Henry Atkinson had gone up the Missouri just three years before, making treaties and smoking the peace pipe with tribes along that stream clear to the mouth of the Yellowstone. Joe hoped those treaties would stick.

But most amazing of all, Bill Sublette's partner, Jedediah S. Smith, had gone all the way across the desert to San Diego only two years before, had spent the winter there, and returned. Now he was gone to California again. Sublette, Joe heard, expected him back for rendezvous next summer. Everybody in St. Louis, it seemed to Joe, faced west.

With glee and gusto early travelers have described St. Louis in the springtime, when pack trains and wagon caravans, keelboats and steamboats carried away most of the able-bodied citizens into the wilderness. And all that was exciting enough, no doubt.

But Joe Meek arrived in St. Louis at a far more interesting time—the autumn—when all those far-flung expeditions were coming home laden with wealth from the mountains.

Then, after the hot, stagnant summer, the men were back, the town came to life—a gay, reckless life—to celebrate their safe return, their successful ventures, their victories over hostile savages.

Long strings of pack mules scuffled in, each wearily plodding under 150 pounds of prime beaver plews. Caravans of rolling, rumbling prairie schooners lurched by behind their slow oxen or straining eight-mule teams, each bulging with buffalo robes, Mexican bar silver, and leathern bags of gold. Mackinaws, keelboats, and steamboats from as far up the Missouri as Teton River tied up at the St. Louis landing to disgorge bale after corded bale of choice peltry, barrel after barrel of pickled buffalo tongues and tallow.

And with these came the men who had brought home the bacon—lank Missouri bullwhackers in checked wool shirts, profane mule skinners and teamsters in heavy boots and homespun, French *voyageurs*—gay, singing—and lively, swaggering keelboat men, loud and violent, tall hunters in fringed buckskins and low-crowned beaver hats or coonskin caps, wealthy fur traders, bankers and merchants in their white ruffled shirts, high beaver hats, their long-tailed coats and brass buttons, twinkling through the streets in carriages drawn by high-stepping trotters, driven by their Negroes.

Of all these, the mountain men caught and held Joe's attention. Those Kentucky fellows, those boys from Tennessee and Virginia, whose grandpappies had fought Indians before them—those men with heavy rifles and swinging fringes of Indian hair on their leggings, their tall tales and familiar lingo—*they* were the men for Joe Meek.

Young, friendless, and poor, Joe could only look on from a distance at the gaiety and carousing in the town. He must have had a hard time to keep going through the winter while he waited for his chance.

But Joe hung on.

The ice in the river went out, yet it was still cold and snowy. Then one day he learned that William Sublette was back in town, buying goods to pack to the mountain rendezvous of the Rocky Mountain Fur Company. Joe heard that Sublette needed men for his pack train.

It was tricky business for a boy of his age to be talking up to an old-timer like Bill Sublette. Happen a young fellow got turned down, it might be he'd have to hang around the settlements another year—and then not be sure of a job. But Joe Meek never lacked cheek or underestimated his capacities. After all, his brother Stephen had made it. Why not Joseph L. Meek?

Joe put on his best bib and tucker and headed for the office of the Rocky Mountain Fur Company, drew a long breath, and boldly knocked.

Someone shouted, "Come in." Joe opened the door.

Burning logs glowed in the fireplace.

"Well?" A big, fair-haired, hawk-nosed man, with a scar on his chin, turned from the desk. That must be Bill; the Indians called him Cut-Face.

Hurriedly Joe Meek introduced himself and made his purpose known.

William Sublette sat silent, sizing the boy up. Joe reckoned those piercing blue eyes could count the knuckles on his backbone.

"How old are you?" Sublette demanded.

Joe licked his lips. "Goin' on nineteen."

Still those piercing eyes scanned him. "Humff—and *you* want to go to the Rocky Mountains." Sublette stood up. He was over six feet—but no taller than Joe, at that.

Joe looked him square in the eye. "Yes, sir."

Sublette snorted. "You don't know what you're talking about, boy. You'd get killed before you got halfway there."

Joe straightened up, squared his broad shoulders. His eyes flashed. Then he relaxed and grinned winningly.

"Well, if I do, then I reckon I can die."

Bill Sublette laughed. He liked the boy's spunk. "Well," he said, "That's the game spirit. Maybe you'll do after all. . . . Only, be smart and keep your wits about you."

Joe laughed in triumph. "Where else would they be?"

He was hired! Sublette brought out articles of agreement, and Joe laboriously made his mark on the foolscap. Eagerly he listened to instructions. Then he shook hands with his new booshway *(bourgeois* or boss) , and marched off to get his outfit, feeling twice as chesty and two inches taller than ever before.

The Trail to the Mountains

JOE BOUGHT his outfit on credit from the fur company, its value to be deducted from his wages for the coming year. Had he realized how much those goods would cost him in furs at mountain prices, he might not have been so happy to get them.

His outfit certainly included one possible sack or war bag; a sack containing six steel beaver traps with chains attached; two Mackinaw blankets; a belt; a sheath with a skinning knife having stamped upon the bright blade the trademark G. R. (according to the trappers for Green River; according to the British for *Georgius Rex*), a regular mountain rifle, sturdy enough for the wilds, of heavy metal, carrying thirty-two balls to the pound, stocked to the muzzle, and mounted with brass, with a trap in the stock to hold patches, a worm to clean it, and a hickory wiping stick; a bullet pouch with several pigs of Galena lead and a mold in which to run bullets; a pound or two of fine glazed DuPont powder to fill his new powder horn; one gaudy capote, with hood, made of a four-point Nor'west blanket; a comb; a tin cup; an awl; flint and steel; a tobacco pouch and pipe; a hatchet; a pair of spurs with enormous rowels, and a rim-fire Spanish saddle.

The saddle, a California tree, was bound tightly together with thongs and rawhide, and had a low saucer-sized horn, the whole shebang being covered with a thick square sheet of sole leather, the *mochila,* with a hole through it for the horn, a slit for the cantle, and wide skirts to carry saddlebags. The *mochila* could be lifted from the tree. The saddle had one hair cinch, and huge wooden stirrups with broad flat treads comfortable to moccasined feet, and with trailing tapaderas. With the saddle went a picket rope of hemp (which wolves would not gnaw), a pair or two of hobbles, an apishamore or saddle blanket, and a bridle with a Spanish curb bit.

One saddle mule completed Joe's outfit. To keep it safe Joe carried an iron-headed picket pin two feet long, and a wooden mallet with which to drive it. Hard up as Joe then was, he probably wore the hat and clothes in which he came to St. Louis.

Perhaps he purchased a few pounds of flour, some sugar and salt to ease his transition to a straight meat diet—or even a cake of soap. More likely, happy-go-lucky as he was, Joe neglected that.

While getting his outfit together, Joe made the acquaintance of another green hand, Robert Newell of Ohio, nicknamed "Doc." Doc was three years older than Joe, and better educated. From the start the two boys hit it off.

Day by day the company increased until the camp numbered about sixty men, with some two hundred and fifty saddle and pack animals. When Joe joined them, it was still cold weather, with occasional snow flurries, sleet storms, and chilling rains. There were no tents or waterproofs in camp. Meek soon learned to spread the *mochila* from his saddle under his blankets to keep the cold down. But when icy rains and sharp winds chilled his shivering marrow, he crawled miserably under some farmer's corncrib or sought snug refuge in the nearest haymow.

Then, while the raindrops pattered on the packs around the sleeping camp, the miserable mules, hating the cold and wet as much as he, stood over their picket pins, with heads down, forlorn ears drooping, and backs arched against the rain, dismally waiting for daybreak.

Every day the green hands were kept busy learning to tame horses and pack mules. Their day began at four o'clock, with cooking a hasty breakfast of salt sowbelly and hominy, or a pot of mush and tallow, while the rain hissed on the fire. Joe was no great shakes as a cook, nor Doc neither.

His prancy saddle mule, Joe found, was as touchy as she was tough, with a strong mind of her own, hard heels, and more evil tricks than Satan himself could have taught her. Joe spent weary hours learning to corner and rope her, choke her down, get the bridle over her sensitive ears, saddle up, mount, and then try to hang on until she became reconciled—temporarily—to the man on her back.

During this process Joe's genial disposition suffered, while his boyish vocabulary rapidly increased. He and Doc were thrown forwards, backwards, sideways, into dust, snow, mud, until both were black and blue all over, with skinned knees and elbows, torn clothes, abraded cheeks, and bloody noses. Still, such rough adventures gave them enormous appetites: even salt pork and boiled corn tasted good.

But the tricks of Joe's temperish saddle mule were few, simple, and tame compared to those of his pack animals. Now Bill Sublette was very particular that none of his mules should be so packed as to get saddle sores: "Thar's only one way to pack a mule—the *right* way!" So Joe explored the deviltry peculiar to each of the three pack mules of which he was in charge—to say nothing of Doc Newell's.

Mule packers were then known, facetiously, as Knights of the Cross. Joe supposed his new title referred to the crossed markings on a mule's withers. But before he was through Joe realized that it was the muleteer, not the mule, who bore the cross!

All his animals behaved like perverse children of the Devil. When Joe laid a packsaddle on a mule's back, it straightway shook itself like a dog coming out of the water, throwing the saddle into the mud; when Joe put one foot on its ribs and tugged to tighten the girth, the ornery beast swung around its ugly head and bit his leg; if Joe went to its head, the mean critter stamped on his foot; if he went to its tail to adjust the crupper, he got a kick on the shins. If, at length, he got the three cowhide-covered bales on the saddle, the mongrel brute would suddenly flounce and caper and buck, tossing them off before he could lash them fast. And when, finally, he got all lashed snugly on, like as not the cussed critter would bolt, running off to pitch and twist and wallop around until the girth slipped and the saddle was under its belly. Then it would paw and squeal and pitch, and kick the packs to pieces.

If too obstinate to bolt, the mule would balk, absolutely refusing to lead or drive. Cordelling a keelboat, Joe heard, was nothing to dragging a balky mule. Sometimes a mule would simply lie down and refuse to get up. Joe lost all patience: "Hell's full of pack-mules!"

But Sublette was firm: No matter how wicked your mule was, you dasn't kill it! Joe warn't going to be left behind this trip. He had to make good!

The two boys worked shoulder to shoulder, until none of their stubborn, cantankerous, spraddle-legged animals could fool them by bellying out with a deep-drawn breath, to be released only after the cinch had been drawn tight. The pair planted their boots on the padded aparejo and tugged with all their might until the cinch was snug. They learned to make up packs of equal weight and to balance these, stowing a third pack on top in the middle, and then throw a hitch over all. Sublette kept them at this by the day until they qualified as packers. It was hard work—and good conditioning for the long trek ahead.

On March 17, 1829, the company hit the trail for the West through that sparsely settled country. By that time Joe was so sick of camp fare that he dreamed nightly of feasting on antelope steak and buffalo hump-ribs, of which old-timers talked so eagerly. When they could, Joe and Doc knocked down a rabbit, coon, or 'possum to add variety to their monotonous diet. And whenever they passed a farm they lost no time in begging for eggs or a drink of milk.

Once day Joe saw an old woman bringing home the milk in a big gourd. Newell who, like Joe, had come from settled country where such vessels were seldom seen, laughed at her primitive container.

Then the old lady gave him a piece of her mind.

"Young chap, I'll bet you run off from your mother! Who'll mend them holes in the elbow of your coat? You're a purty-looking chap to go to the mountains, among them Injuns! They'll *kill* you and cut you to pieces. You'd better go back home!"

After that sound advice the two boys returned, somewhat sobered, to their mules. Like enough the old woman knew what she was talkin' about. On the frontier only men who died in sickbed looked pretty in their coffins. . . .

But in time the company crossed most of Missouri and reached Independence—then a mere hamlet, consisting of one dwelling house, one cotton gin, one grocery. They halted there to organize for the trail.

It was Sunday, and Sublette announced a day of rest. The natives challenged his men to a shooting match. As nobody had any cash money, the stakes were coonskins, deerskins, beeswax and wild honey. To Joe's chagrin, the woodsmen with their long squirrel rifles outshot him.

Joe was a mite uneasy about shootin' on the Sabbath, and he had not yet got the hang of his heavy mountain rifle.

As a town Independence was small potatoes. But Joe and Doc knew they were taking their last look at the settlements for years to come. When they headed West next day, they were two homesick boys, with mighty little to say to each other.

Sublette expected to find the trappers of his Rocky Mountain Fur Company encamped on the headwaters of Wind River, in what is now Wyoming. From Independence, Missouri, his most direct route would have been up the Platte River. But ever since Colonel Henry Leavenworth had made his fruitless attack on the Ree villages six years earlier, those warlike Indians had made the Platte unhealthy. Moreover, that was mostly Sioux country—always dangerous—and Sublette preferred to get into it by the back door. There was as yet no Oregon Trail.

But on the Santa Fe Trail wagons had been rolling for eight years. Uncle Sam had surveyed it, and recently the New Mexicans had come east and made a treaty with the Pawnees to stop raiding on that highway. Farther west the American traders, Bent and St. Vrain, kept the Cheyennes and Arapahoes friendly. Only Kiowas and Comanches south of the Trail were apt to make trouble.

Yet so many atrocities had been committed that President Andrew Jackson (no lover of redskins) that very spring sent Major Bennett Riley, with four companies of the Sixth Infantry, to escort the annual caravan of wagons four hundred miles from Missouri to that point on the Arkansas River where the trail crossed the Mexican border. There it would be met by a Mexican escort. The previous year the caravan had carried goods to the value of $150,000—goods worth several times that in Santa Fe.

These conditions may have led Sublette to choose the Santa Fe Trail. He may even have planned to travel with the troops and wagons, though they would slow his pack mules up. Yet in any case he and his men would have to part company with the troops and ride 150 miles alone before they reached Bent's Fort and turned north along the foothills of the Rockies, heading for the Platte, the Sweetwater, and Wind River.

Sublette's camp was made for defense. The packs formed a barricade all round—or on three sides, if a riverbank was handy to form the fourth. The men lay just inside the barricade, and the hobbled animals stood tied in the middle.

The first night out of Independence, Sublette posted a guard. At intervals Joe would waken to Sublette's call, "All's well!" and hear the reassuring reply, "All's well!" showing that the guard, too, was wide awake. Finally Joe fell sound asleep.

It seemed only forty winks later when he heard a persistent Frenchman calling over and over in rapid singsong, "Levé, levé, levé!" From the sudden stir which followed, Joe knew that call meant "Get up!"

Sublette was already up, rifle in hand. Joe watched him jump upon the bare back of his bay saddler, head out of camp a quarter of a mile, and then gallop all around it, scouting for sign of Indians. For though the Kaws, Osages and Pawnees on the border were friendly tribes, their young braves were always ready to make away with a stray horse or run off a few mules whose owners were not watchful.

When Sublette rode back to camp, the Frenchman began to yell again. The men untied the lariats from the picket pins and loosed their animals. Then the horse guard mounted and herded them out on the prairie to graze, swinging one end of a rope around his head.

While the animals were feeding, the men had time to pack their plunder, wash up and cook breakfast. For by this time the men were organized into messes, each with

its own fire. The booshway, the little booshway, and the
three hunters for the train messed together at one fire.
Some free trappers riding with the train to get—and give
—protection, messed together. The other—hired—men
were four or five to a fire.

Breakfast over, the horse guard brought the animals
in. Joe caught, saddled and packed his mules. When
everybody was "all set," Sublette, the booshway, mounted
his horse, yelled "Put out!" and headed west. Behind
the booshway rode his clerk, leading a plodding mule
packed with two small trunks which held the company's
books, cash, papers, mail, and articles of agreement with
the men. Behind, double file, rode the others, each with
his string of pack animals. Joe had learned to put his
steadiest mule in front, tie the second to its tail, and the
third to the tail of the second. The halter shank of each
was carried forward to the saddle ahead so that a rearing
or balky animal could not injure the one to whose tail it
was tied. Once the animals were accustomed to traveling
together, of course, they would follow faithfully along
without lead ropes.

Meanwhile the hunters left the pack train, riding on
ahead to kill meat. Later, if they were successful, Joe
would see them waiting on the trail with the choice parts
of whatever animals they had killed.

Joe soon discovered that his booshway meant business
—that what they had been through already was only a
picnic compared to what lay ahead.

Captain William Sublette, called Bill—or more often
Billy—by the mountain men, came of a family of Kentucky pioneers. Billy's grandfather had gone into that
country with Dan'l Boone, and on that Dark and Bloody
Ground the Injuns had killed and scalped him. Bill himself had gone up the Missouri River with Henry and
Ashley in 1822. Major Henry had always organized his
fur brigade like a military force and now, Joe found,

Sublette was stepping right in Major Henry's tracks. He wouldn't stand for any foolishness.

The second day out of Independence, during the midday halt or nooning, Joe and another green hand were sitting under a tree whittling sticks. Sublette came striding along, picked up the other fellow's rifle, and inspected it.

"Your gun's dirty," he declared sternly. "Get to work and clean it, *pronto!*" He shoved the gun into the arms of its owner.

Joe was glad his own weapon was clean.

Turning to go, Sublette was halted by an old-timer leading a horse with a saddlesore which he wanted the booshway to doctor. For a minute Joe guardedly watched the weather-beaten mountain man, in his greasy, smutted elkskin hunting coat and moccasins, wagging his beard at Sublette from under his old wool hat.

When Joe looked round again, the fellow with the dirty gun was still whittling, slashing at the stick in a way to show his resentment. He sure was taking his time about obeying orders. Joe reckoned he didn't like being bossed around thataway.

Sublette glanced back then and saw the shirker sulking, with the rifle across his lap, still whittling the stick.

The booshway frowned, and Joe expected him to lash out with hard words. But Sublette ignored the culprit. Instead he suddenly turned on Joe to demand, "Can you clean that gun properly?"

"Yes, sir," Meek said. "I reckon I can, if you back me out to do it."

"I'll give you ten dollars to do it," Sublette declared, and strode off.

Ten dollars! That was real money—nearly a month's wages for a green hand like Joe. The shirker laughed and handed his rifle over.

"Here, Joe, take it. I never hankered to clean the old

shootin' iron. The booshway's mighty particular. But I'll say one thing for him—he shore is free with his money!"

Picking up his knife, he leaned back against the tree and began to whittle again, grinning contentedly, as if he had put something over on the booshway.

The mountain man with the sore-backed horse grinned gloatingly down at the whittler, then suddenly snorted. "You pore greenhorn! In Injun country a man's got to keep his eyes skinned and his powder dry. Them ten dollars comes out of your wages. That'll l'arn ye! Maybe next time you won't be so all-fired brash!"

Joe cleaned and polished that rifle until it shone, then rubbed up his own again afterwards, just in case. Thereafter he took care most times to do his work well, whether he was washing a horse's back, splicing a hair rope, packing a mule, or rustling buffalo chips for the fires.

We have no details of Meek's adventures on this journey to the mountains. But one thing is clear: by the time the pack train reached the foothills of the Rockies, Meek and his comrades formed a compact, disciplined and well-trained company, fat and sassy from the buffalo meat they had eaten. They were good riders, good shots, and hard as nails.

Of an evening, while the dying mess fires flickered in the twilight and pipes were glowing, old-timers taught the green hands the tricks of their trade and how to meet the dangers ahead. Then one or another of the men, snarling his prelude like an angry bear, began:

"*Wagh!* Injuns are the most unsartainest varmints in all creation, and I reckon they're not more'n half human. For you never seed a human, after you'd fed him and treated him to the best fixin's in your lodge, jist turn around and steal all your horses, or ary other thing he could lay hands on. No, not adzackly. He would feel kinder grateful, and ask you to spread a blanket in his lodge if ever you passed thataway. But the Injun don't keer shucks for you, and is ready to do you a heap of mischief as soon as he quits your feed.

" 'Tain't no use to talk about honor with them, nohow. They hain't got no sich thing in 'em, and they won't show fair fight, any ways you fix it. Don't they kill and scalp a white man when-ar they git the better of him? The mean varmints, they'll never behave theirselves until you give 'em a clean out-and-out lickin'. They can't understand white folks' ways, and they won't l'arn 'em; and if you treat 'em decent, they think you air afeard. Nope, you kin depend on it: the only way to treat Injuns is to thrash 'em plenty first. Then the balance will sorter take to you and behave theirselves. . . ."

Speak of the Devil and he appears. Next morning early, before the mules were packed, the top of the ridge suddenly sprouted war bonnets, lances, guns, and horses' heads. "Injuns!" Hundreds of them in line of battle came sweeping down the slope on the dead run.

Joe and his friends sprang up from their mess, grabbing their rifles. Sixty men looked a mighty small handful against all those mounted warriors; there were hundreds, maybe a thousand. Their line looked a mile long!

All around was bare prairie. There was not a smidgin of cover anywhere, not even a clump of grass. Joe could not run; a mule would have no chance against those fleet Indian ponies. It was fight or die.

Sublette lost no time. In a minute he had his whole force drawn up to face the charge. A man could never tell whether Indians were charging in peace or war, for it was their custom to "charge" on their friends and, as it were, "capture" them as a kind of military compliment. For all Sublette knew, those tribesmen were coming to wipe him out; even if they were not, they would surely take advantage of any show of weakness and help themselves to his packs and animals—to say nothing of his hair.

But Sublette showed no fear. He ran out in front of

his line, then turned and called back, "When you hear *my* shot, then *fire!*"

Still the Indians rushed on. When they were only fifty paces away, Sublette glanced back. Every man was drawing a bead on the redskins. Sublette threw up his own rifle.

Rendezvous

THE BOLD stand of the white men had its effect. As suddenly as they had charged, the Indians reined up. The chief jumped from his pony, laid his weapons on the ground, and walked quietly forward, holding up his empty palms in sign of peace.

Sublette likewise laid down his rifle and walked forward for a powwow. The two men shook hands and hugged each other, then parleyed in the sign language.

Sublette learned that the Indians were a war party of Sioux, Arapahoes and Cheyennes, out looking for their enemies.[1]

Sublette opened his packs and made the chief a substantial present of tobacco, blankets, powder and ball, vermilion, and brass rings. There was more handshaking, more hugging. Then the chief, distributing the presents he had received among his leading warriors, mounted and led them away. After all, the presents had cost the chief nothing, whereas the capture of the train must have cost him a good many dead warriors.

Sublette rode up on the ridge to watch his unwelcome

[1] In *The River of the West* (Hartford, Conn., 1870), Mrs. Victor asserts that there were Kiowas in this party. I suspect this is an error, as the Kiowas did not make peace with the Cheyennes until the year 1840. See G. B. Grinnell, *The Fighting Cheyennes* (New York, 1915) Chapter VI.

visitors safely out of sight. By the time their booshway
returned, the packers had the train ready to move.

Joe met with no further adventures until the outfit
reached the rendezvous of the Rocky Mountain Fur Company.

That year Sublette expected to find his trappers encamped on the Popo Agie.[2]

One morning as they rode up the stream, Sublette
halted on top of a spur coming down from the hills and
scanned the grassy, flower-spangled valley ahead. From
his place in the double line of pack mules, Joe saw the
booshway point and then lay the quirt to the flanks of his
horse. The word drifted back that Sublette had seen
smoke.

But when Joe and Doc in their turn reached the top of
the ridge, and swept the country ahead with their eyes,
they could see nothing. Everything up there looked hazy.
Yet as the day wore on and the booshway made no noon-
day halt, the boys knew that rendezvous could not be
far off.

They followed the stream with the funny name, Popo
Agie—"Head River" in the Crow language—until, early
in the afternoon, far off against the naked red sandstone
bluffs, they themselves saw columns of smoke and, a little
later, the sawtooth pattern of Indian lodges underneath,
surrounded by scattered dark shapes like buffalo.

Joe reckoned it was a good place for a camp, with clear
mountain water, timber for fuel along the stream, and
grass belly deep for the stock. From the sign he had seen

---

2 There is considerable difference of opinion among historians as to how
many rendezvous were held in 1829. Robert Newell's "Memorandum of
Robert Newell's Travels in the Territory of Missouri, 1829-1841" (Manuscript
on file at Oregon Historical Society, Portland, Oregon), confirms Mrs.
Victor's account up to the rendezvous. She quotes Meek as reaching rendezvous
on the Popo Agie on July 1; Newell says it was at the foot of the mountains,
on the Sweetwater, July 17; Milton Sublette and David Jackson met on
Priest's Fork, August 20; and Bill Sublette finally found Jedediah Smith in
Pierre's Hole. No doubt each of these meetings might be, and be called, a
rendezvous, since each afforded opportunity for a fur fair.

he judged there was no lack of game in the valley and the hills around.

His long march was nearly over. It was July 1, 1829. They had been three and a half months on the trail. Even the mules quickened their pace. Joe's heart beat faster. Soon he would be among the mountain men. There, if the booshway had not found him too triflin', he hoped to make his home.

As they drew nearer, Joe saw that his "buffalo" were ponies and mules, grazing around the camp. And now he noticed a sudden movement there, as men caught up their horses, saddled, mounted.

In Indian country you never sneaked up or rode quietly into a friendly camp. And when Sublette had come within three hundred yards of the nearest lodge, he suddenly let out a bloodcurdling war whoop, fired his rifle into the air, set spurs to his horse.

All the old-timers with the pack train joined in, stretching their lungs in the racket, slapping their open mouths with one hand as they whooped. Joe and the green hands lost no time in following suit. There was only one thought in all their minds *thar's rendezvous!*

They all charged in on the dead run, shooting, yelling like devils.

By that time the men in camp came rushing to meet them—a long ragged line of horsemen, far outnumbering Sublette's little band, shouting their welcome, half blotted out by the smoke which foamed from rifles along their front.

At first Joe wondered if Sublette had made a mistake and charged a hostile Indian camp. It looked like a regular battle. But Joe had learned to rely on his booshway, and plunged on like the rest through clouds of powder smoke.

The two forces melted together as the campers wheeled their horses, falling in alongside old friends to shake

hands, hug each other, and shout greetings. Together
the whole kit and caboodle rushed into camp, plunging
on through the smoke, to stop, rearing, in a cloud of dust
before the big buffalo lodge of the booshway, headquarters of the partners of the Rocky Mountain Fur Company.

The moment the horsemen stopped and began to
dismount, people came running from the tents on all
sides, preceded by a chorus of barking dogs—Indians,
trappers, breeds, squaws and camp keepers—in a great
babble of greetings, news, queries, handshakes, hugging
and back-slapping.

"How, John, old coon! I was afeared you'd gone
under."

"What's beaver worth to St. Louis?"

"Five dollar a pound, Gouge Eye."

"Hell! Well, it mought be less. . . ."

Joe could have looked and listened forever, but as the
dust drifted away the little booshway gave orders to un-
pack the animals and stow the packs in the booshway's
lodge. That kept Joe and Doc busy until the horse guard
jogged off, driving their animals before him.

By that time Joe had got his bearings. Near the booshway's lodge stood other tall tipis belonging to the Indian
wives of well-to-do free trappers: while all around clus-
tered the improvised camps of the hired trappers, skin
trappers and camp keepers—wickiups, huts, or mere un-
sheltered bedrolls on the ground. Joe tossed his own
plunder with that of the other men in his mess. Then,
warily curious, he stuck his hands in his pockets, and
drank it all in.

By that time nearly everybody in camp had gathered
round the booshway's lodge, waiting impatiently. And
presently, having opened the trunks containing the company's papers, Sublette came out, followed by his clerk
with both arms full of mail.

Sublette called name after name of those to whom letters or newspapers were addressed, tossing the pieces to the claimants until all had been distributed. While the men pored over their mail or begged some better educated man to read it, Joe was free to look over the camp at his leisure.

All around, the valley was dotted with hundreds of grazing animals. But the camp itself was what caught Joe's eye—the big taper Indian lodges with their small, domed kitchen shelters alongside, and racks of meat drying in the sun. Here and there an old squaw with her dubber stooped over a buffalo hide pegged flat on the ground.

Two young squaws, their faces gay with vermilion, in fringed and beaded buckskins, with bright blankets about hips wedged between the high curving pommel and cantle of rawhide saddles, jogged by, the hawk's bells on their saddlery clashing and chinking in tune with their self-conscious giggles as they caught the tall, young white man's eager stare.

Farther on he saw some half-grown Indian children tossing one of their group in a blanket. Three little pot-bellied boys, naked but for a string around their middles, were chasing a snake through the grass. A few old chiefs sat gravely smoking in the shade, passing their long pipe around the circle.

A young warrior squatted under a tree, tapping rhythmically on the stiff rawhide before him on which his two-year-old son was learning to dance. In the other direction a young buck lay with his head in the lap of his sweetheart, while her fingers searched his black locks for the lice she was cracking between her even white teeth.

But it was not the Indians who fascinated Joe.

Those mountain men! They filled the bill for Joe. He had heard of their exploits, how they trapped beaver, killed b'ar, and made the cussed Injuns "come." And now here he was, spang in the middle of 'em, wishing with all his heart to be one of them.

He did not know what he was getting into.

But the crowd still hung around the booshway's lodge, jostling and craning, impatiently waiting for trade to begin.

Sublette was not long in opening his packs. The trappers stood in line, and as each came up with his beaver plews (as prime skins were called from the French *plus)* and other peltry, Sublette's clerk checked them in until the man's last-year's debt was paid, crediting him with it on the books, and then swapping whatever the man needed for the coming year.

First of all the trapper wanted arms: maybe a new rifle, certainly powder and lead; a butcher knife and whetstone; a new hatchet. After that, maybe so, traps to replace those broken, lost, or dragged off by some varmint; a brass camp kettle, red blankets or a blanket coat; a flannel shirt or, failing that, one of calico, costing five dollars at mountain prices and selling at St. Louis for fifty cents or less. Other luxuries from the States sold at even more outrageous prices—blankets at twenty dollars, sugar and coffee one dollar a pound, tobacco two dollars a pound, and "fofurraw"—as the trappers called all fancy goods, from the French word *fanfaron*—at a profit sometimes of two thousand per cent.

But that did not stop the trappers from buying fofurraw galore. Some bad Indian wives, who gloried in their exalted position as a white man's woman. Those who had not womaned generally had friends among the Indian girls. For them scarlet cloth blazed in the sunshine, striped blankets dazzled the eye, bales of calico were flung open, beads glistened, hawk's bells and sleigh-bells tinkled, ribbons fluttered, awls and butcher knives flashed, and there were tin cups and cakes of Chinese vermilion. To do them justice, the Indian girls and the

married women were on hand to receive whatever their
men might buy.

Once a trapper had paid his debt he felt free to
squander his credit, and it was a reckless booshway who
dared refuse anything to a free trapper, or even one of
his hired hands who had proven that he was "up to
beaver." Hell's full of money. And in the mountains,
what else could you spend it for? Some of them blew a
thousand dollars worth of beaver a day.

For, once debts and women were taken care of, the
booming business of the trade began. Sublette brought
out the kegs he had packed in from the States, kegs
purposely made flat to fit on a pack saddle, and knocked
in the bungs with a tent peg and a stone mallet.

The trappers came swarming with tin cups and camp
kettles, eager to "wet their dry," a thirst which had been
building up, like enough, for a whole year of hardship,
danger, and exposure. They had worked hard. They
had seen numbers of their fellows frozen, killed by a
horse, or shot and scalped by Injuns. They felt it was
time to cut loose and raise a little hell. This might be
their last rendezvous.

So, at a time when seventy-five cents would buy as good
a meal as New York City afforded, they gladly paid four
dollars a pint in prime beaver skins for diluted raw
alcohol, potent enough to curl the hair of a grizzly. They
were all dry as a buffalo skull, all set to take a horn or
two with their *companeros*—half froze for galore of drink.

"Hyar's the beaver. Whar's the likker?" was their
slogan.

By that time Joe had begun to size up the various types
in camp and to distinguish among them. He had kept
his ears open on the trip in. It was not difficult to spot
the camp keepers, those pork eaters—*mangeurs de lard*—
who subsisted on salt sowbelly because they could not
hunt, and were condemned to do the dirty work around

camp while better men threw buffalo and trapped beaver.

Joe was glad himself to be classified as a trapper—one who was paid wages by the company and who, though he might be "hired" and so called on for any duty by his booshway, had after all a chance to show his quality among the beaver trappers.

A more fortunate class were the "skin" trappers who, though not paid wages, were in debt to the company for their equipment and were pledged to sell all their furs to the company at company prices—assuming that they were able to take more than would pay off their debt.

But it was the free trappers who fascinated Joe and filled him with awe and envy. They owed no man anything, and bought and sold when and where they pleased.

It had been a good year. Most of the men were young, in good health and spirits, and ready for a blowout. The spring hunt was over. From mid-June until September was the holiday season, when trapping was unprofitable and the weather was fine.

A few of the men were Dutch, or French, Scotch, Irish, English, Delaware Indians, Iroquois, or breeds of various kinds. But most free trappers were Americans. These were the cavaliers of the mountains, game birds, cocks o' the walk, with a bold look on their dark, sunburned faces, aping the cussed Injuns, and mighty proud of it.

They were no hirelings, and, with no intention of returning to the settlements, had adopted the manners, habits, dress, and even the walk of the redskins. Their long hair, combed out, floated down over the collars of their hunting shirts, or, plaited into braids, was swathed in sleek otterskin or bound with colored ribbons. They wore gay shirts of ruffled calico and golden-brown hunting coats of smoked buckskin, fringed and beaded or with quillwork patterns on the sleeves, and with diapers of sleek black velvet adorning full skirts reaching to the knee. Such a coat—with brass buttons and a fur collar—

was a swagger garment. But the leggings, with ample flaps heavily fringed and adorned with hawk's bells, thimbles, and trailing Injun hair, carried broad bands of beadwork. The heels of their brightly colored moccasins trailed tassels of buckskin fringes a foot long and thick as a man's wrist. Some carried a four-point Nor'west scarlet blanket, and in the particolored sash round the waist packed a pistol, a knife, and the stem of an Indian pipe.

When they strutted by, all dressed up for this gala occasion, Joe saw the sun flash from the brass tacks on the stocks of their rifles—the tally of their coups in battle— or marveled at the long buckskin cover of a gun adorned from end to end with fringes three feet long.

But if the trapper himself when on a spree was so decorative, his favorite horse—for war, buffalo running, or racing—ran a close second to its master. For on his horse the trapper lavished a love passing the love of women. His success and standing, his safety, even his life depended on the speed, spirit and endurance of his saddle animal.

He loaded his running animal with the finest horse jewelry he could buy—a silver-mounted Spanish bridle, a saddle adorned with silver plates, tooled leather and elaborate beaded saddlebags. He adorned the mane, tail and forelock of his horse with lustrous black-and-white eagle tail feathers (the blue ribbon of the wilderness) and painted the animal itself with vermilion or white clay, or whatever other paint offered best contrast to its natural color.

That afternoon there were feasts at every mess fire, much talk of past doin's, of many a tight fix, with jokes and hearty laughter, tall tales and mighty brags on this horse and that rifle, which led immediately to challenges, pony races and shooting matches. Each marksman boasted that he could outshoot his fellows any way they liked it— offhand or layin' to a chunk.

There were plenty of buffalo, elk, and mountain sheep in the neighborhood, and the camp was merry. They indulged their hearty appetites, washing down the meat with potations of watered alcohol that cooked their throats as well done as the roasted meat. They gnawed hump-rib after buffalo hump-rib bare and flung it over their shoulders, chuckled as they raked the deep ashes of the fire and drew therefrom a pair of tongues, admirably baked—sweet, soft, and of exquisite flavor.

Yet, stuffed as Meek and the others were on fat cow and prairie oysters—having eaten, as it seemed to him, almost his own weight in meat and marrow—he was not logy, but felt as easy as if he had supped on strawberries and cream. Having wiped their fingers on their long hair and cleaned their butcher knives, by thrusting them two or three times into the ground, the trappers got out their pipes and began the initiation of the greenhorns.

Every free trapper had a circle of admirers about him, and filled them up with tall tales of his own mighty prowess, wild adventures, and the tricks of his trade. Meek unexpectedly made himself a favorite at once by confessing to his particular hero, "I tuk ye for an Injun!"

Joe could have stared and listened forever, but a bow-legged trapper in an old wool hat swaggered up to the group, slapped down an armful of furs, and squatted cross-legged on the ground. He displayed a pack of greasy cards and challenged, "Hi, boys! Hyar's the deck, and hyar's the beaver. Who dares set his horse?"

There had been nothing like this on the trip out. Sublette was not the man to issue grog or permit gambling in a small party on the trail. Joe's pious stepmother had taught him that gambling, cards, and drinking were sinful, stepping-stones on the road to Hell.

Yet so far as he could see, nobody there was any the worse for it—yit. He had thrown in with these men, aimed to be one of them, and reckoned he would take things easy and overlook it. After all, there were no preachers at rendezvous, and Joe was glad of it.

All over camp men were playing Old Sledge. A few were still running races, jumping against each other, wrestling—but those on whom the liquor had taken hold began to sing Injun, sitting on the ground, beating a camp kettle or slapping their bellies to knock out the vocables more forcibly.

As the liquor went down, the bragging went up. Profanely each swore that his own rifle would shoot plumb center, and made many an Injun come, and never failed to throw the meat cold; that his horse was faster, braver, and could run farther and longer than any other, that his woman—or women—were the handsomest in camp. These brags passed harmlessly enough.

But when the trapper began to brag about himself, his feats of arms, his strength and daring, that was a challenge not to be endured. Competition grew fierce and bitter as each exalted himself and belittled his comrades. Then fists began to fly, and the good spirits and high jinks of the mountain men turned suddenly to violence and bloodshed. Then there were black eyes and bloody noses galore in the camp, as the friends of each champion rallied to his support and the bullies of each company went for their opponents.

For the most part, Joe saw, it was a pleasant, friendly fight of lusty young men with too much liquor under their belts. But that day, whether from too much straight alcohol or too hard a blow, one man was killed.

This sobered the brawlers sufficiently to bring their combat to an end, and they went back to milder forms of competition with cards, or playing Hand with the Indians.

Joe Meek was horrified to see four trappers using the carcass of their dead comrade for a card table. Callously they slapped down the cardboards on his cold back with never a sign of revulsion—except another swig of booze from the camp kettle.

Their callousness, and the laughter it inspired in others, shocked Joe even more. Though astonished and alarmed by the gambling, swearing, drinking, and fighting, Joe, unsophisticated as he was, had found something to admire in those, something congenial with his own carefree disposition. He admired the fearlessness, the scorn of sordid gain, the wholehearted merriment and frolicsome abandon all around him. He longed to be brave as the bravest, gay as the gayest, and tough as the hardiest.

But now, apt scholar though he wished to be, he found the lesson too hard for him. He puked—only to be laughed at for his pains.

Revolted and numb at heart, he went off to his blankets and lay there miserably under the stars, a lonely, homesick boy who had to wipe away some tears and could not sleep until he had said the prayers his dead mother had taught him.

That night, Joe—like Jedediah Smith before him—"felt the need for the watch and care of a Christian church." As Smith put it in a letter to his parents, "You may well suppose that our society is of the strangest kind. Men of good morals seldom enter into business of this kind."

But Joe Meek was no such strict Methodist as Smith, and was willing enough to call the trappers friends, if he could only get the hang of it.

Moreover, Meek was not a man to be downhearted long, much less endure ridicule from those he was bound to emulate. In the morning, though not too peart, he felt some better.

To Newell, sitting up soberly in his blankets alongside, Joe said, "Well, hyar we are, Doc. I reckon the green will rub off afore long."

PART II
TRAPPER

The Grand Teton

BY THIS time, Joe's boots were worn out, and the clothing he had worn on the long trail from the settlements was all in rags. He set about getting a new outfit.

One day Joe carried a handful of beads to the tent of a free trapper, and, with him to interpret, hired the squaw to make half a dozen pair of moccasins, to replace his worn-out boots. The old woman cached the beads in her possible sack, pulled out her sewing kit, and went to work. She produced a roll of soft-tanned buckskins. But Joe, proud of his new knowledge, insisted on moccasins made from the top of an old tipi, for such lodge skins, having had a year's smoking, would not stiffen after a wetting.

So she rummaged and brought out a roll of browned lodge skin. Then she spread a piece of stiff rawhide down and made Joe stand on it barefoot, throwing all his weight on his right foot while she traced its outline on the hide with a burnt stick from the fire. She cut the sole out, turned it over, and made another to match for the left foot. Then she measured Joe's instep; the old gal had learned from her husband that white men had higher insteps than her own people. She cut uppers big enough to serve, cut a thong to go all round each shoe, and a tongue to shield the ankle. Then, with flying awl, she deftly stitched sole to upper, using thread of twisted sinew. In half an hour, the first pair was ready. The trapper showed Joe how to put on the moccasin, pulling the toe well up before slipping the heel on.

Joe stood up, walked around the lodge, stretching his toes, shaping the new shoe to his foot. It was a heap better than going barefoot, but just as free and easy. Why, his feet had gloves on, a regular second skin!

But there was more to it than that.

No longer could he go stamping around roughshod like a man in boots; now he found himself treading cat-like, feeling his way, sensitive to the surface he walked on. Mother Earth took on a new significance for him; now he was close to her, aware. He had to be. It was as if he handled the ground he walked on!

As time passed, he learned to gauge, unconsciously, the character of the sand or mud or gravel on which he was about to set foot, as a man gauges the feel of an object before he takes it in his hand. And so he seldom slipped or stumbled, as he sometimes had in boots. And when night sent him back to his mess fire, Joe discovered, to his delight, that he could follow the trail through the dark; his feet felt his way, instantly warning him whenever he stepped out of the narrow path. He reckoned he was going to have to live *with* this country, not just in it. . . .

Rendezvous was soon over. Captain William Sublette, the booshway, was becoming anxious. His two partners in the fur company, David Jackson and Jedediah Smith, were to have met him thereabouts and had not turned up. Sublette was anxious to learn what luck his partners had had, how many beaver were in their packs. It would soon be time to start the fall hunt, and Captain Sublette was not the man to sit still when there was work to do.

The seasoned trappers, now poor again and in debt for new outfits, were, as they put it, "half froze for the trail" and "ready to put out." And when Joe Meek saw the squaws pulling down the booshway's big lodge, and the pack mules being driven in, he thrilled with keen anticipation. Now he was heading into the mountains to set his first trap.

Captain Sublette sent his younger brother, Milton, with Fraeb and Gervais, scouting down the Big Horn looking for the partners. The Captain himself led the main party towards the headwaters of Wind River and soon found Dave Jackson in Jackson's Hole. Meek traveled with him.

Then the question was, "Where is Smith?" Jackson had seen nothing of him. The anxious partners sent runners west to see if they could cut his trail.

Diah, as they called Jedediah Smith, had headed west into California and Oregon. Diah was a great explorer; and when he did not turn up, Sublette and Jackson began to suspect that their British rivals had done away with him. That got their dander up, and while they waited impatiently for the report of their runners, they began to plan reprisals on the redcoats.

As it happened, the search party with which Joe Meek rode had got clear over the pass into Pierre's Hole when they saw four men coming, leading a single pack horse. On the pack horse were a few moose hides, a few beaver plews and a few sea-otter skins—apparently all that Diah had to show for his year's expedition to the coast.

Smith brought bad news. One day, he said, while he was absent from his camp, the men had admitted a large number of Umpqua Indians. Smith's men had carelessly laid aside their guns. Suddenly the Indians attacked and butchered twenty-four of them, stole Smith's horses, furs, traps, and all. Now Jedediah was back, with the survivors and a single horse.

The news of this heavy loss of life struck Joe Meek hard, and he waited to see how the old hands would take it. To his surprise they gave no sign of grief. Their simple comment was, "Out of luck."

Joe began to understand how it was that those men at rendezvous could play cards on a dead comrade's back. Though they warmly welcomed Smith and the other sur-, vivors here in Pierre's Hole, they had nothing to say about those who had "gone under."

Trappers lived dangerous and lonely lives, always in peril of the claws of a grizzly bear or the sudden arrow of a skulking savage. They dared not dwell on past tragedies. They had present problems to solve. They never knew when a horse might cripple them with a kick or make a misstep on some mountainside, or when they might be drowned, frozen, starved, or die of thirst. War, work, and weather were trouble enough for them, without adding the evils of worry.

And so, Joe realized, he and his comrades must be gay, forget the dangers and the death which threatened them. They would keep their hearts strong by ignoring all that menaced them. Their motto was, so far as Joe could see, "Keep your heart big today, or tomorrow you die." As Joe Meek later put it, "Live men war what we wanted; dead ones war of no account."

So all three partners camped together there in Pierre's Hole—that lovely valley under the towering peaks of the Tetons. There it came out that Diah Smith had not come off too badly. He was not nearly so poor as he looked. The British had recovered most of his stolen furs and had bought them from him at current prices. Smith had brought back a draft on London for $20,000, besides four thousand dollars in cash received in San Francisco. He had, moreover, explored country no white American had ever seen before.

In fact, Diah's account of the Oregon country to the west and north made his partners' mouths water. The Hudson's Bay Company, he told them, had been shipping beaver pelts from Fort Vancouver by the hundreds of thousands, and Vancouver was only one of their posts. Sublette and Jackson were eager to carry out their plan to make their fall hunt west of the mountains and trap in that hunter's paradise.

But Smith objected. He was a man of principle, who always carried his Bible in his pocket and kept the knees of his buckskin leggings bagged out by kneeling to say his prayers. Diah always played fair with the other fellow, even with the Indians—who finally murdered him. The British, Smith declared, had befriended him after his hard luck. But for them he might have gone under. They had recovered his furs, paid him a fair price for them, and disciplined the Indians who had massacred his men. Therefore, Smith demanded that his partners leave the Oregon country west of the mountains to the redcoats, and go back over the divide to make their fall hunt in what was definitely American territory.

While the partners wrangled, the trappers celebrated another rendezvous. Though Smith had brought few furs, they celebrated his return with their usual manly outdoor sports.

There in Pierre's Hole, Meek found himself at the very heart of the country of the mountain men, the paradise of the beaver trapper. For just east of the Hole rose the imposing Teton Range, sweeping up abruptly from the valley in a mighty, tumultuous wave of bare rock, its tossing crest white with snow. Three peaks—*Les Trois Tetons*—flung themselves up above the range, incredibly close, incredibly remote. And of these three, one towered above its rivals, thrusting its sharp spire into a sky scarcely bluer than the peak itself. That peak, the Grand Teton, was the central landmark, visible from afar in all directions—the pivot and pilot knob of all that vast welter of mountains and uneven plains, of winding valleys and rushing streams where beaver made their homes and trappers their hunting grounds. From that central point flowed the headwaters of four mighty rivers—North, East, South, West—towards the Atlantic and the Pacific, the Gulf of California and the Gulf of Mexico. As time passed, Meek was to know them all. Which would he get to explore first?

To the north, beyond the geysers, and the boiling springs and lakes of what is now Yellowstone Park, the Gallatin, the Madison, and the Jefferson met at Three Forks to form the Missouri River, which flowed away northward, east of the Continental Divide, turning eastward. at length to receive its tributaries, Judith River and the Musselshell. Dangerous country that, but rich in fur. East of the Divide later stood Fort Piegan, and, later still, Fort McKenzie, posts of the American Fur Company. West of the Divide was the range of the peaceful Flathead tribe.

From the Grand Teton, east and northeast, the swift gray Yellowstone River rushed away, dodging the lofty Absaroka Mountains, picking up the waters of one after another of its many tributaries streaming up from the south and west: Clark's Fork and the Big Horn, the Rosebud, the Tongue, until it reached Powder River, the extreme range of most beaver trappers, where buffalo abounded. On the Yellowstone, at various times, stood Fort Cass, Fort Sarpy, Fort Manuel, and other trading posts serving the Crow Indians. East of the Big Horn River, the Big Horn Mountains stretched north and south beyond the Big Horn Basin, and far beyond them the Black Hills, haunt of hostile Cheyennes and Sioux. In those days the Black Hills included also what are known now as the Laramie Mountains, and extended all the way down from the Belle Fourche of Cheyenne River to Fort Laramie on the Platte. Crow country ended at the Oregon Trail and South Pass.

To the south from the Grand Teton flowed the headwaters of Green River, heading for its lower, desert, reaches known as the Colorado of the West. Green River had many forks, all famous in trapper history. Fort Bonneville stood near the mouth of Horse Creek, Fort Bridger on Black's Fork below, and Fort Davy Crockett in Brown's Hole farther along, in the country of the Utes. West of all these, across the Uintah and Wasatch ranges lay Great Salt Lake, Utah Lake, Cache Valley, Bear River, and Ogden's Hole. That was ranged over by Snakes or Shoshones, Bannocks, Paiutes, and Digger Indians.

From the Grand Teton westward flowed the headwaters—Henry's Fork, Lewis' Fork, Pierre's Fork, and the rest—of Snake River, draining the hunting grounds of the tribe from which it takes its name, and—farther northwest—those of the friendly Nez Percés, until beyond the Blue Mountains, the Snake reached the mighty Columbia River near the country of the tricky Cayuses. On Snake River, Fort Hall and Fort Boisé became the chief posts for trade. All that country, as well as the sources of Green River, lay west of the Divide, and so formed part of Oregon, then occupied jointly by the British and Americans, pending a settlement of the international boundary. It contained many rivers, some teeming with beaver, some unexplored; the Salmon, the Malade, Payette River, Blackfoot River, the Clearwater, Godin's River, the Owyhee. Hearing talk of these rich trapping grounds, knowing the British coveted them, Joe Meek was eager to explore.

In September Joe was ordered off with other trappers to make his first hunt. Now at last he was to be amongst the fur, to try his apprentice hand and see, as the mountain men put it in their lingo, whether he was "up to beaver."

Up to Beaver

JOE CAUGHT up his mule, tied his trap sack on the saddle and rode with the rest downstream "towards where the the forks unite to form Snake River." But the trappers had scarcely reached the beaver dams when one of them discovered Injun sign—and Blackfoot sign at that—near their camp.

Beaver trapping was done in groups of two or three men who turned off from the main line of march to work on their own hook. Each one was looking for a good place to set his own traps. For, though each was hired by the company, he had to earn his own wages and pay his own debt with the furs that he himself brought in. And now that the Blackfeet, or—as the trappers called them—"Bug's Boys," were hovering around, Joe understood better than ever why his comrades were so laconic about losses. It took a bold heart to ride off alone or with one companion on a slow mule into strange country swarming with hostiles and there muck around on foot in swampy, open valleys where the beaver had gnawed down all the trees and a man could be seen from any hilltop or thicket for miles around.

Worst of all, they told Joe, you never saw hide nor hair of a hostile till he jumped you. It seemed like a hostile could hide in his own shadow, or lay under a wolfskin so quiet you might walk up and step on him afore you saw him. One moccasin print or pony track or one small pile of warm gray ashes where his fire had burned might show sign of only one hostile in the neighborhood, but you could lay your bottom dollar that wherever *one* redskin left sign, a dozen others lurked near by. Blackfeet, like other troubles, never came alone.

Of all the redskins in the mountains, the Blackfeet were most feared and hated. John Colter, Joe learned, traveling with a band of friendly Crows, had had to defend himself when the Blackfeet attacked the Crows. He was a good shot and so was the first American to shoot down a Blackfoot. Ever since that day, men said, Bug's Boys had been relentlessly hostile to all Americans. They were indeed the Devil's Own.

The Blackfoot Confederacy was made up of several big tribes: Blackfeet, Piegans, and Bloods—all closely allied with the Big Bellies or Gros Ventres of the Prairie, or Atsina, sometimes called Grovants for short.

These Indians fought for glory, for horses, for enemy hair—and for the sheer fun of it. They generally went to war on foot, and so could easily choose their own trail and cover it. They lay in wait in thickets, in gulches— as tricky, sudden, and dangerous as a rattlesnake without a rattle. Many of them had been well armed with fusees by their traders. Sometimes, it is true, these Indians waited for the white men to fire the first shot: but it was all they could do *to* wait. But Blackfeet or no Blackfeet, Joe and his friends had to trap the fur. Joe rode out with the rest looking for sign of beaver.

Now Captain Sublette saw to it that each green hand hunted with an experienced trapper so that he would quickly learn the difficult, skilled trade of a mountain man.

The beaver is a big water rat who builds his dams to protect his lodge and runways and to cover and guard the chunks of aspen buried under water for his winter provender.

Of course, a swift mountain torrent plunging down its rocky bed would defy all efforts of beaver to build a dam. But given a mountain meadow or gentle valley where the stream flowed slowly, a single pair of beaver has been known to build as many as six dams in one summer. So, when beaver were plenty— as they were in that unspoiled wilderness where Joe Meek learned his trade—dams were plenty too, sometimes stretching for hundreds and hundreds of yards, each with its mounded lodge and quiet pool, along the marshy stream.

The party rode rapidly along, and when Meek's mentor turned off to the left, Joe followed without a word. They rode hard to get away from the main party, looking for some hidden patch of grass where they could safely stake out their mules to roll and graze while they went to set their traps.

The sun was setting when the older man reined up, off-saddled, and then hid his plunder in a clump of willow brush. Then he staked out his mule, hobbled her, sat down and lighted his pipe. Meek followed his example in every detail. Not a word was said. It would be time enough to set their traps come dusk. Joe noticed the old trapper had a mighty strong stink.

Meanwhile, they found time to cut and peel a dozen six-foot stakes of dry wood as thick as a man's thumb, small enough to slide easily through the ring at the end of the five-foot chain attached to the steel trap with a swivel. The stakes had to be dry so that a trapped beaver could not gnaw one in two and so free himself before he drowned. Each stake had a short spur or fork about a foot above the pointed end.

When the sun had set and the hills threw their deepening shadows over the valley, Joe and his friend heaved their trap sacks to their shoulders, and taking their stakes and their rifles, plodded upstream towards the nearest beaver dam.

Some distance below, the old trapper, with Joe at his heels, halted, and, setting his moccasined feet on the springs, spread wide the jaws of one trap and set the trigger. Then picking up the trap, a stake, and a twig a foot long he stepped into the water and waded quietly upstream. The water would leave no human scent to frighten beaver from the trap.

That water looked very cold. Gingerly, Joe stepped into the shallow creek, then drew in his breath sharply. *Wagh!* That water was cold! And at every step of his moccasined feet it grew colder, deeper, slowly inching up his shins, his knees, his thighs, soaking his leggins. Trapping was evidently wet work, and Joe foresaw a dismal future of rheumatism and kindred ailments of the joints for him. But he could not turn back now. If the older man could take it, surely he could.

But Joe's companion only laughed at his discomfort. "Son," he admonished, "Wait till a beaver drags your trap to the bottom of the pool and drowns and you have to dive for it. You *will*, too. You might let the beaver go, but you can't afford to lose your trap when there is none nigher than St. Louie to take its place. Mountain water ain't never warm. It frosts every month of the year in high country. So grit your teeth and l'arn to put up with it."

Looking from bank to bank the trapper soon found what he wanted—a gnawed aspen tree, chips or shavings, a log partly cut in two, tracks in the mud. In short, fresh beaver sign. Then moving to the right bank, he pulled his skinning knife from its sheath and excavated a shelf or bed four or five inches under water on the bank, upon which he firmly seated the trap, the jaws spread wide, which he had already set. Then he slipped the ring at the end of the chain attached to the trap over the end of one of the six-foot stakes they had cut, and planted the pointed end deep and solid in the muddy bottom of the stream bed about as far from the trap as the chain would easily reach.

Then, opening a small horn bottle attached to his belt, he dipped the end of his peeled twig into the creamy, brownish, smelly "medicine" which it contained—the castoreum found near the preputial glands of the beaver. Afterward he stuck this twig into the mud between the open jaws of the trap so that the end bearing the "medicine" stood directly above it. This was his bait. Then Joe knew what made the trappers stink the way they did. He reckoned he'd stink the same as long as he lived in the mountains.

It was explained to Joe that, if he wished to catch the beaver by a forefoot, he should use a short twig; if by the hind foot, a longer one that would make the beaver rise on his hind legs to sniff it.

"When your beaver whiffs that medicine, he gets plenty wrathy. He don't like the smell of a strange beaver near his lodge. So up he comes to sniff it and puts his foot square in your trap. More 'n likely when first he feels the trap snap on his foot he'll turn a somersault diving for the bottom. Then the ring on the chain will slip down the stake and lodge under the fork near the bottom. Your beaver cain't bite through the chain nor gnaw his feet off nuther under water nor come up for air. Fust thing he knows, he's drowned. And there he lays under water, safe from coyotes and painters, jest waiting for you."

"Happen the stake pulls out and he gets to air, he won't go far dragging that float. Still, you might have to trail him for a mile."

When all their traps had been set in this manner, Joe and his instructor walked back, dripping wet, to their mules, saddled up quickly and rode fast to camp. With

Blackfeet around, it was no time to linger or to camp alone.

Before he rolled up in his blankets, Joe started to peel off his soaked moccasins. But the old-timer, gesturing with his pipe, stopped him. "Boy, if you take 'em off wet, they'll shrink so you'll never get 'em on again. Happen they dry and pinch your feet too hard in the night, you can always get up and step in the crick again. Then you can go back to sleep."

"So now," Joe thought, "I'll not only have my feet wet all day, but sleep with 'em wet all night."

But he could not work barefoot, or buy a new pair of moccasins every day. He found the advice given him was sound.

It was still pitch dark when Joe heard the trappers about him stirring. He got up stiffly, saddled his mule, and rode off to raise his traps before sunup. That morning Joe caught his first beaver—a big, fat, slick fellow with a broad, flat, scaly tail like a paddle. He reckoned it hefted twenty-five pounds.

Fearing that the sound of gunfire might bring Blackfeet upon them, the trappers in the party did not hunt for meat, but subsisted on the flesh of the beaver they caught. Joe learned to skin his beaver, cut off the tail, and hang it on a stick by the fire to roast. The heat, he found, peeled off the skin, leaving the meat ready for his eager appetite. Joe could not tell whether beavertail tasted more like marrow or boiled perch—though it was more oily than either. Anyhow, he found it mighty tasty, as good as any meat he had eaten in the mountains so far.

But the men could not subsist on beavertail alone. They dressed the whole carcass and hung it up by the fire on a thong. Twisting this thong, they soon set the beaver turning by his own weight until the flesh was nicely roasted.

So day after day, Joe set his traps until the beaver along

that stream became wary, were "up to trap" and could not be "brought to medicine." Then the men abandoned the "medicine" and set their traps at the foot of beaver slides, in runways, and the subterranean passages leading to the lodge. Thus they caught a few, but soon found their traps empty and moved on to another part of the stream or over the divide to another stream.

Meanwhile in camp, their camp keepers stretched the fresh beaverskins, all ruddy on the flesh side, on hoops eighteen inches to three feet across, depending on the size of the hide, and hung them out in the sun to dry. The whole camp was decorated with those red disks, trophies of a successful hunt.

Back at the main camp in Pierre's Hole, Joe learned that the partners had finally yielded to Jedediah Smith's demand. Captain Bill Sublette gave in "for the present." However, "the present," according to Sublette, did not begin at once; since certainly some of the men made their fall hunt that year west of the Divide. All agreed that winter quarters should be on Wind River. They all packed up to make the fall hunt in American territory.

Sublette himself planned to go up Henry's Fork of Snake River towards the North Pass to Missouri Lake, where the Madison Fork of the Missouri River rises. There would be plenty of beaver on Henry's Fork, and (Joe Meek hoped) on all the streams from there on. All that was dangerous Blackfoot country, much of it unexplored. And even before the camp on the forks of the Snake could pull out, Joe had his baptism of fire—his first Indian fight.

It was early one morning, still twilight, when Meek heard the call to turn out. He was just ready to loosen the lariats and hobbles of his mules when he heard a high-pitched yelp, a chorus of war whoops, the banging of fusees close at hand, and the beat of hoofs on the hard, dry prairie, coming on the run. While Joe clung to the lariat of his rearing mule, he saw the flash of gunfire, the ragged silhouette of a hundred warriors, half-hidden in white powder smoke, tear by, waving blankets as they tried to stampede the horses.

As the smoke drifted away, Joe saw that most of the horses were still hobbled and staked out securely. As it happened, some that had broken loose, terrified by the noise, the smoke, and the smell of the Indians, came tearing right back into the trappers' camp and were caught. The Blackfeet had jumped the camp a little too quick. Had they waited a few minutes longer until all the animals had been turned loose, they might have swept off the whole herd.

It was all over in a moment, before Joe knew what to do, or could do anything but hang on to his mule. As suddenly as they had come, the Indians were gone.

By that time Tom Fitzpatrick was yelling to his men from the bare back of his best horse, leading them out to circle the camp on a dead run and head back the strays which had jerked up their pickets. All the way as Tom rode yelling, the Indians kept popping at him. Joe saw Tom's horse go down. But no! At once Tom was up again, caught another animal, and dashed on after the stock. While Joe watched, tying his mule securely, hammering down the picket and setting his triggers, he saw Tom unhorsed again. But Tom, undaunted, kept on with his men and brought back the loose horses under the very gun muzzles of the Blackfeet. It was as daring as anything Meek had ever seen.

Then, leaving camp keepers to guard the animals, all the trappers put out afoot to l'arn the pesky Blackfeet who that country belonged to. The warriors, now seen to be one hundred or more in number, quickly took cover in a narrow gulch near by—no easy place to storm. Disgruntled by their ill success, the angry Blackfeet fought off all attacks of the mountain men, who did not attempt a charge. Joe Meek, lying among the rocks with the rest, set his triggers and watched his chance to fire at the puffs of white powder smoke which bloomed from time to time along the gulch, hoping to "bring an Injun." He knew his heavy rifle was a heap better than a light fusee, but could not tell whether he hit anyone or not. One thing sure—the Blackfeet hit two of the whites.

Still Joe stuck to his post, hot, tired, thirsty, his shoulder sore from the kick of his gun, through what seemed the longest day of his life. He could not believe it was still only about noon when the fight ended. After the Blackfeet pulled out through the canyon, Meek was among those who entered it to inspect their position. The Indians had carried off their dead and wounded—if any. Meek, however, was lucky enough to pick up a trophy—a pair of moccasins some brave had dropped. Joe naturally thought the rest of the day would be spent in idleness. But Captain Sublette soon put his tired men to work building a big pole corral to hold the stock that night. The Captain's anxious scowl and elaborate precautions seemed foolish to Meek. None of the trappers had been killed. Joe felt sure they had seen the last of the redskins. And he found that building a corral big enough to hold all those animals was some job.

After supper, when night fell, Joe relaxed about the fire with the others. At about eight o'clock the booshway came around to tell Joe, who was about to turn in for the night, that he was detailed for guard duty. When his watch came and they awakened him, Joe and an old-timer named Reese took up their blankets and rifles and stumbled to the far side of the camp.

Both were tired out. It was cold that night—and a guard could not hang around a fire. The intervals between the booshway's warning call, "All's well"—a call every guard repeated around the camp to prove he was alert—dragged on interminably under the slow stars. The first thing Meek knew, Reese was sound asleep. By this time Meek knew better than to advise an old-timer; he did not disturb Reese. It seemed simpler—and smarter maybe—to follow suit. The horses seemed safe enough in the corral. Joe snuggled down into his blanket and closed his eyes.

The next thing Joe knew, he heard Sublette snorting and swearing, coming round the corral to inspect the guard—mad as a wet hen.

Joe saw his beaver going up in blue smoke. He wondered how big a fine the booshway would put on him. One thing was sure, a guard caught napping would have to walk all the next day—and maybe carry his saddle too. Joe guessed at once that the Captain's last call, "All's well," had not been answered.

But as Sublette came a-r'aring up, Joe heard Reese, that sly old-timer, call to the Captain in a loud whisper, "Down, Billy! Injuns!"

Suddenly Sublette's tall figure vanished as he bellied down beside Reese. Meek heard him answer, "Where? Where?"

Reese whispered back reproachfully, "They war right thar when you hollered so."

Still angry, Sublette demanded defensively, "Where's Meek?"

Raising his voice a little so Meek could hear, Reese replied, "He's trying to shoot one."

Before Sublette could move to see what Meek was doing, Reese hastily crawled over to Joe to make sure that Joe was awake—and knew what was up.

Meek crawled carefully back to Sublette. The Captain demanded to know how many Injuns were out there.

Joe said, "I cain't make out just how many thar are, Captain."

Then there was a time of watchful waiting. But at last Sublette went back to bed. From then on Joe and

Reese kept their eyes peeled and their thoughts busy. They weren't out of the woods yet. Come sunup the Captain was sure to look for Blackfoot sign around camp, and if he found none, there might be hell to pay.

But then Joe remembered the pair of Blackfoot moccasins he had in his possible sack. Before daylight, he sneaked them out and tossed them away on the far side of camp where somebody would be bound to look.

Sure enough. When, soon after sunup, the horse guard found the moccasins and brought them to Sublette, the booshway publicly praised the two poker-faced guards for their vigilance the night before.

Lost in the Snow

THE BRIGADE pressed on, into and through the endless forests they called the Pine Woods; fine scenery, but few trails. But with snow falling and more snow to come, those magnificent mountains seemed merely so many big rocks in their way. It was already November when they left Missouri Lake, crossing that rough and broken country beyond the Gallatin Fork. At length they reached the high ridge overlooking the valley not far from Cinnabar Mountain,[1] and crossed the Yellowstone River.

There they made camp, to rest a few days on the riverbank, for both men and animals were nearly played out. Luckily, as was usual in winter, the Blackfoot war party was afoot.

But that halt gave the Blackfeet time to catch up. Meanwhile the hired trapper, Joe Meek, was sent hunting. Game was scarce in that snowy wilderness, and he rode out some distance on his weary mule. Finding nothing, he was heading back to camp when he heard a great banging of guns and yelling in that direction. Joe

---

[1] Though Meek, as quoted by Mrs. Victor, does not name this mountain, I have followed the authoritative suggestion of Hiram Martin Chittenden as to Meek's route, as given in his book *The Yellowstone National Park* (Cincinnati, 1903), Chapter V.

hurried to a bunch of pines where he could see towards the river.

The camp was in confusion, with animals running about and much white powder smoke drifting against the dark pines. The Blackfeet were all around his comrades. Joe knew he could not reach them. Before long he saw Sublette and the others hightail it out of there, with the redskins hot on their trail.

So there he was, cut off from his friends by Bug's Boys, who were dogging Sublette. He could never fight through the Blackfeet to rejoin his fellows—that was certain. He thought he would follow along as soon as it was safe and try to reach them.

But even a greenhorn like Joe soon realized that to ride on the trail of that camp was sure death. He was on his own hook now. The question was—what to do?

It was bitter cold. The ground was covered with snow, blotting out the trails. Joe didn't know straight up about that tangled country. He had no food with him, and had not seen hide nor hair of game all morning. And with all those Blackfeet in the country, he would have been scared to fire his rifle if there had been an elk under every tree.

Joe forked his mule and quirted the weary animal farther into the hills. There he led it into the thick brush and tied it securely.

"Keep your nose open, old gal. Thar's red skin hyar abouts."

Then Joe warily climbed the nearest hill to take a peek and lay his course to safety.

From the top he could see the Yellowstone River, up which that running fight had disappeared. Every other stream and every mountain within view—and there were plenty—was equally unknown to Joe. He stared and stared, but saw no sign of trappers or trails in all that snowy welter. The scenery was magnificent, and Joe had a taste for the beauties of unspoiled nature. But now, out in the middle of that freezing wilderness, with blood-thirsty enemies all around him and his friends skedaddling to God-knows-where, Joe had no time for admiration.

There he stood, cold and shivering, hungry as a bear in spring, lost, scairt and lonesome. Just then his heart was mighty small and lying on the ground. Joe was only nineteen years old.

If any of the boys had been there to see him he might have kept his feelings under. But now he just let go and busted out crying.

It did him good, and he soon felt better. Anyhow, he said to himself, it was too cold to stand up thar bawlin' over the fix he was in. His heart was stronger as he turned and headed downhill to the thicket where his mule was tied. One thing was sartain sure—wharever Sublette and the boys were headin', it warn't no deeper into Black-footland!

Joe remembered that Sublette had declared his winter quarters would be on Wind River. That would be some-where south, in the country of the Crows. This Blackfoot country was bitter cold.

But cold as it might be, it was now too hot to hold him. He must head south along the Yellowstone, but to avoid the Blackfeet he decided to keep well away from the river.

It was pitch dark by the time he reached his nervous mule. Though chilled to the bone, Joe dared not light a fire, and he knew he would surely freeze, lying or sitting in the snow. Stiffly he climbed aboard and kicked the old gal into a walk. Neither one knew where they were going. But all night long they blundered among the pines, sliding and stumbling over rocks and fallen trees, plunging down hills, scrambling up again. Joe took the precaution of tying the end of the mule's trail rope round his waist, so that when the animal fell or a bough swept him from the saddle, he could wind up the rope and get into the saddle once more. Some how mule and man got through that miserable night without parting company.

When daybreak came at last, Joe guessed he hadn't made thirty miles on a very crooked course, but he was still on the east side of the Yellowstone. And with the morning sun he felt a little easier. After all, he still had his mule, his rifle, his knife, his flint and steel. Those little fixin's made a man feel right peart, all alone in the snow amongst the wild Injuns.

But as Joe rode on, keeping to the timber, covering the trail as best he could, dreary mile after dreary mile, he saw nary sign of meat. The bears already slept snug in their winter hideouts; elk and deer and sheep had left the high ground for better grazing below. The cold kept small game snuggled in their holes and forms, and nary a bird flew over big enough to eat. Even if Joe had seen game he didn't dare shoot it, much less build a fire to cook: one rifle shot or one puff of smoke would surely bring Bug's Boys swarming on his trail. Joe warn't ready to swap his hair for one square meal yit!

For two days he plodded on. Apparently his trail lay some distance from, but more or less parallel to, the course of the Yellowstone River. In all that time neither Joe nor his mule had had a bite to eat. For drink, Joe could eat snow, but the frozen streams provided no water for the mule. Finally the stumbling animal balked and stood weaving in the snow. Kicks and blows fell unheeded on its gaunt ribs. It could go no farther.

Joe Meek's recollections, as recorded by Mrs. Victor in *The River of the West*, might have made a better book if that first biographer had been a man instead of a woman. It is evident that the presence of the lady somewhat cramped Joe's style, sometimes tempting him to stretch the blanket "a leetle too fur," and at other times to pull his punches and avoid raw details.

Joe told Mrs. Victor that after he and the mule had gone hungry for two days he "abandoned" the animal.

Some have scoffed at this story, declaring that no mountain man, after carrying empty paunch for two freezing days through the snow, would have left the mule alive. Any mountain man, they say, would have cut its throat and stayed his hunger with the raw flesh. In that bitter cold the meat would not spoil, and what a man could pack along would keep him going until he was safely rid of the red devils. Moreover, they say, no mountain man would leave a live mule behind for the Blackfeet to pick up.

Yet Joe's story is probable. He was a young fellow, without experience of such emergencies or any real bitterness against Indians—as yet. Probably he felt sorry for his poor mule, long companion of his wanderings, and never dreamed of killing it.

Moreover, that mule belonged to Bill Sublette, his booshway, who might turn up to reclaim it. Then what?

Next day Joe plodded south another twenty miles, or what seemed like twenty miles, over rough country. Towards evening his heart leaped up to behold a band of mountain sheep. So far he had seen no sign of Injuns. Might as well be scalped as starve to death. It was now or never. His old shootin' iron threw a fat ewe, and the long days of fasting were over.

Warmed by his campfire, filled with fat meat, Joe rolled up in his blanket and had a good night's sleep, until at daybreak a cold north wind drove him to action.

With the wind at his back Joe hurried on, lugging all the mountain mutton he could carry. He had never seen so much empty country. He got so lonesome he would almost have welcomed a hostile Blackfoot, just for company.

At the end of his fourth day Joe made camp in a deep gulch, out of the wind, where his fire of dry sticks would not show. Again he roasted meat and had a good sleep. After breakfast next day he felt like himself again, and climbed the nearest hill to take a look around. It was a sharp, clear, frosty morning.

Before Joe had run off to the mountains, the preacher at home had warned him that some day civilization and Hell would surely catch up with him. Yet when Joe took one look from that hilltop, he was astonished. He hadn't expected Hell would catch up with him first!

Far as he could see ahead, that whole level rolling country was smoking and fuming, with burning gases and vapor rising from huge boiling springs. Geysers whistled and belched, tossing their spume and scalding waters far into the air.

It minded Joe of that smoky town, Pittsburgh, Pennsylvania. But Pittsburgh was small potatoes compared to this steaming, boiling plain, stretching for miles and dotted with cone-shaped mounds and large craters or basins, then vomiting—it seemed to Joe—blue flames and molten brimstone.

Joe said to himself, as he stood there shivering with cold, "I have been told the sun would be blown out, and the earth burnt up. If this infernal wind keeps up, I shouldn't be surprised if the sun *war* blown out. And if the earth is *not* burning up over thar, then it *is* that place the old Methodist preacher used to threaten me with. Anyway it suits me to go and see what it's like."

Joe went downhill to explore the roof of Hell. Underfoot the earth sounded hollow, and in places the crust broke under him and each track he left behind quickly filled with boiling water.

There was no cover and no game in that bare, steaming country.

But after the freezing cold of the mountains, Joe found

the warmth delightful. He said to himself, "If this *is* Hell, it's a heap better climate than the one I just left."

Joe Meek had reached the hot springs country in what is now Yellowstone Park.

Standing there in the open, looking round him at many marvels, suddenly Joe heard a shot fired—then another—then an Injun whoop! Thar he stood right out in the open, in hot water agin!

Hardly knowing whether to run or throw himself down for a stand-off fight, he heard someone yell, "It *is* old Joe!" He looked around and saw he had found his *compaueros*.

Two seasoned trappers out scouting for him came up, grasped his hands, slapped him on the back. As Joe told of his hard scrape and how he had pulled through, he sensed a new respect in them. He might still be just a hired trapper, but he had rubbed the green off. The other men didn't say much, but treated him like an equal. For the first time they had called him "old" Joe. That made his heart big.

They told Joe the Blackfeet had killed two of his comrades in that attack on the camp beside the Yellowstone.

Joe went with them towards Sublette's camp. Three days later, they caught up with it.

Colter's Hell

MEEK FOUND Sublette's camp in the Absaroka Mountains. They were heading for the plains along the Big Horn River.

Joe thought he had seen hard times while wandering alone. But now he found the whole brigade starving. There was not a bite of meat in camp, and no game in that high country. In the passes the snow lay deep. Men had to break trail for the wallowing animals. Meek took his turn with the others. Leading the march was heavy, back-breaking work—especially as neither man nor beast had anything to eat.

Yet, no matter how hard they worked, they made only a few hundred yards a day, and one by one the mules and then the gaunt horses began to flounder and founder in the endless drifts.

Day after day it was the same—only worse. Even small game was hardly to be found.

However, Jedediah Smith strictly maintained his mild, Christian manner. Though he rarely censured, he never could approve the profane language of his employees.

Diah had with him a slave, a Negro boy, whom he treated with the same consideration he gave white men. One day that boy was the luckiest fellow in the brigade. Scouting through the trees he spied a porcupine in one of them, climbed up, knocked it down with a stick, and came lugging his spiny prize to camp.

That was the first wild meat anyone had seen in days. The grinning Negro gutted the carcass and laid it flat on its back on hot coals. Then he squatted alongside to watch the fire burn off the quills and roast the rich fat meat for dinner.

Meek, now feeling his oats, was ready for any deviltry that might win a laugh from his comrades. The odor of that rich, dark red, roasting meat floated through the starving camp. It was more than Meek and Reese could stand. Watching their chance, they waited until the boy happened to turn from his fire to watch something going on in the camp. Then the two of them, careless of burned fingers, snatched the roast and ran off among the dark pine trees.

It did not take long for them and their ravenous friends to make away with the half-roasted porcupine. They felt hungry enough to eat the quills too, if the fire had not destroyed them. As it was, the fat scorched skin of the animal was rich and tasty as bacon rind.

By the time the boy discovered his loss and began to holler, there was nothing left to holler about. The poor lad suspected Meek and Reese. But no white man there would peach on another, "to save a nigger's rights." The boy never really knew who had robbed him. All who shared in the feast found Meek's theft amusing.

One mean trick inspires another. One day Craig, a trapper, caught a rabbit, skinned it and hung it up on a stick to roast before the fire. Seeing that Craig showed no intention of sharing his meat, some of the boys decided to see how it tasted. Someone called out that the booshway wanted to talk to Craig. Completely taken in, he left his rabbit at the fire and walked over to the booshway's lodge. By the time he discovered the hoax and ran back, his rabbit was gone.

Furious, Craig whipped out his Green River and swore he would cut the rabbit out of the stomach that held it. His difficulty lay in discovering the guilty stomach. Naturally enough, since Meek had stolen the porcupine, Craig suspected him. But Meek insisted he was not the guilty man. After many blistering threats Craig had to give up, put up his knife, and go to bed without his supper.

For, after snatching the porcupine, Meek had become ashamed of his trick, and always described it as "the meanest act of my life."

Jedediah Smith apparently shared Meek's opinion, for when he reached St. Louis the next summer he gave the little slave his freedom and a present of two hundred dollars, so that it became a saying in the mountains that the Negro "got his freedom for a porcupine."

Within a few days the Rocky Mountain Fur Company lost a hundred head of mules and horses, which fell exhausted one by one in the drifts and could not get up again. When the train had floundered past, Meek or some other would go back, shoot the fallen animal and butcher it for food.

Looked like they would *never* get out of those mountains. One day Diah sent Black Harris to climb a high peak near by, take a look, and find out where they were.

Harris was "a free and easy soul, especially with a belly full." But it was a long, hard scramble to the top; a bitter wind was blowing, and he came back down cold, empty, tired and surly.

Anxiously Smith asked, in his mild accents, "Well, Harris, what did you see?"

Regardless of Smith's scruples, Harris swore a mighty oath. Then bitterly he declared, "I saw the city of St. Louis—and a feller takin' a drink!"

Whether Smith took Harris' hint about the grog is not of record. Nobody knew where they were, or even where they had been. But they did know that going downhill might take them where they were going.

And so at last, without the loss of a man, the brigade came to the forks of the Shoshone River. Because of its sulphurous waters the stream was then known as the "Stinking Water," and all that volcanic region was known to the trappers as "Colter's Hell," after John Colter, who had first traversed it.

They wasted no time in that unsavory region, but pushed on to the Big Horn River. There, after some scouting, they found Milton Sublette with his trappers comfortably encamped.

Even then, they had so few animals that the Sublettes decided to cache their furs where they were and then go into winter quarters.

It was hard digging in that frozen ground, but eventually, at the foot of a high cut bank, they dug out a hole like a well, six feet deep and big enough for a man to stand in and swing a pick. Taking turns standing in this hole, the hands excavated a hole back under the cut bank, a room big enough to pack their furs in, stowed on a floor of poles. Then they packed the door tight with poles and earth, climbed out, and filled the "well," tramping down the tight-packed earth.

After that they built a big fire where the hole had been dug, and then tied horses over the cold ashes, hoping by these means to conceal all signs of digging. Luckily no redskins turned up until the job was completed.

They had hardly cached the furs until someone yelled "Injuns!" and a war party was seen on the ridge. Some of the men cried "Shoot! Shoot!"

But Sublette soon stopped that, made signs of peace and beckoned the Crows to come in. The chiefs and the booshways smoked the long pipe together. Sublette gave the Indians a twist of tobacco as a pledge of good will, and the Crows rode away.

Then the combined camps traveled through the snow to Wind River, the name given the headwaters of the Big Horn River. The booshways were well satisfied with their fall hunt. Besides, they had explored a new route into that rich fur country west of the Rockies on which Bill Sublette kept his eye.

Bitter cold it was when they made camp at winter quarters. But it was Christmas, and they celebrated as best they could with what cheer the Captain provided and such game as they could kill.

As for Captain Sublette himself, he made snowshoes and set out for St. Louis afoot with Black Harris. A horse was no good for fast travel on the snowy plains. They carried their plunder in packs on wolflike Indian dogs. There was one thing Meek could say for Bill Sublette: he was always ready for the toughest and most dangerous job of all.

After the Captain left, things went from bad to worse. The weather grew ever colder, and there was no more game on Wind River. Dave Jackson cached his furs, then he and Smith left winter quarters, heading for buffalo country on Powder River. That was no time of year to be traveling a hundred and fifty miles through the Big Horn Mountains and over wind-bitten prairies. But they made it.

Their nearest way would be through the pass between the present towns of Ten Sleep and Buffalo.

The snow was too deep for those gaunt mules and ponies to paw it away and find enough grass to keep them going. The men fed their animals on cottonwood bark, felling trees along the frozen streams and chopping up the pale smooth limbs into short lengths like firewood. Then, sitting by the fire, they pulled out their skinning knives and, holding a chunk between their knees, pulled the blade towards them like a drawknife to shave off the sweet green bark, which they carried to the animals

in a blanket. Some horses could peel a chunk of cottonwood themselves, holding it down with one forefoot and
gnawing it as a dog gnaws a bone. The animals gained
flesh as if they had been fed on oats; soon they were all
seal-fat.

But in that bitter winter, while the cottonwood groves
helped shelter the camp and feed the ponies, Meek found
it had other advantages. Buffalo kept swarming in for
shelter, bringing their meat to the very doors of the
lodges. There they could be shot down and butchered,
and their meat prepared, without once using a pack
saddle. That winter, Powder River was a hunter's paradise, where a man could live fat and keep sassy.

In fact, buffalo became such a nuisance that the booshways had to station guards to keep them out of camp.
Wherever buffalo were, that was the place for redskins,
and they soon came riding to join the trappers. What of
that? There was meat aplenty, and the redskins brought
along their women.

In an Indian camp there was never any lack of fun.
Every night the thump of tomtoms and the *shish-shish*
of rattles could be heard under the high-pitched Indian
singsong and the whoops and yelps of warriors and trappers, dancing in some big lodge, or maybe in the open
on the moonlit snow. And when there was no dancing,
there were always the taunting chants and chances of
the Hand game, while the two teams faced each other,
making their bets, trying to guess whose hand held the
"button," in a clamor and excitement that might last the
night out.

Through the day hunters were going and coming,
camp keepers butchering, cooking, drying meat, or
making moccasins. Men were cleaning their weapons,
wrestling, jumping, racing, playing games, smoking with
Indian men or making friends with their daughters. At
night they told marvelous tales of adventure around the

bright fires, and sang old songs in chorus. Some, better educated than others, read or recited passages from their favorite authors. Jedediah Smith had, besides the Bible, nearly twenty books in his library.

So Joe Meek did not spend all his time dancing, "singing Injun," gambling, bragging, or shooting at a mark. By this time he realized how handicapped he was by his lack of book l'arnin'. Joe was ambitious, and he didn't aim to let any man have the better of him. In camp he discovered a dog-eared copy of Shakespeare and a worn Bible. He paid a fellow named Green to l'arn him, and afore the winter was out he could read Shakespeare, leastways whar the lingo warn't too highfalutin'. The old Elizabethan language rang familiarly in the ears of a Virginia mountaineer.

Bible stories gave Joe something to think about, too. Them old patriarchs, he found, had as many wives as a Crow chief, and the wisest man of all, King Solomon, had more than ary one of 'em!

Besides the reading, Joe heard many a debate and discussion—of history; of the internal politics or international relations of this tribe or that, which chief or band was rising to power, which losing it; of the geography of the mountains, the passes, trails, and hunting grounds.

About the first of April, 1830, the camp divided into companies and they set out on the spring hunt. Dave Jackson took half the men and started for the territory of the Snake Indians.

Jedediah Smith led the rest, with Jim ("Old Gabe") Bridger for pilot or guide. Meek traveled with them.

They headed straight for that rich fur country of the hostile Blackfeet!

Buried Alive

JOE WAS glad to be off on the spring hunt. There
was sure to be plenty fur in Blackfoot country, and,
like enough, plenty buffalo, elk, and b'ar. By this time
he knew the routine. Since such a large camp cleaned
out the beaver and scared off the game from any one
valley in a few days' time, the camp was always on the
move, even when meat was plenty. Hunters and trappers,
knowing the direction the camp would take, could ride
out, clean out a beaver colony, and be back with their
comrades within two or three days. If they saw sign of
Bug's Boys, they spent every night in the main camp.

At first the weather was fine, but on Bovey's[1] Fork of
the Big Horn River they were caught in a heavy fall of
snow which slowed them up and, when it melted, suddenly filled all the streams bankfull. They might have
waited to let the rise go down. But the booshway was in
a hurry.

The stream hardly seemed wide enough to require
bullboats. The company tried to swim their pack animals
over. But the water was deep, swift, cold. Thirty head
of horses were swept away and drowned, with the loss of
all the plunder on their saddles. The horses and the

---

1 Correctly, *Beauvais*.

furs could be replaced, but there were no beaver traps nearer than St. Louis, and in this disaster the party lost three hundred—a loss of three thousand dollars. Luckily no man was drowned.

The loss of the traps meant that the men would sometimes have to drain the dams, break open the lodges and kill the beaver with clubs. Even the hard-boiled, seasoned trapper sometimes hated that. Meek found it a tough assignment.

"They are the most harmless things in the world. Catch a beaver and touch it and it will just turn up its head; a little one will just turn up and cry like a little baby. I hated to kill them, but, says I, 'It's five dollars.' Sometimes I would take them out and put them in my pocket and take them to camp. They are just as nice as any pet in the world.[1]"

In fact the booshway, Jedediah Smith, kept a dozen live beaver kittens in camp. His favorite pet wore a red collar and a chain. The Negro boy looked after them. One day Red Collar disappeared. Hastily Jedediah assembled his eighty trappers and announced, "Boys, whoever gets that beaver will have ten pounds of coffee, ten pounds of sugar, and two pints of rum!"

For bait like that the boys hunted beaver as never before, but the little fellow with the red collar was too slick for them. He was never found.

Smith's brigade kept moving, passed through Pryor's Gap to Clark's Fork of the Yellowstone and on to Rosebud River.[2] They followed it down to its mouth, where it flows into Yellowstone River.

One day Joe, Mark Head and Mitchell were out to-

---

1 See, Maurice S. Sullivan, *Jedediah Smith, Trader and Trail Breaker* (New York, 1936) , p. 203.

2 This refers, of course, to the Rosebud River which flows into the Yellowstone above Clark's Fork, a stream formed by the Big Rosebud and the Little Rosebud, and not to the Rosebud River far down, which flows into the Yellowstone below the Big Horn River.

gether on the Rosebud. Having set their traps, they shot a fat buffalo cow and, after eating all they could hold, made camp on the snow in a grove of young aspens. They divided the remaining choice cuts, put these, for safety from wild varmints, where they would serve as pillows, and got into their bedrolls. Their loaded rifles, of course, lay in their blankets alongside them.

Full of beef, they slept soundly under the frosty stars. Just as day broke, Joe dreamed that something heavy was walking over him, snuffing in his ears. Suddenly he wakened to find that the creature standing over him was no dream, but a grizzly bear after the buffalo meat under Joe's head.

"You may be sure," says Joe, "that I kept very quiet, while that b'ar helped himself to some of my buffalo meat, and went a little way off to eat it. But Mark Head, one of the men, raised up, and back came the b'ar. Down went our heads under the blankets, and I kept mine covered pretty snug, while the beast took another walk over the bed, but finally went off again to a little distance. Mitchell then wanted to shoot; but I said, 'No, no; hold on, or the brute will kill us, sure.' When the b'ar heard our voices, back he run again, and jumped on the bed as before. I'd have been happy to have felt myself sinking ten feet under ground, while that b'ar promenaded over and around us! However, he couldn't quite make out our style, and finally took fright, and ran off down the mountain."[1]

"Don't tread on me" was Joe's motto. After such a scare and so much tromping, he could not wait to get even. Joe grabbed his rifle and went after him. When the bear slowed up, Joe drew a bead and threw him cold.

"Then," says Joe, "I took my turn at running over *him* a while!"

---

[1] Unless credited to some other source, passages quoted in this book are taken from *The River of the West* by Mrs. Frances Fuller Victor. S.V.

Indians might swim the gray waters of the Yellowstone when it was rushing bankfull with melting snows, but after Smith's lesson on Bovey's Fork, the booshway decided to ferry his goods across that glittering and resolute stream and let the animals swim bareback. Accordingly the hunters rode out and brought back raw buffalo hides to make bullboats.

These hides they sewed together and stretched over stout frameworks or baskets of willow sticks lashed together with rawhide, smearing the seams with elk tallow and ashes. Such a bullboat would carry the heavy plunder.

The rest they ferried over in a lodge-skin float. They spread the lodge skin on the ground and put light articles, saddles and war bags in the middle. A rope was then run through the holes in the edge of the tent (made for tent pegs) and then drawn up like a purse or reticule into a regular ball. The women piled the children on top and swam behind, pushing, while a man hanging onto his horse's mane and with the end of the rope in his teeth towed the whole shebang across.

Smith got all his plunder and animals across that swift river in less than an hour.

Now they were across the Yellowstone, in the country of the Blackfeet. The booshway tightened up discipline and rode to the Musselshell River and so on to Judith River, both tributaries of the Missouri. Plenty beaver, plenty buffalo—and plenty Blackfeet!—so many that a man hardly dared leave camp to set or raise his traps. The brigade was pestered by continual raids and thieving, daily losing traps and horses until Smith, unable to do any hunting and tired of that endless warfare, ordered an about-face and headed south again.

Joe and his friends were ready enough. They had made a big hunt and had heavy packs of furs which they were eager to take to rendezvous. And every day they stuck around in Blackfootland they ran a great risk of losing all their beaver—and their own topknots!

So back they went through Pryor's Gap and up the Big Horn to Wind River, to the cache made the winter before. Tullock was sent to raise the cache on the Big Horn while Diah was busy pressing his furs for packing to the settlements. Meek and a Frenchman "named Ponto" were among those who followed Tullock.

The men went to digging to get out the furs. In their turn Meek and Ponto got into the hole under the big cut bank and dug away. Suddenly Meek heard a yell of warning, and looked up. The whole bank was crashing down upon him.

There was no time to get out of the hole. He could only throw up his arms and stagger back against the wall of the excavation as tons of earth and gravel crushed the breath from his body and flattened him where he stood.

After that Joe did not remember anything until he found himself lying in the open, gasping for breath, with his comrades standing around. He was sore all over and weak as a cat. But no bones were broken, and when the furs were finally dug out the men spread him on a buffalo robe, picked up the corners, and carried him to camp.

Ponto, who had been taken out dead, was "rolled in a blanket and pitched into the river."

When Meek was able to travel, the party packed him back to the main camp, bringing in the furs.

That summer of 1830 rendezvous was on the head-waters of Wind River, probably not far from South Pass —perhaps on Popo Agie. The winter before the boosh-ways had decided on the daring plan of hauling their goods from the settlements in freight wagons, and all the trappers were anxious to see if Bill Sublette could really make it. So far nary a wagon had ever rolled into that wilderness.

But sure enough, when Captain Sublette turned up

about the middle of July, 1830 thar they war—ten spanking big schooners, behind their five-mule teams, every wagon loaded chockablock with 1800 pounds of goods for the fur fair of the trappers. The Captain had two fancy Dearborn carriages along, four head of beef cattle —and a milch cow! Looked like civilization would catch up with Joe yit.

Sublette had brought two hundred new hands along, and from them the mountain men soon learned all about the trip out. The wagons had left St. Louis early in April, crossed the Kaw River, rolled up the Platte, the Sweetwater, and so to rendezvous. They had killed and eaten eight steers on the way to buffalo country.[1] The rest they had brought safely through.

Meanwhile the trappers and their women waited impatiently for the goods to be unloaded, trading their furs to buy a new rifle at fifty dollars, a pair of blankets at twenty-five, a pound of tobacco or of coffee at two dollars, a gallon of rum for twenty, and as much powder, lead, sugar, red cloth, face paint, wire—as many mirrors, beads, files, rings, handkerchiefs, shirts and all such fixin's as they could wangle credit for.

When the trading and carousing were over, the partners of the Rocky Mountain Fur Company sold out, taking a note for some fifteen thousand dollars signed by the new booshways: Tom "Broken Hand" Fitzpatrick, Milton Sublette, Henry Fraeb (or Frapp, as the trappers called him), Jean Baptiste Gervais, and Jim "Old Gabe" Bridger.

It was high time. The American Fur Company, chartered by John Jacob Astor, was moving into the mountains, determined to monopolize the trade. From its new trading post, later called Fort Union, at the mouth of

---

[1] See Hiram M. Chittenden, *The American Fur Trade of the Far West* (New York, 1935), p. 294. Also see the letter written in 1830 by Smith, Jackson and Sublette to the Honorable Secretary of War, John H. Eaton, at Washington, which gives route followed by wagon caravan.

Yellowstone, it was about to send Jacob Berger to open trade with the Blackfeet, and was preparing to build Fort Piegan at the mouth of the Marias, where the Blackfeet could buy guns and ammunition.

Early in August Bill Sublette, Dave Jackson and Jedediah Smith loaded their furs, 190 packs of beaver, worth fully seventy-five thousand dollars, into the empty wagons and hit the trail for the settlements. The trappers who had harvested those furs gave the three a rousing cheer as they put out, for their old booshways had worked and suffered like the others, and there was no envy in the men at their success.

Indeed, Meek and many another of the trappers left behind were luckier than the men with the wagons.

Back they went into that dangerous Blackfoot country for the fall hunt. It was too rich in furs to be let alone. They moved north through the Big Horn Basin and crossed the Yellowstone River. This time there were two hundred men in camp, more than Bug's Boys cared to tackle in pitched battle.

The brigade went on to the Great Falls of the Missouri, then headed south to Three Forks, and up the Jefferson Fork to the continental divide. They were making a good hunt. Beaver and other game were plentiful.

Now that Jedediah Smith was no longer a partner of the Rocky Mountain Fur Company, there was no one to object to their hunting on the west side of the mountains. The new booshways held all that region to be American territory. They were unwilling to share it with trappers of the Hudson's Bay Company, who were rapidly stripping the streams of beaver. Accordingly the new booshways crossed the Divide, led their men down the west side of the mountains to the forks of Snake River, and some time later went on south to Ogden's Hole, a beautiful, sheltered cove in the mountains on the northeast shore of Great Salt Lake.

There, sure enough, they found Peter Skene Ogden with a brigade of Jonathan Work's trappers of the Hudson's Bay Company. Each party resented the presence of the other.

The Fight for Fur

OGDEN'S HOLE on the shores of Great Salt Lake was a long, long way from the western head quarters of the Hudson's Bay Company at Fort Vancouver on the north bank of the Columbia River. But the boundary between the British possessions and American territory had not yet been determined. The Oregon country was to be jointly occupied until the boundary was fixed, and the British expected that boundary to run down the middle of the Columbia River. While the country was jointly occupied, the Americans saw no reason why they should not hunt south of the river.

From the beginning the Hudson's Bay Company conserved the fur-bearing animals in their territory, never taking or buying more peltry than the year's increase. But for some years past they had been alarmed by the presence of American trappers in Oregon. Jedediah Smith had managed to obtain furs from Hudson's Bay Company trappers on Snake River as early as 1824, and in 1825 orders had come to Governor Simpson from the Company, directing him to "work the southern portion of the country as hard as possible, while it continues free to subjects (sic) of both nations." Again, in 1827, the Company wrote to Sir George Simpson: "It is extremely desireable to hunt as bare as possible all the country south of the Columbia and west of the mountains."[1] And when Jedediah Smith turned up at Fort Vancouver to report the massacre of his men on the Umpqua River, the Hudson's Bay Company really became alarmed. The Americans were hunting and exploring west of the Cascade Mountains and along the Columbia, even in California! The British policy of killing off all the game animals in southern Oregon only incited the Americans to hunt farther north. And when it came to cleaning out beaver from a given area, nobody could compare with the American mountain man. He was not interested in conservation; he wanted to make a killing and quit.

And so they found Ogden, trapping on that British mission with his Cree and Rockaway Indians, busy as a buffalo's tail in fly-time.[2]

Ogden was a person of high moral character, but ruthless in competing for furs. He had no reason to love Americans, though once employed by Astor, since——though born in Canada—he was descended from an American refugee royalist. So, carrying out his orders,[3] he had moved far into what American trappers regarded as their own territory, methodically killing every beaver in his path. When Meek and his comrades ran into Ogden that year, they found his packs bulging with rich furs.

Tom Fitzpatrick knew that Ashley had got the better

---

1 See Frederick Merk, *Fur Trade and Empire* (Massachusetts, 1932, pp. 252, 286.

2 Rockaway (Regawihaki, "Sandyland") Indians, a tribe formerly living about Rockaway and Hempstead, on the southern shore of Long Island, New York. They formed a local division of the Lenape or Delaware Indians of southern New York. By 1770 most of them had moved to Indiana or Canada, and about 1835 to a reservation in Kansas. The Delawares were numerous among employees of the fur companies, and the Bureau of American Ethnology reports "It is quite possible that some of them [the Rockaways] were in the employ of the Hudson's Bay Company." Some of those with Ogden appear to have been of mixed blood.

3 Some surmise that Ogden's encounter with Fitzpatrick took place in 1829, not 1830. We follow Meek here.

of Ogden some years before, relieving him of most of his furs, so it was said, not far off at Cache Valley, north of Great Salt Lake. The story went that Ashley got back to St. Louis with furs worth $70,000—or as some claimed, $200,000—which Ogden had harvested. Some thought Ashley had "lifted" these furs from Ogden's cache, others that he had somehow compelled Ogden to sell them for a song. . . . If Ashley could get the best of Ogden, why not Tom?

The Hudson's Bay Company seldom used liquor in trade with the Indians, and then only along the border in competition with American traders. The Rocky Mountain Fur Company had no such scruples. Moreover, it had the liquor. So Broken Hand invited Ogden's Indians to his own camp, and knocked in the bungs of a keg or two. He soon acquired all their furs and even inveigled Chief Gray and seven of his Rockaways and some Crees to throw in with the Americans. At mountain prices Tom's rotgut was expensive, and Ogden, in order to save what furs he could, was compelled to pay the free trappers, in more expensive goods, or cash, all of three American dollars a plew. On top of that, he came near losing his horses—and his wife.

By that time the feeling of hostility between the two camps was keen. One day the horses in Ogden's camp were stampeded, perhaps by accident. Three of them ran galloping into the rival camp. One pack horse was saddled with a load of furs. Another animal had a saddle on it, with a papoose cradle hanging from its horn, and in it Ogden's own child by his Indian wife.

The motto of the American trappers was "Finders, keepers," and it may be that Ogden's diminished force could not have compelled the return of the stray animals, if it ever came to that.

But before anyone could catch and unsaddle the pack horse loaded with beaver, the Indian mother came running after her baby, went right into the American camp, caught her horse, and mounted. The baby was none the worse for its adventure.

With her mind at rest on that point, she soon spied the stray pack horse. Fearlessly she seized its halter shank and headed out of the camp.

Angry at this raid on what they felt belonged to them by all the laws of war, some of the men yelled, "Shoot her! Shoot her!"

But others objected, "Let her go! Let her alone! She's a brave woman: I glory in her pluck!"

While her enemies argued, the mother galloped off with her baby and her pack horse.

As the winter of 1830-31 set in, Tom Fitzpatrick's brigade set out on its long, long ride to winter quarters in the buffalo country on Powder River . . . six hundred miles as the crow flies from Ogden's Hole to the mouth of the Powder on Yellowstone River,[1] and much farther by the mountain trails. Fraeb and Gervais were hunting meanwhile far to the south. Tom decided that an express must be sent to St. Louis without delay. It would be a dangerous trip, a task for trusty men.

Though only twenty years old, Meek's qualifications already distinguished him among the hired trappers. The booshways chose him to go, sending a Frenchman, Legarde, along as his only companion.

We have few details of the journey. But when the pair reached the Pawnee villages, they found those Indians unfriendly. The Pawnees held Legarde. But Meek, more cautious or more lucky, evaded them and went on alone with his letters.

After several days' travel through the snow, he fell in with another express heading for the settlements, turned

---

1 Newell says winter quarters were on the Yellowstone. This is not necessarily a contradiction of Meek's story, as the Powder is a tributary of that stream.

over his papers to them, and with a Frenchman named Cabeneau headed back to Powder River. Soon after he got in, preparations for the spring hunt of 1831 began. This time the plan was to head north for Blackfoot country. But now that Bill Sublette had left the company, bad luck seemed to dog them. The third day out, while their horses were turned loose to graze, a Crow war party sneaked up. Before the horse guard knew it, they stampeded and ran off three hundred head.[1] The trappers stood and cursed.

There they were, afoot in Blackfoot country. There warn't enough horse beasts left to outfight the Crows. Anyhow, most of the remaining horses belonged to free trappers who flatly refused to risk their own animals to recover those stolen from the company.

But those horses had to be recovered, and the booshways decided to send a party of one hundred picked men after them on foot. Antoine Godin, a brave half-breed, was put in command. Meek and Newell were among the men he chose.

The sign showed that the Crows numbered about sixty warriors, and were losing no time in getting the stolen horses out of reach of their owners. They rode hard day and night, driving the stolen herd ahead of them.

There was nothing for the trappers to do but to push on day and night afoot, hoping to catch up with the thieves whenever the Crows should stop to rest. "For two hundred miles, traveling day and night," according to Joe Meek's first biographer, they pushed on, following

---

[1] Newell's "Memorandum" mentions this raid. He reports they (perhaps his own "squad") "lost fifty-seven head to Crow Indians." He says it was the first time he ever went to war on foot. He may, of course, mean that, of the three hundred head stolen, all but fifty-seven were recovered. It is not clear how sixty Crows could run away with only fifty-seven horses, or how one hundred trappers could ride home on them—unless the thieves were mounted in the first place and lost one hundred head to the trappers. The inaccuracy here seems to be Newell's, not Meek's.

the trail. "On the third day they came up with them on a branch of the Big Horn River."

Quite a hike—at the rate of seventy miles a day—in moccasins, through the snow! But no doubt it *seemed* like two hundred miles.

They found the Crows, evidently confident that they were safely away with their booty, sitting around campfires just across a little stream over-looked by an overhanging bluff, within easy rifle shot. While the Crows gloated, Meek and the trappers lined up on the bluff, lying hidden until darkness fell and the Crows had rolled up in their blankets inside a hastily built log fort.

When all was silent, Godin and Newell sneaked across the creek and into the encampment. It was a simple matter, knowing the animals as they did, to cut the lariats, mount the bell mare and ease the herd down the creek to the ford.

But the Indians, though caught napping, heard the animals moving. They seized their arms and ran out of the fort. This was just what the trappers on the bluff had been waiting for.

They fired one volley, knocking over seven warriors (as they learned later). Then, hurrying to the horses, they mounted bareback and raced away, leaving the Crows to walk in their turn.

But the trip home was hard. Sleepless, tired, raw from riding on the sharp backs of their hard-driven ponies, they were also plagued by weather which turned snow to slush and earth to mud. They reached camp worn out. But the booshways, fearing another raid, gave them no rest. Next morning they all pushed on more rapidly than usual.

Soon after, Tom Fitzpatrick started for St. Louis with one companion to buy the goods for the summer rendezvous. Meek heard that rendezvous would be held that year of 1831 on Green River.

The Rocky Mountain Fur Company made a good hunt that spring, without much loss of men or animals. They hunted along the Yellowstone, then southward and over the mountains into Pierre's Hole, on to Snake River, Salt River, Bear River, and so to rendezvous.

Impatiently they waited for Fitzpatrick to return. The company had now so many employees that its stock of goods was exhausted. There was nary a blanket in Bridger's packs, no powder or lead, not even a Green River knife or a sure-fire beaver trap. Well, they could wait for those. But how could a mountain man keep going without a chaw of tobacco or a drop of alcohol to wet his dry? Hard doin's on Green River that summer. Where in hell was Broken Hand and his goods?

Jim Bridger and Milton Sublette waited and waited until they could wait no longer. The morale of the brigade, no less than its equipment, was at stake. Old Fraeb, the Dutchman with the yellow teeth, who had lived long enough in the wilds to pick up Indian ways, decided to appeal to "medicine." In camp was a Cree Indian whom they had lured away from Ogden.

This man had the reputation of possessing supernatural power, with gifts of divination, prophecy and healing. Fraeb gave the Cree two good horses and requested him to find out what had become of Broken Hand.[1]

After heroic efforts, the medicine man announced that he had learned from the spirits: "Broken Hand is not dead. He is traveling on some trail; but not on the right trail."

This information cheered old Fraeb, spurred him to

---

[1] Mrs. Victor calls this medicine man a Crow in one passage, a Cree in several others. For Crow methods of divination see: R. H. Lowie, *The Crow Indians* (New York City; Farrar and Rinehart, 1935). For Cree methods of divination see: D. G. Mandelbaum, *The Plains Cree* (New York City: American Museum of Natural History). Anthropological Papers, Vol. 37, II, 1940.

action. He called for volunteers to go with him and find old Tom. Meek, Reese, George Wood Ebbert and Nelson offered their services.

Blackfoot Scrape

FRAEB, with Joe Meek and the other volunteers, rode towards Wind River, but found no sign of the lost booshway. They crossed to the Sweetwater and followed the wagon ruts down to the North Fork of the Platte. Still no sign of old Tom.

They went on into the Black Hills, that beautiful country, then swarming with game. But still they found no trace of Broken Hand. Finally they all went back to the North Platte. There at last they met with the impatient booshway and his lagging pack train.

By that time they all knew well enough that Bridger and Sublette were no longer on Green River, so Fraeb and Tom Fitzpatrick headed for winter quarters. Before they reached it cold weather had already set in.

Old Tom had a long tale to tell. Bridger, Fitzpatrick and the other partners, having just bought the Rocky Mountain Fur Company with a note, had no capital with which to buy goods. Fitzpatrick had counted on Bill Sublette to supply them. But when at last he found Sublette and Smith, they had other plans. They urged him to go on with them to Santa Fe. There, they promised, they would furnish him and hire men to take his pack mules north to rendezvous.

Well, Diah and Bill had the money; there was nothing

Tom could do but go along. It was a slow trip and a long one, and when he got to Santa Fe he was still about as far from Green River as he had been in Missouri.

On the way out, the train had had a terrible dry scrape on the Cimarron Desert. Diah Smith, always thinking of others, had gone off alone to find water. He never came back. Afterward Mexican traders in Santa Fe, who had purchased Smith's weapons and equipment from some Comanches, told Bill and Tom how those Indians had killed him.

But at Santa Fe, Tom said, Bill Sublette had been as good as his word, and so Fitzpatrick had finally got started. And now here were the goods, and certainly no lack of customers. Winter quarters on Powder River were usually agreeable enough, but that year of 1831 the trappers really had high jinks—Christmas and rendezvous rolled into one.

Joe Meek was not allowed to celebrate long. His recent success as an express to St. Louis had singled him out. One day Legarde, his companion on that trip, who had been captured by the Pawnees, showed up. The booshways promptly sent him and Meek on snowshoes to the Bitterroot River to look for a party of free trappers whose beaver they wished to buy. Meek knew that was well over three hundred miles each way; he reckoned the two of them would be gone more than two months—if they got back at all.

By this time Meek was an old hand at winter travel in the mountains. He could run on snowshoes all day, carrying his pack, and knew how to camp in the snow in comfort. At night, if camped in open country where there were no boughs to make a bed, Joe would dig away the snow, clearing away a space of bare ground, and on that spread grass, weeds, or sage, if he could find any, as a foundation for his blankets and buffalo robe. If lucky enough to kill a bull where the snow was deep, he did not bother to clear the ground, but spread the warm rawhide down on the snow and made his bed on that.

When thirsty in camp, he could heat a rock in the fire, fill his hat with snow, drop the rock into the hat, and so melt the snow to drinking water.

When in a hurry, Joe and Legarde did not bother to melt snow, but wolfed down their supper, sitting with a chunk of snow in one hand and a piece of meat in the other, taking first a bite of one and then a bite of the other.

In summer, when the sun dance or some other ceremony was going on or in prospect, all the bands of a Plains Indian tribe pitched their tents together in one great tribal camp circle. But in winter the bands scattered, each seeking some sheltered valley where game, grass and wood abounded; there each family pitched its tent in the most convenient spot along the stream. One day Meek and Legarde, following a creek through the hills, stumbled upon a Blackfoot camp square in their path. They were almost among the tipis scattered through the brush before they saw them, for the snow and sleet had so glazed and disguised the Indian tents that only the smoked, brown tops and rakish poles betrayed them. Luckily, no dog barked. Meek and his friend quickly backtracked and slipped around the hostile village through the cold night, unseen.

On the Bitterroot Meek found the trappers and secured their furs for his company.

Meanwhile, John Jacob Astor was steadily extending the operations of his American Fur Company into the mountains. Already he had overcome the reluctance of some St. Louis traders to join with him, and his Western Department, with headquarters in that town, was thriving. Already it had absorbed the Columbia Fur Company, hiring its best men—among them Kenneth McKenzie, now "king" at Fort Union—and busily reached for the Blackfoot trade. Besides Fort Piegan, building on Marias River, McKenzie laid plans for Fort Cass on the Yellowstone, in Crow country, and another post at Three Forks. And the brigades under Drips and Vanderburgh were crowding the Rocky Mountain Fur Company as hard as they could. Monopoly was on the march.

Drips and Vanderburgh were new to the mountains, and had no idea where to find the best beaver streams. So they adopted a simple plan: to follow the Rocky Mountain Fur Company's brigade around the country, and thus make certain of a rich harvest in furs.

The first thing Meek knew, the trappers of the American Fur Company were encamped near by, watching and waiting for Fitzpatrick and Bridger to start on the spring hunt!

Meanwhile, Vanderburgh and Drips bribed and tempted the trappers of the Rocky Mountain Company in order to learn where their rivals planned to hold their summer rendezvous. With that information, they hoped to be on hand with a supply of goods before William Sublette could bring out the Rocky Mountain Fur Company's goods from St. Louis!

What was worse they were already trading with the Indians, and even secretly swapping goods for the furs of their rivals' hired trappers! Feeling grew so bitter among the old hands, that any man who went over to the other company was "gone beaver!"

The booshways of the Rocky Mountain Fur Company determined to slip away from winter quarters, head for the forks of Snake River, and so leave Drips and Vanderburgh behind. On Snake River, at any rate, they could trade with the Nez Percés and Flatheads. They passed the word that rendezvous that summer of '32 would be in Pierre's Hole, west of the Tetons. The move was urgent —they dared not delay.

But that winter it seemed that Meek was hardly ever to travel with the main camp.

Chief Gray of the Rockaway Indians, who had abandoned the Hudson's Bay Company at Ogden's Hole and attached himself to the Rocky Mountain Fur Company, was still in camp with his family, on Bear River.

One of the trappers apparently offered the chief's daughter some indignity, and there was trouble in camp. Milton Sublette was on hand, and in the fracas Gray stabbed him. He was so badly cut up that he could not travel.

Sublette asked Joe Meek to stay with him when the brigade pulled out—"to take care of him while he lived and bury him if he died."

So Joe Meek moved into the booshway's tipi, to act as doctor, nurse, cook, hunter, guard, companion and entertainer. Meek was handy at all these roles—particularly the latter. It would be hard to find a man better fitted to cheer a convalescent, and the fact that Old Milt chose Meek to stay with him shows that they were already fast friends. Milton knew that, though Meek was then only twenty-two, no man in the brigade was more capable, big-hearted, courageous, cheerful and loyal.

Of course, as Milton Sublette grew better, he found their lone camp boring. In spite of all Joe Meek's jokes and stories, the convalescent complained of lack of excitement. For forty days Meek tended the complaining invalid. At the end of that time, once he was helped into his saddle, Milton was able to ride.

Slowly they set out, following the trail of their brigade. Vanderburgh and Drips had pulled out long since.

On the headwaters of Green River Old Milt's hankering for excitement was more than satisfied. Riding out from the timber, Meek suddenly saw a bunch of warriors seated together in a grassy bend of the river, and their loose horses grazing round about them. "Snakes!" Meek groaned.

It was too late to turn back. Already the warriors had

seen them. They jumped up, screaming the war whoop, and ran to catch their horses.

Ordinarily, mountain men and Snake Indians rocked along together well enough, though the Snakes had a great reputation for stealing everything not nailed down even in the camps of their friends; but it was clear enough from the actions of the warriors sprinting to mount their ponies that they were hostile now. What trouble they might have had with other white men to make them so, Joe could not know and did not wait to ask. He knew only that two men with single-shot rifles had no chance against all those warriors, and certainly, Old Milt was in no shape to outrun them.

Farther down the stream Joe saw the Snake camp There lay their one chance of safety. "Let's go," Meek yelled.

While the warriors were catching and mounting their ponies, Joe and Milton raced past them on a dead run straight into the village. There in the middle of the circle of lodges they saw a big tipi standing alone, and never slackened rein until they jerked up their horses at its door.

Both men threw themselves from the saddle, ducked quickly through the slanting door-slit of the tipi, turned to the right, and immediately sat down side by side facing the fireplace in the center.

Joe knew well enough that this big lodge in the middle of the camp was a kind of tribal headquarters, either a "soldier lodge" occupied by the warrior society then in charge of the camp or else a sacred tent where a medicine man kept some powerful bundle or talisman. Having found sanctuary in that lodge, they might have a chance for their lives.

They heard the thunder of hoofs as the warriors galloped up to surround the tent. A moment later they came crowding in, seating themselves all around, scowling and making threats. Some carried guns, some bows—or war clubs, with the blades of two or three butcher knives set in the business end. All wore knives in their belts. Outside, Meek could hear the voices of a crowd gathering. But through it all, Joe and Milton sat quiet, taking good care to show no fear. They knew well enough how Injuns despised a coward—and how extremely likely they were to kill one.

If only the Horned Chief had been there! He had been always friendly to the whites. Even Iron Wristband, that tricky rascal, might have been friendly—for a price. Instead, Joe found himself facing a treacherous old man, Bad Left Hand, known also to the trappers as "Goche" or "Gotia" from the French translation of his name, *Mauvais Gauche*.

Only six or eight years before, Bad Left Hand had treacherously attacked the brigade of Etienne Provost not far from Utah Lake. Bad Left Hand had invited the whites to smoke the peace pipe with his party. When Provost agreed, the chief explained that it was "against his medicine" to have any metal near by while he smoked. Provost and his men obligingly stacked their weapons at a distance from the council. The Snakes also put their few guns away. While all were smoking, Bad Left Hand suddenly gave a signal.

At once the warriors whipped out hidden knives and hatchets and jumped on the unarmed trappers. Provost, strong and active, managed to save himself with three or four of his men. All the rest were murdered. Bad Left Hand was not the kind of chief Joe Meek had hoped to find.

Most of the warriors favored killing the two men, but to Meek's surprise "a good old man" (as Joe calls him) argued long and persistently in favor of letting them go. What inducements Sublette offered or what reward Joe may have promised, the old man said he could see no good in killing two harmless travelers. This "good old man" was none other than Bad Left Hand!

All day the two sat in the lodge while their fate hung in the balance and the warriors, weapons in hand, sat opposite scowling and blustering.

Suddenly, along about dusk, Joe and Milton heard a great noise. Peering out, they saw a commotion that looked like horses stampeding at the far end of the village. Everybody ran out of the lodge and hurried off to see the excitement. Meek and Milton were left alone.

Then Bad Left Hand, who had probably arranged this diversion, hurried in, and beckoned Joe and Milton to go with him. The three splashed through the ford and took to the brush. There they found an Indian girl holding their horses ready saddled.

Meek declares he had never seen an Injun gal so good looking as that Snake Pocahontas. But just then he had no time to make her acquaintance. He helped Milton into the saddle and quickly forked his own horse, while the chief gave them the wholly unnecessary advice, "Ride, if you hope to live; ride all night without stopping, and keep going tomorrow."

During all this time Meek's comrades had been making a very successful spring hunt. West of the mountains they had followed up the valley of Snake River to the mouth of Salt River, then up that stream and across the divide to John Day (then John Gray) River, which they traced to its headwaters. They crossed the mountains to Bear River. There, to their intense disgust, they found the camp of Vanderburgh and Drips, the camp of the American Fur Company, their bitter rivals!

There, apparently, Joe Meek and Milton found them preparing to head for Pierre's Hole.

It was nearly time for the rendezvous of the Rocky Mountain Fur Company. Unable to get rid of Drips and Vanderburgh, who followed them like shadows, the booshways of the Rocky Mountain Fur Company finally offered to divide the trapping territory with their rivals so that each could operate independently of the other.

But Drips and Vanderburgh had done very well following their rivals. Knowing so little of the mountains, they feared that in any such bargain they would be cheated. They refused.

After that, there was only one thing to do—send an express to meet Bill Sublette, who was bringing their goods, and hurry him up before the American Fur Company had a chance to hog the trade. Already the trappers were gathering for rendezvous.

The matter was so urgent that Tom Fitzpatrick resolved to go himself. He found Sublette and his pack train, with Robert Campbell, on the Platte below the mouth of the Laramie, only four hundred miles away. He also found some stray and impoverished hunters belonging to the company of Gant and Blackwell, bargained for their furs, cached these, and then induced the men to go along with him.

With Sublette was a Yankee, Nathaniel Wyeth, a very intelligent man—though a greenhorn—heading into the Rockies to try his luck in the fur trade. Says Meek, "It looked like everybody war a-hornin' in."

When Tom Fitzpatrick reached the Sweetwater, he rashly decided to hurry along alone and bring his partners the cheering news that Bill Sublette was making all haste to arrive in time. This news he hoped would enable the Rocky Mountain Fur Company to keep their trappers and Indian friends from trading with their rivals, the American Fur Company, even though Fontenelle's pack train got to rendezvous ahead of Sublette. Tom was out to win that race.

When Bill Sublette reached Pierre's Hole early in July, he naturally expected to find Old Tom waiting with everybody else. "Where is Tom?" he demanded.

None of the partners had seen hide nor hair of him. Maybe so Broken Hand had gone under.

Bill Sublette shook his head; he himself had had a brush with the Blackfeet on the way in. Nobody had been killed and he had lost only a few worthless horses. Bill confessed he had not expected to find Blackfeet on Wind River.

Not long after, two Iroquois hunters rode in bringing an emaciated scarecrow whom his partners could scarcely recognize as their old friend, Tom Fitzpatrick. The story goes that his long hair had turned white as a result of the cruel hardships and dangers he had passed. Certain it is that he was thereafter known as "White Head" rather than "Broken Hand" among the Indians.

Tom said that he rode unmolested for three or four days after leaving Sublette on the Sweetwater, making good time. Then for two days the weather was so cloudy that he could not see the sun or stars and lost his bearings. He found himself in a rough, rocky, wooded country. There he had an adventure with a bear, which he killed. Tom got into a valley hemmed in by rocky hills.

The first thing he knew, he was among the hostiles. His pack horse escaped with most of his possibles; but he had a good saddler and took refuge in a small canyon where he waited for several hours in hiding. When he sneaked out again, a bunch of young warriors saw him and gave chase. In level country he might have run away from them, but here he found it much too steep and rough. The Indians, dismounting, kept on his trail. Unwilling to give up his horse, Tom kept whipping it up the rocky hillside until the animal played out. Taking his gun and blanket, Tom ran on afoot until he saw that the young Indians swarming up the bluff were sure to catch him.

By good luck he found a hole among the rocks where some varmint had made its den. He crawled in and blocked the opening with sticks and leaves. All around, Tom could hear war whoops and the cheering of the Indians when they captured his horse. And all that day the young warriors scoured the hillside passing and re-passing the hole where Tom lay without chance to run or fight.

Long after dark, Tom slipped out to make his getaway and found himself in the middle of the Blackfoot camp.

Once more, back in his smelly hide-out, he starved and waited until they gave up searching for him. When finally he dared to look out, he saw them running races with his fine horse. After darkness fell, he crawled out again and hid in the brush along the creek. All the next day he was still never out of sight of Indians. Finally, he came to the mouth of the creek, recognized Pierre's River, and knew where he was.

To get away from the Indians he decided to cross the river. Putting his plunder on a raft, he started for the other bank; but the swift current swept his flimsy raft against a rock and tore it to pieces. Tom's rifle fell in the water along with everything else he owned except his knife. He had no blanket now and had thrown away most of his clothing while running away from the Indians up the mountain. For days he lived on nothing but rose-buds and roots.

Wolves began to follow him. He climbed a tree, and after his fright told how the wolves dug at the roots and tried to gnaw the tree down! Once he found a dead buffalo with some flesh still on its bones, but finally was starved into insensibility. In that state, the Iroquois hunters had found him, roused him, and brought him in.

That was Tom's story, which created much excitement in camp. According to Zenas Leonard[1] some wanted to re-taliate on the Indians and recapture Tom's horse; others

---

[1] Zenas Leonard, *Narrative of the Adventures of Zenas Leonard* (Clear-field, Pennsylvania, 1839), p. 109.

doubted his story—and certainly, that part about the wolves gnawing at the tree was a leetle mite hard to swallow.

Anyhow, most of the trappers felt that while they were in camp at rendezvous was no time to go lookin' for Injuns. Like as not Injuns war a-lookin' for them!

Battle of Pierre's Hole

THAT WAS the biggest rendezvous held in the mountains up to that time. Fur trade in the Rockies was at its peak, and more things happened that year of '32 than in any other during the heyday of the mountain men. Never was such a rendezvous. With the raw New Englanders of Wyeth's brigade for audience, all the trappers—and especially the free trappers—outdid themselves in all manner of mad pranks. The mountain men were on their spree.

To start with, there were the usual races, wrestling, jumping, shooting matches, and exhibitions of horsemanship. But when they began to pass the camp kettle filled with raw alcohol around the circle, trouble started. For the trapper never sipped his liquor; he gulped it down "to make drunk come."

As Meek puts it, "When the pie was opened the birds began to sing." They were ready for anything. One of them, in mockery, profanely baptized a redhead with raw alcohol, drenching his friend's hair and clothing. While the victim staggered, blinded and gasping, another drunken wag picked up a lighted stick from the campfire and set the soaked wretch afire.

Meek saw him capering around all ablaze. He and some of the others who were still sober snatched up aparejos and beat out the fire. But what with the beating and the burning, the poor devil almost died.

Bill Sublette had arrived at Pierre's Hole on the eighth of July, and on the seventeenth rendezvous broke up. His brother, Milton, with thirty men (of whom Meek, of course, was one), set out to the southwest to explore new country as far as Ogden's River, since called the Humboldt. With them marched Wyeth's dwindling company of greenhorns and Sinclair's fifteen free trappers, making a total force of about sixty men, most of them green hands, besides Indians.

That first day they made about six miles.

Next morning early, while the men were raising camp and the booshway looked on, smoking his pipe, Meek saw far-off dark objects moving down from the hills. Fontenelle had not showed up at rendezvous, and at first Milton thought it must be Fontenelle's pack train. Well, if so, this time the American Fur Company was sure out of luck. That was a laugh on Fontenelle! Bill Sublette had all the beaver!

Meek thought it might be buffalo. But Wyeth got out a long brass spyglass, took one look, and shouted "Indians!"

The redskins were in two bunches: Wyeth counted 150. And they were heading straight for the trappers' camp, the women and children trailing, the warriors in advance whooping and quirting their horses. They left the hills and rode out into the valley. There they halted, beyond rifle range.

For a while nobody was sure just who those Indians were. One of them carried a Union Jack, which might be a present from the Hudson's Bay Company—or a trophy taken from them. While the leaders stood staring and the men made ready for defense, one of the warriors left the band and rode forward.

Meek could see that along his left arm rested the long

stem of an Indian pipe, and knew he must be a chief. Still Joe could not identify the tribe.

"Mought be Crow," Sinclair offered. But when the chief came near enough to yell across to them, all doubt vanished. Meek knew then—"Blackfoot!"

Bug's Boys again! The Yankee greenhorns with Wyeth asked questions which showed how little they realized what lay ahead. But Meek and other mountain men foresaw there would be war.

These Indians were allies, not members, of the Blackfoot Confederacy. They were neither Piegans, Bloods, nor Blackfeet, though all four tribes were thick as thieves can be.

Meek knew these were the Atsina, or Gros Ventres of the Prairie, "Grovants"—blood brothers of the Arapaho, whose language they understood and who called them, aptly enough, "Spongers." About a dozen years before the Atsina had rejoined their Arapaho cousins who, living far south on the Arkansas, had many more horses than the northern Indians. But some dispute had sent the Atsina north again, where a disastrous encounter with the Crows had driven them on into Blackfoot country. The trappers called them Blackfeet like the rest.

The powerful tribes of the Blackfoot Confederacy hated the whites quite as much as their allies, the Atsina, did. Only the winter before they had burned Fort Piegan, the trading post near the mouth of the Marias River. But the American Fur Company kept wooing them, and had already begun to build a new post in the same neighborhood.

Meek had heard how these Indians had run off some of Bill Sublette's pack horses only two weeks back. The chief had a lot of gall, riding out with a peace pipe thataway asking for a council.

"Maybeso he takes us for Fontenelle's men."

Of course the Indians outnumbered the trappers.

Milton Sublette had fifteen men; Sinclair, partisan of the free trappers, the same number; Wyeth, twenty raw hands; and a few other whites and some Flatheads had joined the party at rendezvous, not caring to travel alone.

The Blackfeet numbered 150 or more, nearly half of whom were men and boys old enough to bear arms. They had a good many Mackinaw guns, for Kenneth "Redcoat" McKenzie, booshway of the American Fur Company at Fort Union, had supplied them.

Still, it seemed strange that the chief would bring his women and children out of the hills into the open prairie if he planned to attack, more especially as not a few of them were afoot.

But too many of Meek's comrades had lost their top-knots to the Blackfeet in the past few seasons for the survivors to put any faith in the Atsina, though they had been down on the Arkansas River for three winters past. Surely the Blackfoot chief could see his enemies, the Flatheads, with Sublette's party. More than likely the chief had brought his pipe forward just to learn what he could before the scrap began, or to gain time while more of his people came along. Anyways you fix it, a Blackfoot was a Blackfoot, the orneriest skunk in the mountains.

Milton Sublette, Meek's booshway, still convalescent, was in no fix to lead a charge, Wyeth, like his men, was a greenhorn who had never fought Injuns. Sinclair, brave partisan of the free trappers, having lost some toes to frostbite, could only fight horseback or in the brush. The booshways and the Flathead chief sent two horsemen riding hell-for-leather to rendezvous to bring up reinforcements. Meanwhile they would stand on the defensive. They were not yet ready to fight.

But Antoine Godin, the Iroquois half-breed hunter, was ready enough. Those Blackfeet had killed and scalped his father on Godin Creek. He stared grimly at the lone chieftain.

"Looks like the cussed Injun wants to talk," someone suggested. Nobody offered to go forward for the parley. Godin spoke up, grimly: *"I'll* talk to him."

Turning to the Flathead who stood at his elbow, rifle in hand, Godin snapped out a brief question: "Is your piece charged?"

The Flathead glanced quickly at his Iroquois friend. "It is," he answered.

"Then cock it and follow me," Godin replied.

The two of them mounted and rode out abreast to meet the chief halfway: Godin, lithe and swarthy in his fancy buckskins and wool hat, the stocky Flathead with two eagle feathers in the long black hair which flowed down over the shoulders of his fringed scalp-shirt. They rode poker-faced.

Baihoh, the Gros Ventre chief, must have had misgivings as he saw the Flathead coming forward. But if he did, he scorned to show them. He sat his pony, swathed to the waist in a scarlet blanket, with the broad band of bright quillwork across it. On his left arm rested the long stem of the peace pipe.

Godin rode up on the chief's right hand, the Flathead rode up on his left. Baihoh extended his right hand in friendship. Godin's eyes never left the chief's face. He reached out, grasped the Indian's hand, held it tight. Without looking round he shouted, "Fire!"

Instantly the Flathead threw up his barrel, gloated for a split second over the shock in Baihoh's face, then fired. Baihoh tumbled from his saddle in a cloud of white smoke. The Flathead whirled his pony round and galloped away. A great howl of grief and rage burst from the throats of the Gros Ventres. Their bullets whistled angrily around the Iroquois.

But Godin, in bravado, whooped in triumph, and, leaning from his saddle, snatched the corner of the dead man's scarlet blanket up, dragged it from under him, and loped away, trailing the blood-red trophy. Triumphant, he and his Flathead accomplice both regained their own party unhurt.

By that time Meek and other mountain men were returning the fire of the enraged Indians. And as soon as the redskins had recovered from the surprise of seeing their chief shot down, they scuttled for the nearest cover. This was a wide swamp, caused by beavers damming the stream. The swamp was overgrown with brush, willows and cottonwoods, vines and weeds, all thickly entangled and matted together. Within this thicket the Indians found cover: the men covering the retreat of the women and children; the women hastily raising a "fort" of logs and branches, and digging trenches with their knives behind that rude breastwork. The mountain men, finding the Indians all armed with McKenzie's fusees, and good shots, took shelter in a ravine which ran across the front of the Indian position, and kept firing into the brush.

The down-Easters with Wyeth were wholly unused to such warfare, and exposed themselves recklessly, without being of the least use. Wyeth promptly got them out of the way. He caught up all his horses, tied them up at a safe distance, under cover and out of sight. Then he made a breastwork of his packs, made his men lie down behind it, and ordered them not to leave their post under any circumstances. He himself took his rifle and went off to join the fray.

Joe Meek knew well enough that those few men could never drive the Blackfeet from cover, much less charge in and rub them out. All they could do was to wait while their two runners rode those six miles to rendezvous, lashed their lathered horses through the encampment, yelling to Flatheads, Pierced Noses, trappers, "Blackfeet! Blackfeet! Get your guns and come a-runnin'!"

Once Bill Sublette and Robert Campbell had forked

their horses and brought their fighters into battle, it would be a different story.

And so it was.

For when the Blackfeet saw all those enemies riding in, they covered their mouths with their hands in astonishment, abandoned the brush covert where they lay, and fell back into their flimsy fort and foxholes. Most of the women and children had already taken to the tall timber on the mountainside, heading back to bring up the main camp of their people. The warriors left behind could only stand off the whites while their families escaped.

As for the trappers, nobody as yet showed any eagerness to rush blindly across the open at their invisible enemies. Already one half-breed had been severely wounded; the men waited in their ravine.

But Bill Sublette was a man of action. He had come to fight. He flung himself from his saddle, stripped off shirt and leggings, and made a verbal will, appointing Robert Campbell his executor.

Captain Sublette did not order anybody forward. He led the way. Campbell and Sinclair emulated his courage. Then, somewhat more reluctantly, about thirty whites and as many Indians advanced through a grove of willows. Joe Meek was with them.

Struggling through the brush, the three leaders found themselves facing the open space beyond which the Indians had entrenched themselves. Their improvised "fort" was simply a breastwork of logs and branches, and its low shelter was extended upward by a curtain of buffalo robes, scarlet blankets, and lodge covers, which concealed, though it could not protect, the warriors behind it. The brush was so thick that every movement of the white men disturbed it, and so the Indians could see them coming.

Sinclair by this time was in the lead, gently parting the branches as he crept forward. A puff of smoke bloomed from a crevice in the Indian fort. Sinclair jerked back, shot through the body. Campbell lay nearest, and Sinclair, turning to face him, begged, "Take me to my brother." Then he fainted.

Campbell crept forward, caught hold of Sinclair's leg, and dragged him back. When he reached the men behind, he let them take the wounded man. They carried him out of the swamp. Then Campbell rejoined his friend Sublette.

All this time Bill Sublette had been snaking his way to the front. Made cautious by Sinclair's disaster, the Captain lay still and studied the Indian defenses, trying to find the loopholes through which the warriors were firing. Suddenly he saw an Indian peeping through one of these. Quickly he raised his rifle, fired, and struck the Indian square in the eye. With a grin he turned to Campbell, pointing to the opening. "Watch that hole," he whispered, hastily reloading, "and you'll soon have a fair chance for a shot." He stood behind a cottonwood to ram home the charge.

Before he could reload, an Indian fired. Sublette was hit in the shoulder. He moved his arm up and down, making sure that the bone was not broken. Then he grew faint, and sagged to the ground. Boldly Meek and Campbell risked death to carry him out of the swamp. Strangely enough, the ball that passed through Sublette's shoulder also wounded a man behind him in the head.

Warmed to their work by the courage and by the wounding of their leaders, the mountain men began to pour a steady fire upon the Indian fort. They surrounded it, firing from every side. Wyeth, who was leading a group of Nez Percés, found himself endangered by the cross fire of his own comrades. One of his Indian allies was shot down at his elbow—and the bullet had come from the rifle of a trapper beyond the fort. The hostile Indians did not fire often; they were running short of powder:

but when they did fire, somebody was hit. They kept doggedly inside their fort; they gave no quarter, and they expected none. All that day the siege went on.

All day long more men came riding from rendezvous. Most of them, camp keepers and packers, were of no use in the fight. Meanwhile both sides were running short of ammunition, and some of the men, as John Wyeth records, "recoiled from" the "idea of a barbed arrow sticking in a man's body."

Some who could roll logs ahead of them got into position to fire into the Indian fort without much danger. One, relying on Dutch courage, charged the fort and was killed.

Suddenly there was silence in the Indian fort. Meek guessed the Blackfeet were reserving their powder and lead—if they still had any—to stop the charge they must have felt sure was coming. But now that Sinclair lay dying and Bill Sublette had been wounded, there was nobody to lead an attack. Those men who still had Galena pills in their bullet pouches and powder in their horns lay around in the hot sun, firing into the brush. The Blackfeet, lying low in their foxholes, waited for darkness.

But Bill Sublette had got his dander up. He was spunky. A brisk wind was blowing, and he determined to fire the grass and brush and burn the Blackfoot fort. "Burn 'em out, boys! That'll fix 'em!"

The Flatheads and Nez Percés, however, objected earnestly to that scheme.

"No, no," they said. "Those Blackfeet are rich. They have been visiting, and are bringing back presents. If we burn them out, all those fine red blankets and things will be burned up too. We've got them licked; that loot is as good as ours right now. It would be foolish to burn up our own property."

While the friendlies and the whites argued and

wrangled about the matter, the Blackfeet in the fort had seen the squaws gathering grass and brush. They knew what was doing. They were desperate, and being desperate, began to taunt and threaten their enemies. Their chief began to yell.

"While we had plenty of powder and lead," the chief shouted, "we fought you on the open prairie. It was only when our powder ran low that we hid in the brush. We came here to die with our women and children. We are only a handful, and you are many. We know you can kill us all. You can burn us out and shoot us. What do we care? We have thrown away our bodies. But if you are hungry for fighting, just stay beside our ashes here, and you will soon get your bellyful. There are four hundred lodges of our brothers headed this way. We have sent for them. They are brave, their arms are strong, and their hearts are big. They will avenge us!"

"What are they yelling?" the mountain men demanded.

Then everyone with a smattering of the Indian tongue tried to interpret. The translating went on for some time. It was never very clear, passing as it did through so many Flathead, Nez Percé, and Creole mouths before it was turned into broken English. But out of all that confusion of tongues one statement rang clear: "Blackfeet! Blackfeet comin'! Heap Blackfeet! Heap big fight!"

That news was bad enough. But suddenly someone called out: "The cussed Injuns are thar a'ready. At rendezvous! They're raidin' our camps!"

That struck alarm to the besiegers. Back there at rendezvous were their wives and children, their horses and mules, their outfits for the coming season, their clothes, their tents, their priceless "beaver." If the Blackfeet captured those, all would be lost!

It was late in the day. Everyone was tired, sore from the kick of the guns, powder-marked, hungry, and dry. Casualties had been heavy: Sinclair and four other mountain men had been killed, along with a half-breed and seven friendly Indians. There were at least a dozen seriously wounded; it had been a hard fight. But when the mountain men heard that danger threatened their camps at rendezvous they did not falter. They threw themselves into their saddles, and rode hell-for-leather to meet the—by then—"eight hundred" savage warriors thirsting for their blood.

Campbell and Fitzpatrick led the mountain men back to rendezvous on the dead run. There they found everything just as they had left it. No Blackfeet had been sighted thereabouts. The mountain men scoured the country around their camps, looking for fresh Blackfoot sign. They found none, and, as darkness fell, jogged in and unsaddled where their women were at work about the dancing little cook-fires. That night the battle-weary men remained on guard at rendezvous. There was no attack. Come sunup, they knew that the Indians in the fort had been lying, had lured them away from the fight with an empty threat, a false alarm. Angry at the deceit, they dashed back to rub out the tricky Blackfeet in the fort. Some of their men had been left there to watch it.

They all surrounded it once more, yelling defiance, and shooting into the logs and earthworks. The Blackfeet did not return their fire, and when one of the whites, bolder than the rest, went up and looked inside, he saw that the fort was empty. The Blackfeet had slipped away in the night, leaving nine dead warriors and twenty-four dead horses behind them in this fort. Other bodies were found outside.

The mountain men and Flatheads rushed in, ripped off the scalps, looked for the packs. But they found no scarlet blankets, no abalone shells, nor any other plunder. The Blackfeet had got away with most of their valuables.

Enraged, the disappointed Flatheads, tireless and relentless as so many wolves, set out on the trail of their enemies, determined to let none escape. Many of the mountain men went with them. Here and there they came upon an abandoned, broken-down horse, a dropped pack, or the body of a warrior who had died of his wounds. The Flatheads counted coup on these poor relics, while they or the mountain men lifted the topknots to tie in their belts.

Suddenly they came upon a striking figure. A dead warrior lay at the foot of a great pine. Beside him, leaning against the tree, waited his woman.[1] She beckoned the mountain men. "Come on, kill me!" she called. The trappers hung back, astonished at this pitiful picture.

But the Flatheads and Nez Percés never dreamed of sparing a woman, who might become the mother of an enemy. They rushed in, screeching, and shot her dead before the whites could interfere. Farther on they killed a second Blackfoot woman, overtaken while running for her life. It was not often that the Flatheads had a chance to shed Blackfoot blood with such impunity.

This pursuit brought the known loss of the Blackfeet up to sixteen dead, all told. (Actually, they said, they had lost twenty-six men.) But seeing that the fugitives were heading towards the main Blackfoot camp, the trappers and friendlies turned back. That night they rested once more in their camps at rendezvous, in Pierre's Hole.

To Meek and the rest it seemed likely enough that the Blackfoot chief had been yelling the truth and that their main camp was somewhere around. The Atsina were a small tribe, and would hardly have risked the long ride

---

1 Though he admits that he had "heard this anecdote discredited by one of the leaders who had been in this battle," Washington Irving, always the romanticist, in his *Adventures of Captain Bonneville* (London and New York, 1843), Chapter VI, attributes the Indian woman's failure to fly either to "grief . . . or a proud spirit." But Meek (see Mrs. Victor's biography, page 117) points out that "the woman's leg had been broken by a ball and she was unable to move from the spot." She may have begged the trappers to kill her for fear of falling into the hands of her Indian enemies, or *because* of the pain she suffered.

from the Arapaho camp to Blackfoot country in small bands. So everybody remained in rendezvous for a few days before breaking up for the fall hunt.

No Blackfeet came to bother them, and the booshways prepared to put out. Captain William Sublette, however, had to rest and allow his wound to heal. Impatient at this delay, a small party of seven men, two of them said to be grandsons of Daniel Boone, started for Missouri on their own. Stephens, having been one of Gant's and Blackwell's band picked up by Fitzpatrick, was disgusted at his treatment by the Rocky Mountain Fur Company. After some hard words he lit out, on July 25, for the Laramie River, to lift his cache of furs before Sublette could get there. His anger made him rash.

With him rode a young Bostonian, More, eager to get back to civilization.

A few days later, five of them came back to rendezvous. Stephens was mortally wounded. As they got into Jackson's Hole, they said, twenty Gros Ventres had jumped them. The war whoops terrified More's horse, which whirled and threw him. Everybody fled back up the slope.

More, afoot, left behind, scrambled up the hillside too, but at the top seemed to lose his head and stood as though paralyzed, watching the warriors rushing at him. The other whites spurred on for their lives. But when Daniel Boone's grandsons saw More's danger they turned back, leaped from their saddles, and rallied to his defense. But the Gros Ventres were too many. They struck More down, shot Foy dead, wounded Stephens. The Gros Ventres had got off unharmed.

These Indians, particularly those who had lost relatives in the battle of Pierre's Hole, were eager to avenge them and tried to enlist their allies for the fight. But the Blackfeet, having been none too successful in a campaign against the Flathead tribe and fearing the wrath of

Kenneth McKenzie, held out against it. Finally all agreed to let white men alone for a while and slake their thirst for blood among the Crows. A big war party headed up Wind River.

But the Crows were not asleep. They ambushed the Blackfeet, and killed forty warriors. The remnant scattered and made their way home in a very ugly mood.

On July 30 William "Cut Face" Sublette and his pack train headed for the States. He too was unlucky, and ran into the main camp of the Gros Ventres. But Cut Face bluffed and bought them off, avoiding a fight. He arrived at Lexington, Missouri, on the second of September, richly laden. On his way in, Washington Irving met and described the "long cavalcade, stretched in single file for nearly half a mile." Sublette still wore his arm in a sling.

As for Joe Meek, he rode with his favorite booshway, Old Milt Sublette. They headed for Snake River. Wyeth's men kept them company as far as the headwaters of the Humboldt—then called Mary's River.

Meat's Meat

BEFORE Wyeth left Meek and his company on the headwaters of the Humboldt River, they were already in that barren, inhospitable waste inhabited by the Digger Indians. The lowly Diggers with their miserable diet, arid country, and alternately blistering and chilling desert climate were nearer to the natural man than any tribe in America; they had practically no industry, no arts, no ceremonies; their lives were, to use the words of the philosopher, solitary, poor, brutish, nasty, and short!

Half starved, stark naked, nesting in a hole in the ground, the Digger was perforce omnivorous. Occasionally he killed a beaver, a rabbit or a mouse. The rest of the time he lived on insects. He owed the worm no silk, the beast no hide, the sheep no wool, the cat no perfume. Other tribes, by comparison, were sophisticated, but the Digger was the thing itself—unaccommodated man, hardly more than a poor, bare, forked animal.

Despicable as he was, however, he could yet be dangerous; for he carried arrows poisoned with rattlesnake venom.

One day while Meek was out alone raising his traps, four of these Diggers jumped out of a ravine and took after him. Not hankering for a poisoned arrow in his guts, Joe lit out, and being longer-legged than the short little brown men, kept ahead for half a mile. But the Diggers were enduring; they hung on his trail like so many skinny coyotes. They spread out and would have caught him or shot him down had not one of his comrades come unexpectedly to the rescue.

The Diggers were not mighty warriors like the Crows and Blackfeet; but they could steal and murder when the chance came their way.

One day Joe saw a Digger hanging around, following him along the stream where he was setting his traps. Joe tried to warn, then scare the man away; but the rascal kept hanging around, waiting for the white man to leave, until finally Joe lost his temper, threw up his rifle and shot the Digger down.

Wyeth, who was pestered in the mountains by his New England conscience, could not approve of such actions, and demanded, "Why did you shoot him?"

"To keep him from stealin' my traps," Joe replied.

"Had he stolen any?" Wyeth inquired.

Meek grinned disarmingly, "No; but he looked as if he war goin' to."

Wyeth did not understand what Meek and other mountain men had learned the hard way: that war is not just fighting, but in fact exists wherever there is a known disposition thereto and no assurance to the contrary. In the mountains where all men of one tribe were held responsible for the crimes of any of his kind, no man—white or red—could ever be sure that a stranger was not his enemy. They believed every man an enemy until he was proven friendly.

For a time, Milton Sublette and his men wandered about in the barren country between the Humboldt and the Owyhee rivers. They found no game or beaver, no grass or cottonwood bark to give their horses. At last, when they did succeed in killing beaver, they found the flesh poisonous and were all sick; for even beaver could not find proper food in that region, and had been reduced to eating wild parsnips.

Both men and animals grew gaunt and irritable. Sublette decided to turn north and look for better hunting.

In that dreadful desert Meek and his comrades began to starve, and soon found themselves reduced to the same loathsome diet as the Diggers whom they had so despised a few days earlier. There was nothing they did not eat that could be swallowed.

Long afterwards, Meek declared, "I held my hands in an ant-hill until they were covered with ants, then greedily licked them off. I took the soles off my moccasins, crisped them in the fire, and ate them. In our extremity, the large black crickets which are found in this country were considered game. We used to take a kettle of hot water, catch the crickets and throw them in, and when they stopped kicking, eat them. That was not what we called 'cant tickup ko hanch' ('good meat, my friend'), but it kept us alive."[1]

Parched by the hot winds, burned by the blazing sun, they also suffered all the torments of great thirst. Some drank their own urine or that of their horses. At night when camp was made, messmates would debate whose mule was to be bled. Having chosen an animal by vote, they cut a vein in the mule's ear, drained off a pint of blood and drank this—the only food they had.

Yet those men could not afford to bleed their mules to death—mules which were already famishing—for the men were too weak to travel far by shank's mare. Moreover, the veneer of civilization (which consists, for the most part, of a layer of fatty tissue) had worn thin, and the men were so grouchy and cross that, when a mule was

[1] The expression, cant tickup ko hanch, is from the Shoshone language and means literally "good food, my friend." Phonetically, saunt-den-tickup, hintz; "good meat," saunt-den-duke. S.V.

chosen to be bled or killed for meat, the owner was likely to pick a fight with his comrades. It was all a question of whose mule was gored.

Finally, the famished men picked out the poorest mule, killed it and ate the flesh. Several times they had to do this, as the stricken party pushed slowly northward towards Snake River.

But at last, after weeks of interminable days of famine and four days of absolute starvation, one afternoon their haggard mules started running. The men knew they were heading for water.

They struck Snake River about fifty miles above the "Fishing Falls" as those rapids were then called. All plunged in and soaked themselves inside and out.

Now they had water, but still no food. The swift, clear water was alive with mountain trout, but they had no fishhooks. The booshway decided to kill one of the horses. He selected an animal no longer serviceable because of saddle sores.

The man who owned the animal prepared to transfer his saddle to another animal, and, in order to avoid injury to his new mount, began to pick the stuffing out of his saddle, trying to make a softer, smoother surface.

All at once he pricked his finger on a long brass pin that had accidentally gotten into the saddle when it was being made in the settlements. Then his gaunt face lighted with a triumphant grin. He let out a croak of joy and held up the pin so that the other boys could see. It was that pin which had made the horse's back so sore.

When Joe Meek and the others saw that big brass pin, no words were needed. They all knew at once what could be done with that. Quickly they bent it into a hook, pulled hair from their horses' tails and twisted these into a line, cut a pole from the nearest thicket, baited the hook with a grasshopper, and dropped it into the water. The fish seemed to stand in line waiting to take the hook.

That night they gorged themselves; and when they hit the trail next morning, every man had half a dozen big ones tied on his saddle. They rode on their way rejoicing, finding the country ever more hospitable as they moved toward the mountains. They passed up Payette River to Payette Lake. There Sublette made camp and sent his men out trapping.

Joe Meek with three others, Antoine Godin, Louis Leaugar [LeGarde?] and Small, headed north towards Salmon River. One day up there while his comrades were out hunting, Meek stayed in camp to cook some meat from a fine, fat deer he had just killed.

Suddenly looking up from his labors, he saw about a hundred Indians coming straight for camp. Odds of a hundred to one looked a little too big to Joe. He reckoned, he says, that running from them would not increase their numbers, while it might help him to defend himself. He took to his heels, ran as hard as he could, and took cover in the brush.

There, panting and looking back, Joe was surprised to see that the Indians were not after him, but had stopped at his campfire and were busy roasting the *whole* deer which he had killed for his own dinner. Joe watched them preparing to eat all his deer meat until he could stand it no longer; then he coolly walked out and joined the party to share in the feast. His visitors belonged to the Nez Percé tribe. Having eaten Joe's deer, they invited him to go with them to their camp not far off. When he got there, he found the other three fellows and their horses already in camp. Soon after, Milton Sublette and the rest of the brigade rode in.

They hunted all that country, trapping on the Malade, or Big Wood River, on Godin Creek, or Big Lost River, finally making camp at the forks of the Salmon. There they found the main brigade of the Rocky Mountain Fur Company, under Old Gabe Bridger and Tom Fitzpatrick, waiting. Not far off was Bonneville's tumble-down trade house.

Meek learned that while he had been with Sublette west of the mountains, Bridger and Fitzpatrick had been doing their best to shake the rival brigade of the American Fur Company led by Drips and Vanderburgh, who kept dogging Bridger, hoping he would lead them to good hunting grounds. Bridger rode to the Yellowstone, then to the forks of the Missouri. But wherever he went, they followed. Unwilling to act as guide for the rival company, Bridger kept on the move, trying to leave them behind, until at last he had come back to the west side of the Continental Divide, where Meek found him on Salmon River.

Here the brigades were reorganized. Meek rode with Bridger and Fitzpatrick. And after them trailed Drips and Vanderburgh.

By this time, the booshways of the Rocky Mountain Fur Company were exasperated. They decided to give Drips and Vanderburgh a run for their money, leading them on a wild-goose chase across the mountains to the Missouri, pushing into Blackfoot country, keeping away from the beaver streams, and killing all the game—if any —they found along the way. Thus they hoped to ruin their rivals.

Ferris, one of Vanderburgh's men, tells how they found the trail and old camps of the Rocky Mountain Fur Company, but seldom any game. Hurrying on, they caught up with Bridger, who blandly assured them that a band of Indians, probably Blackfeet, was trapping and hunting on the trail ahead of him, and killing all the game! The fact that Bridger's eighty men were themselves on short rations kept Ferris and his party from suspecting that they were purposely being led into starving country.[1]

---

[1] W. A. Ferris, *Life in the Rocky Mountains* (Denver, 1940), p. 168.

Finding themselves in the midst of hostile Blackfeet, Drips and Vanderburgh unwisely decided to divide their forces, determined to find beaver somewhere. Though new to the mountains, Drips had long been in the fur trade, and knew he was not "up to Blackfeet." But Vanderburgh, a West Pointer without experience of Indian fighting, on October 8, 1832, recklessly rode out to reconnoiter with only half a dozen men. Not far from the Madison River a hundred warriors jumped him from a small gulch, and fired on him from a distance of only thirty yards. When his horse went down, Vanderburgh stood his ground and died fighting, while his men galloped to safety. Ferris was badly wounded.

This disaster pretty well put an end to the operations of the American Fur Company for that season.

Once rid of his rivals, Old Gabe set his own men to trapping. They could not afford to waste those precious autumn months tearing around country where no beaver could be found. Meek wanted to make hay while the sun shone, and Blackfoot country offered the largest returns.

But they well knew how dangerous that country was and kept close watch on their horses. It wasn't likely they could get to winter quarters without at least *one* fight with the cussed Injuns.

And so it was. On a small lake near the headwaters of the Missouri, Joe Meek and some other trappers surprised a small band of Blackfeet on a little peninsula at a bend in the lake shore. Meek opened fire, and the Blackfeet, who had no guns, were forced to dive into the lake and swim for safety. The trappers then lay on the bank and amused themselves by shooting at their heads, keeping the redskins diving and ducking, having a wonderful time.

While this sport was at its height, lo and behold, a big bunch of warriors from the main camp of the Blackfeet turned up; then it was the turn of Meek and his friends to run for their lives. They headed back for camp. The Indians pursued. But on seeing the camp so big, the Blackfeet warily kept to the rocky hillsides and sent one of their chiefs out into the open carrying a peace pipe.

Bridger and Fitzpatrick took no stock in any treaty made with Blackfeet and saw little point in smoking with them. But one of their men, Loretto, a free trapper with a Blackfoot wife, told Bridger not to worry. He recognized the band as the relatives of his wife. She offered to act as interpreter.

Fitzpatrick, with seven seasoned trappers, walked out to meet the chief and his seven braves and talk things over. They all sat down and then shook hands all around. The talk began and went on for some time—in the sign language.

While they palavered, Loretto's wife recognized her brother among the Blackfeet on the hillside. She called and signalled to him. The commotion which followed alarmed one of the warriors sitting in the council with Fitzpatrick. He stood up and made signs inquiring what was up. A young Blackfoot warrior rode out to explain matters, forgetting to leave his bow and quiver behind.

His coming made the number unequal. Jim Bridger, seeing that the young man had a bow and arrows in his hand, took his rifle and rode out to make the number equal. With him rode Loretto's Blackfoot woman, to act as interpreter. Just as one of the chiefs came up to shake his hand, Jim saw that the young warrior's bow was strung, and so cocked his gun.

When the chief heard the lock click on Bridger's gun, he grabbed the barrel, and jerked the muzzle downward. Bridger's finger was on the trigger and the sudden tug caused him to fire. The bullet struck the ground square between the feet of the chief. Before Jim knew what was doing, the chief wrested his rifle away, struck him at the base of the skull, and knocked him senseless to the ground.

By that time Jim had two arrows in his back from the bow of the young warrior. Then the Blackfoot chief snatched the reins of Bridger's horse, mounted and rode back to his people. The unarmed men at the parley swiftly ran back to get their weapons. The fight had already begun. In the middle of all this hubbub, Loretto's woman's horse whirled and threw her, turned and galloped back to Bridger's camp. The Blackfeet took the woman with them to the hillside.

On both sides the men took cover and fired at long range. Loretto, who heard his wife crying, boldly took their baby in his arms and galloped into the heart of the Blackfoot band to give the child to its distracted mother. Meek was sure the Blackfeet would shoot the foolhardy Mexican; but Loretto's boldness roused the admiration of the warriors, and the chief said he could go back unharmed.

Loretto begged to take his wife and baby along. He told the chief how he had found the Blackfoot woman captive among the Crows, who would have tortured her to death, if he had not ransomed her and made her his wife. But the chief would not give him the woman, and sternly ordered Loretto to skip. It was not until the following year, when the two fur companies united, that he was able to go to Blackfoot country and take his wife again.

In this fight the Rocky Mountain Fur Company lost three men killed, and six horses. They managed to extract one of the arrowheads from Jim Bridger's back; but the other defied all efforts to butcher it out. The Blackfeet lost nine warriors.

After this fight the Rocky Mountain Fur Company brigade continued its trapping, heading for the Beaverhead Valley. They spent Christmas in winter quarters at the forks of the Snake.

But the trappers were not happy in winter quarters. They had not done too well that year, what with their dry scrape in the desert and those squabbles with the American Fur Company interfering with their beaver trapping. Game was not easily found near the forks of the Snake, and the grass was far too scanty to maintain their horses. Towards the end of January they had to pull out, and move camp through bitter cold wind to save their animals.

The main camp moved swiftly against the cold wind, while those with pack horses and lodges to transport straggled along behind. Meek and five others trailed behind everybody else, having been given the duty of rounding up stray animals. It was very cold riding through such bitter weather: the air was thick with fine, sharp ice particles through which the sun shone between two sun-dogs—or as Meek put it, three suns! It was a strange and fearsome day.

Meek, as usual, had no underwear, or even a shirt. Like most others, he wore only a beaver-fur cap, buckskin breeches, moccasins, and his capote—a blanket coat with hood attached. A shirt warn't no good in the mountains —except to dress up in at rendezvous. Thar warn't no warmth in cotton; a man couldn't be bothered to wash it clean, and the seams were always full of lice.

But as Meek rode along, hazing the horses and gaunt mules against the wind, he came up with Mountain Lamb, Milton Sublette's wife. She was riding along with head bent, clutching her baby—which she had wrapped in her own shawl—and shivering with cold. Meek could see from the way she carried her child, shielding it from the wind with her own body, that she was more concerned about her baby than about herself.

Now Joe Meek had always prided himself on his chivalry and consideration towards the fair sex, and the pages of Sir Walter Scott's novels and Mrs. Porter's

Scottish Chiefs which he had heard read in winter quarters, had only made him the more chivalrous. That poor mother, that handsome squaw, his friend's wife, could not be allowed to freeze. Cold as Joe was, he did not hesitate a moment, but pulled off his warm capote, wrapped it around the woman and child, and laid his quirt across her horse's rump. "Hurry," he said. "Push hard; git to camp."

The Indian woman thanked him, then drubbed the ribs of her slow horse to put it to a faster gait.

But poor Meek, naked now above the waist except for his fur cap, could not hurry or keep up with her. He had to herd to camp those reluctant, half-starved ponies lagging into the bitter wind. All that fearful afternoon Joe rode naked, lashed by that stinging icy hail. Perhaps the sting of it kept his blood from freezing.

When he did pull in, nearly frozen, numb, stiff, and blistered with the frost, his friends had to roll him in the snow and rub his white fingers and face until he was warm enough to approach the fire in safety.

As if to celebrate Joe's courage, the heavens that night put on an extraordinary display of blazing Northern Lights. Says Meek, "It was the most beautiful sight I ever saw."

That winter was savagely cold. Not only mules, but men froze to death in the mountains. When Meek wakened in the morning and looked up at the lodgepoles which met at the top of his tent, he could see the frost hanging in great skeins, two feet long, and his blankets and beard were white with it. But Joe was a trapper. He did not have to get up in the cold. He just lay there and hollered for the camp keepers. "Git up and fix the fire."

Within a few minutes a small fire made the snug buffalo-hide tepee warm as toast.

That is, when there was fuel a-plenty. But that winter on Snake River there was mighty little. Such heat as they had was made by burning strips of buffalo fat, in a brief blaze giving a momentary glow.

Yet the Nez Percés and Flatheads were hospitable. When Meek stood by, watching the Indians' fire, not venturing to go near it, some chief would call, "My friend, are you cold? Come to my fire."

But there was not much buffalo fat to burn that winter, because the bison were east of the mountains and other game was hard to find. One day Meek, Hawkins, Doughty and Antoine Claymore (Clement) were out almost two weeks without killing anything more than they needed to keep alive. They could find no elk or deer in the valley, and, in the desperate hope of shooting a mountain sheep, clambered up the side of a mountain covered with frozen snow. They were passing single file under a rocky ledge, when Meek saw grizzly bear tracks—huge ones—leading into a cave. "Hooray," he yelled, "thar's the meat!"

The catch was how to get it. Few hunters cared to beard a grizzly in his den even in the dead of winter.

Doughty quickly offered to get up on the rocks above the mouth of the cave and shoot the bear when it came out—if somebody else would go in and run him out.

At this challenge, Meek spoke up. "I'm your man," he declared.

"Me too," said Claymore.

"Hell," said Hawkins, "I'll be damned if I'm not as brave as you are."

So the three men walked into the cave. It was about twenty feet square and high enough to stand up in. There the three men found three bears standing up to receive them. There was a little bear, a middle-sized bear and a big bear, which stood in the middle. Slowly, step by step, the three hunters, hugging the walls of the cave, crept towards the game. As soon as Meek was near enough, he whipped out his wiping stick and hit the big bear a smart blow over its sensitive snout.

At once the big bear rushed out of the cave. They heard Doughty's gun bang; but the bear, only wounded, came tearing back into the cave growling and snarling, running in a circle, until all three hunters fired and dropped it on the spot.

The roar of those three rifles in the narrow room deafened Meek.

But Hawkins was in high spirits. He began to sing and dance around and joined the others in striking the middle-sized bear to make it run out. Out it went, and this time Doughty killed his bear.

Louder and louder Hawkins began to yell, "We are Daniels in the lions' den—and no mistake!"

It did not take long to drive out the little bear. As it fled from the cave, three of the hunters fired and killed it.

But Hawkins was still shouting. "Dan'l war a humbug; Dan'l couldn't shine in this crowd," said he. "Dan'l in the lions' den! Of course, it war winter and the lions were suckin' their paws! Don't tell me no more about Dan'l's brave deeds. We are as good Daniels as he ever dared to be. Hooray for us!"

Leaving the bears' den, they made sleds of willow sticks and harness of rawhide taken from the bears and so dragged their meat to camp. But Hawkins never stopped talking, never allowed the camp to forget that Daniels, he and Meek, and Claymore had been in that cave with the three grizzlies. . . .

Jim Bridger had a fast running horse—fast and enduring, a Comanche buffalo horse which he called Grohean. One morning Bridger discovered that the Blackfeet had run off most of the horses, including Grohean. Old Gabe was wrathy as a bear.

Kit Carson headed a party of the gamest trappers, of which Joe Meek was one. They trailed the horse thieves through the snow for some fifty miles, and so came up with them. The trappers were afoot and moved a good deal faster than the Blackfeet, on snowshoes, could break trail for the horses through the snow.

When the Blackfeet saw the trappers coming they drove the stolen horses out of the deep snow of the valley onto a bare hillside where they could travel faster and have opportunity to secrete the animals in some canyon until the inevitable fight was over.

Kit and the trappers floundering through the drifts were left behind. So Kit Carson signaled to the Blackfeet to sit and talk it over. The Blackfeet were willing enough; time was on their side. For, while the trappers talked, the horses could be kept moving towards the Blackfoot camp.

Each party posted a guard to watch their weapons and walked forward unarmed to the parley. They sat in two lines facing each other. Both sides wanted to have a good look at the enemy before the scrap began—if scrap there was to be.

The chief was very bland and oily and all his warriors made a great show of being peace-loving and innocent.

The chief said that they had had no idea they were stealing horses from a white man's camp; that they had gone to war against the Snakes! Still, after all their trouble in stealing the horses, the Blackfeet were unwilling to give them back. That would mean a loss of face as well as of horses.

The trappers, on their part, after running through the snow so far after the thieves, were in no mood for foolishness or lies. They never dreamed of admitting that white men had no business in Blackfoot country.[1]

Finally the Blackfeet agreed to give up five broken-

---

[1] Kit Carson gives the number of trappers in this fracas as thirty; the number of horses stolen as eighteen; the number of Blackfoot warriors encountered as thirty. Meek's story is that the trappers numbered thirty, that most of the horses in camp were stolen, and that there were more trappers than Indians in the fight. It is possible that, after the trappers overtook the Indians, the latter divided their forces and sent some of the warriors to haze the horses for home.

down animals, which they could never take home anyway. Seeing that nothing more was to be gained by talk, the trappers broke and ran to get their weapons; the Indians sprinted for their own. Both sides snatched up their weapons, and the scrap began.

Kit and Mark Head led the charge and ran into two of the warriors cached behind trees. Kit stalked one; Mark Head the other. As Kit advanced, he saw Mark Head's Indian about to fire upon his friend. Then, Kit says, "I forgot entirely the danger" and "neglected my Indian for Mark Head's." Kit drew a bead on the redskin, who tried to dodge—but was too late. Then Kit saw his own Indian aiming at his breast. He could not load in time to get the first shot. Mark Head had run on. Kit jumped and danced around, Indian-fashion, to spoil the Blackfoot's aim. But the bullet grazed Kit's neck and passed clean through his shoulder.

Meek and Mark Head carried Kit back to cover in the timber. There they camped for the night, about a mile from the battleground. They dared not sleep by a fire for fear the Indians would sneak up and kill them by the light of it. With only a thin saddle blanket to shelter him, Kit suffered miserably all night from the bitter chill, loss of blood, and shock. It grew so cold that the blood flowing from his wound froze and stopped the hemorrhage.

Next morning some of the Indians were still waiting, full of fight; but the horses were nowhere to be seen. Meek and the rest went back to camp afoot.

Bridger then organized another party to hit the Blackfoot trail, but never caught up with the thieves. He had only the five broken-down nags Kit had brought back. Old Gabe had to buy new mounts from the Nez Percés.

His spring hunt was made on Snake River and its tributaries and on Green River. There, that summer of 1833, the annual rendezvous was held near the mouth of Horse Creek, where Captain Benjamin Louis Eulalie

de Bonneville, the independent operator, had recently
built his fort.

By this time Joe Meek had risen above his status of
hired trapper. He was a free trapper now, no longer
working for wages, but trapping on his own hook. Still
he sold whatever beaver he could take exclusively to the
Rocky Mountain Fur Company, which furnished him
his equipment.

At rendezvous Joe found his own outfit, also the
American Fur Company brigade, and the St. Louis Company of Captain William Sublette and Robert Campbell,
besides a big camp of Indians and Captain Bonneville's
brigade.

But far more remarkable to Meek was the small company of furriners in the employ of Captain Sir William
Drummond Stewart. He had come west with a staff of
servants.[1]

Sir William was a seasoned sportsman, a spare man over
six feet tall with a ruddy complexion, beak nose, black
hair, a handsome mustache and a game spirit. At the time
he was about forty years of age.

Now Meek had a chance to see for himself a real British
aristocrat and to check what he had read in novels by
surveying the thing itself. Joe was not disappointed. Sir
William was as liberal as any mountain man, a crack shot,
a splendid horseman, and a brave soldier. He introduced
Meek and other trappers to certain civilized refinements:
New Orleans brandy, porter and fine wines, coffee, tea,
pickles, and tins of preserved meats. He shared their enthusiasm for Indian women, and, like them, enjoyed
taking a horn.

---

[1] Later, in 1837, he brought along an artist, Alfred Jacob Miller, to make
water-color sketches of scenes of mountain life. Many of these have been
published. See Bernard DeVoto's *Across the Wide Missouri* (Boston, 1947),
"Illustrated with paintings by Alfred Jacob Miller, Charles Bodmer, and
George Catlin, with an account of the discovery of the Miller collection by
Mae Reed Porter." Some had previously appeared in *Fortune* magazine, and
in the *St. Louis Post-Dispatch* for December 1, 1940. S. V.

But, apparently, Sir William was not given to alcoholic excess.

Now Joe Meek was celebrating his recent attainment to the glorious privilege of being independent. No longer a hireling, Joe was as independent as a hog on ice. At rendezvous that summer, by his own account, he indulged himself more than usual. Joe was on his spree. *Wagh!* Now it happened that a mad wolf prowled around the camp. One night it came into camp and bit a sleeping man severely. Poor Holmes sat up bleeding, with one ear nearly torn off. Several other men were bitten, as well as one of the bulls.. The wolf hung around for several nights, so that no creature's life was safe. But Joe Meek, happy-go-lucky, could not postpone the celebration of his rise in the world. He had earned it by long hard years in the mountains. Now he was on his own hook. He knew whar to lay hand on beaver galore, and his heart was big. The bellowing of the bull bitten by the wolf, the screams and shouting, the crack of rifles that night, all failed to waken Joe.

The next day Sir William admonished him. "You were so drunk," he said, "that wolf might easily have bitten you."

Meek laughed. Back in Virginia they had l'arned him that alcohol was a cure for the pizen of hydrophobia. "Shucks," said Joe, "if that wolf had bit me, it would have killed him sure—if it hadn't cured him!"

Ride to Monterey

MEEK WAS trapping east of Salt Lake when, on Bear River, he encountered a company of mountain men in the employ of Captain Benjamin Louis Eulalie de Bonneville, heading for the lake to hunt buffalo. The booshway of the band was that strapping old-timer, Captain Joseph Reddeford Walker, known to all the mountain men. Dark, bearded, and tall enough to carry his two hundred pounds handily, Meek knew him for a noted Indian fighter, Missourian, trader, trapper and trail maker. Though naturally mild, Walker was resolute. Meek had confidence in such a leader. On learning that Walker and his men were heading west from Salt Lake over country never yet explored by white men, Meek and his friends resolved to go along. For Meek, in spite of his recent hardships experienced with Sublette on the Humboldt River, was ready for new adventures out there. Also, his brother, Stephen H. L. Meek, was to accompany the party.

Of course, exploration was a very important part of the fur business, and the man who had ventured into unexplored territory might profit from his knowledge by hiring out as pilot or guide. Beaver should be plenty on unexplored streams. In short, as Meek put it, going with Walker would be "a feather in a man's cap."

Of course, men had gone overland to California before
—Lewis and Clark and the Astorians by way of the Columbia River; Bill Wolfskill had crossed the desert of the
Colorado and extended the Spanish Trail, Ewing Young
had crossed the Mohave by a middle route, and Dave
Jackson farther down. Jedediah Smith had crossed the
Great Basin three times. But no white man had ever
attempted to head directly west through the desert from
the Great Salt Lake.

Captain Bonneville was not only a booshway of trappers, but an officer of the United States Army, on leave.
His leave was so extended that it seems likely our government would not have been so liberal with him merely to
help him make a fortune in furs.

When Bonneville's adventures were recorded by Washington Irving, he wrote that the Captain sent Walker on a
mere trapping expedition to explore the western shores
of Salt Lake; but few historians can now accept Bonneville's version of the matter. The *Narrative* of Zenas
Leonard, Walker's clerk, was published in book form in
1839. Leonard says he went with Walker because he was
"anxious to go to the coast of the Pacific." When Joe
Meek joined the party, he certainly knew where it was
heading.

Walker had forty men when he left Green River July
24, 1833, but since Sublette's recent expedition, Joe Meek
and others had learned a thing or two. Before heading
into the desert again, they had a big buffalo hunt, made
meat, and packed along sixty pounds of jerky for every
man in the party. It was about mid-August when they
headed west into the Salt Lake Desert.

That first night they camped at a spring, where they
found Indians. The chief told them they would find a
snow-capped peak with a large river heading on it. The
river formed a chain of lakes, he said, until at last it sank
into the sand. There was no game in that country, he re-

ported; only a tribe of wretched Indians, probably unfriendly.

They were more than a week reaching that lone mountain. It bore some scrawny pinon trees. Leaving the mountain behind them, Meek and the others reached the headwaters of the Humboldt, then called Mary's River. There was sign of beaver, but no other game. They found a few dirty Indians all stark naked; and from them Walker bought for two awls and one fishhook a robe made of beaverskins worth forty dollars.

The stunted Indians had a few furs to trade, for apparently they lived largely on beaver. Once these wretched people learned how steel traps worked, nothing could keep them from trying to steal some. The traps, of course, belonged to individual trappers and cost twenty dollars apiece in the mountains. But they were priceless in that country. Of course, a trapper with six or eight traps to watch could not possibly prevent this thieving, and bitterly resented it. Captain Walker, however, warned the men not to start trouble with the savages. His men obeyed until one of the Indians tried to shoot Frazer while he was setting his traps. Walker could not watch all his men; and some, though not daring to report it, killed three Indians in retaliation.

These Indians were Shoshokoes, or as Meek puts it, "Shuckers"—more commonly known as Diggers, most backward of all the Shoshone stock.

Walker's men found no fuel on "Barren River," as Leonard named it. Nothing grew along the stream, and they rode for days without finding a single stick big enough to make a walking cane—no buffalo chips, nothing. Yet as they went on they saw more and more sign of Indians, saw signal smokes.

They found grass along the swampy stream and after trailing through a gloomy canyon, saw lakes gleaming on ahead. On these they flushed flocks of ducks, and cranes, trailing their long legs, flew from the reeds along the sullen waters. Here was good grass. Walker dismounted and they made camp. Horses, mules and men alike were easy.

But just before sunset, while taking a look around through his spyglass, Walker saw smoke rising on all sides. They were surrounded. The Diggers had set the grass aflame, and there was no timber in which to make a stand!

Walker and his men acted quickly. Meek and the others thought first of their horses. They led them all down to the lake shore, tied them all together and staked them out there. Around the horses Meek and the others built a breastwork of the packs—a shallow fort against poisoned arrows.

By that time the Diggers were coming—eight or nine hundred, maybe a thousand, singing and dancing in happy anticipation of their victory. Suddenly they all sat down at a distance of about one hundred and fifty yards. Five of their chiefs came forward and talked in signs with Captain Walker. They asked to come into the white men's camp and smoke with them.

Captain Walker was no fool. At close range a bow was better than a rifle. He refused to admit so many Indians to his camp, but said he would talk with them halfway between his fort and their people. The chiefs returned in anger.

Soon after, some of the Indians signaled that they were coming to the fort anyhow. Then Meek and ten or twelve others climbed the breastwork and signed back warning them to come no nearer unless they wished to die. The Diggers demanded to know how the white men expected to kill them. Meek and the others brandished their rifles. This made the Diggers laugh. That was the first time Meek ever saw an Indian laugh at *his* rifle.

But before charging, the Diggers cannily demanded a

demonstration of what a mountain man's rifle could do. Ducks were swimming in the lakes not far from Walker's fort. Walker decided to throw a scare into those ignorant savages and so get rid of them. He told his men to shoot the ducks. They did. At the roar of the guns all the redskins dropped flat on the ground. They hardly noticed the dead ducks.

Later they put up a beaverskin on a bank as a target for Walker's rifles. Finding it pierced by the bullets, the Diggers decided to pull out.

All night the trappers kept guard, but their camp was not disturbed.

Walker's men packed and hit the trail early next day. Shortly after sunrise they found the grass on both sides full of warriors. Walker left the lake and the high grass and travelled over bare desert. This move the savages may have interpreted as a retreat. At any rate they began to tag along, first by twos and threes and then by scores. For several hours they followed like so many wolves, always increasing in number.

Then small parties were seen ahead, each of them begging the white men to stop and smoke. It was clear enough that they merely wanted to detain the trappers until the whole tribe could come up, surround the whites, come to close quarters and kill them all with arrows. Walker repeatedly warned the Diggers and held his fire.

But when a party of about a hundred boldly advanced, Walker acted. "Boys," he said, "thar is nothin' equal to a good start in such a fix. Get ready to charge."

A good many of Walker's men had never fought Indians and were eager to try their marksmanship. The party reined up. Thirty-two men dismounted. Then, after tying up their pack horses, they mounted again to surround the Indians. Closing in, they gave the Diggers a volley or two, dropping a good number.[1]

---

[1] Figures differ as to the number of Indians killed in this affair: Leonard, thirty-nine; Nidever, thirty-three; Stephen H. L. Meek, eighteen; Joe Meek, seventy-five. Rely on Joe to make a good story of it.

The surviving Indians tore off into the tall grass howling in the most lamentable manner, scattering "like partridges from the hawk." Captain Walker then ordered some of his men to take the bows and arrows of the dead and put the wounded out of their pain. No sense in wasting gunpowder.

According to Stephen H. L. Meek the whites captured five prisoners, severely whipped them and then let them go.

"The severity with which we dealt with these Indians," writes Leonard, "may be revolting to the heart of the philanthropist; but the circumstances of the case altogether atones for the cruelty. It must be borne in mind, that we were far removed from the hope of any succour in case we were surrounded, and that the country we were in was swarming with hostile savages, sufficiently numerous to devour us. Our object was to strike a decisive blow. This we did—even to a greater extent than we had intended."

Certainly Walker's "severity" was revolting to his employer, Captain Bonneville, who never tired of excoriating the mountain men and condemning them for what he thought wanton murder of those wretched Diggers. Bonneville had not suffered at the hands of Indians, and lived most of the time with the friendly Flatheads, Nez Percés and Snakes. . . .

And so they came to Battle Lakes, travelling down the south bank of the Humboldt to the point where the river turned sharply into the lake. They found the water alkali, with quantities of pumice stone floating on its surface.

Their buffalo meat was now exhausted. Walker sent hunters out to look for game and trails through the mountains. They found neither; but did bring back a colt belonging to some Indians who had run away when the hunters came in sight. The colt was killed and divided among the men. They had come, they estimated, twelve

hundred miles without seeing any hills except the lone
mountain where the Barren River heads, and no game
but rabbits. Yet the country was full of Indians!

Here Meek and his little party of free trappers, which
included his brother, left Walker's starving brigade and
struck off on their own hook. From Pyramid Lake they
followed the Truckee River, hoping it would lead them
to a pass over the Sierra. For more than three weeks they
scrambled and strained, hastening to get through those
unknown mountains before winter closed down upon
them. They had to blaze their own trail, and sometimes
break trail through newly fallen snow; always tired,
always hungry, always in danger. Sometimes they had to
surmount smooth surfaces of granite on which their
horses slipped and struggled, trying to gain a foothold
in some seam or crevice in the rock; sometimes they
fought their way through dense pine woods clogged with
snow and fallen trees; more rarely, they found a few yards
of easy trail on high ridges swept bare by the wind.
Hemmed in by peaks and spires of rock red as though it
had been singed in hell-fire, the half-frozen trappers
stared across a sea of granite, its fissures marked by stunted evergreens twisted and gnarled by the mountain gales.
With the instinct of seasoned mountaineers, Meek and
the rest kept to the streams, and sometimes found a snug
and grassy valley, set cuplike among the rocks, and like a
cup, containing a pool of water. But at that season, Meek
dared not rest in any mountain meadow, no matter how
inviting.

But at last they emerged, and whooped for joy at the
vision of sunny valleys far below, the valleys of streams
flowing into the Sacramento River. Here once more they
found oaks and alders and willows, springlike climate,
sunshine and plenty. Just where Meek joined forces with
Walker's brigade once more is not clear from the record.
But it was obviously before they met the Spaniards in

San José Valley. There can be no doubt that the two Meek brothers were together and passed along the route described, for Stephen later gave the same story to a newspaper; it was published in 1837. Certainly they must have been glad to see Walker before the Spanish troops found them and led them to Monterey. From Walker's men Joe learned that they had had an even more desperate time than his own party in getting over the Sierra.

One night they camped near the mouth of the San Joaquin River. It was a quiet night; but when the men lay down with their ears to the ground, they were startled to hear a loud noise like far-off thunder. Some supposed it an earthquake and were frightened lest the earth should gape and swallow them; others believed it the roar of a waterfall. But Captain Walker assured them it must be the beating of the waves upon the shores of the Pacific. At this, everyone was happy; their journey was so nearly at an end. They hastened on for two days, and, on November 12, made camp.

But that night, after darkness rose from the ground and filled the sky, they had another scare worse than the first. The sky was suddenly thick with shooting stars and flaming meteors, some exploding in the air, others striking the earth. It was all the frightened men could do to control their terrified horses. Captain Walker again reassured them. They were in little danger from this display of celestial fireworks, extraordinary as it was. But the trappers long remembered that season as the "Winter it Rained Fire."

Next day they reached tidewater and soon went through the swampy country to an arm of San Francisco Bay. They encountered Indians and saw a stranded sperm whale, and, what was more to their profit, found an American ship, the *Lagoda*, of 292 tons, John Bradshaw, captain. Bradshaw entertained them aboard, made great cheer, and gave them information about the country, and good advice. San Francisco, he said, was forty miles north and Monterey, the capital of the province, sixty or seventy miles in the other direction.

Parting with Captain Bradshaw they moved toward Monterey, and, not knowing how they might be received by the Spaniards, took time out to hunt for deerskins to make moccasins to carry them through the winter. The whole country was alive with wild cattle and wild horses. Some Spaniards came along and agreed to act as guides to the mission of San Juan Bautista.

There Captain Walker was granted a campground by the padres, with grass and water; and there he forted. Afterward, obtaining a passport, he took two men to Monterey, seeking permission to remain in California during the winter. Captain Bradshaw, having arrived in Monterey, acted as Walker's interpreter.

The Spaniards made the Americans welcome. There— in winter quarters where they found no winter—the mountain men had a rare holiday. They found the *caballeros* as good horsemen as themselves, and enjoyed their rough sports. They too were fond of dressing up and showing off, yet lived simply and without much fofurraw. Horses were so abundant in California that there was no penalty for horse-stealing. The Americans were regaled with *aguardiente,* attended fandangos and watched battles between horned bulls and grizzly bears. The *senoras,* in their bright-colored shawls and gaudy dresses, were friendly enough. Meek, like the rest, thought California "some punkins."

But, by the middle of February, Walker decided to start east again.

His party had almost as desperate a time going back as they had had coming out, getting lost in the desert, and having to return to the mountains and head north until they cut their old trail along the Humboldt to Salt Lake. Bonneville's men returned with Walker.

But Meek and some other free trappers followed up the San Joaquin to its source, turned southeast to the Colorado River and traded with the friendly Mohave Indians.[1] Thence they followed the Colorado to the mouth of the Gila, then back to William's Fork and up that stream, until they met with a company of sixty trappers of the Rocky Mountain Fur Company led by Fraeb and Gervais. These two partisans regularly hunted in the Colorado River country, along the Gila and in the mountain parks of Colorado. It was a joyous reunion, and Meek traveled with them, heading back towards Green River where rendezvous was to be held in '34.

They moved from William's Fork to the Colorado Chiquito and visited the village of the Moqui or Hopi Indians.

These were Pueblo Indians, farmers, who irrigated and cultivated small fields.

But the mountain men, who as boys back in the States had been in the habit of raiding melon patches, did not offer to buy the garden truck of these industrious Indians. Instead, they walked right in and helped themselves. The Hopi, who called themselves *Hopituh,* "Peaceful Ones," swarmed out and protested. At that the mountain men, in no mood to take back talk from redskins, raised their rifles and shot down fifteen or twenty of the men they had robbed.

"I didn't belong to that crowd," says Joe Meek. "I sat on the fence and saw it, though. It was a shameful thing."

From the gardens of the Hopi the brigade headed northeast. And so at last, after his prodigious journey, Joe Meek arrived on the Rio Grande.

Soon after, Meek had his hardest fight.

---

[1] *Crede* Mrs. Victor, *The River of the West,* pp. 152-53.

Mule Fort

ONCE MORE in New Mexico, the main party followed up the Rio Grande del Norte towards San Luis Park and the Bayou Salade, the present South Park in Colorado. On the way Kit Carson, then ambitious to become a partisan, persuaded Meek to join him on a hunt in Comanche country, south of the Arkansas River. Meek had never been down there, but Bill Mitchell knew it well, and would act as guide. He had once married a Comanche woman and ranged with that tribe, hoping to find gold in the mountains there.

The Cimarron desert was desolate, waterless country. Bill Mitchell warned thar war a turrible dry scrape ahead. But mountain men scorned to carry water on their saddles—there was nary a canteen or even a beaver-skin pouch of water among them. They could ride to water, if they wasted no time.

Besides Joe and Bill, Kit had recruited three Delaware Indians, Tom Hill, Jonas and Manhead. "The Delawares were typical members of their tribe, which had taken over the white frontiersmen's weapons and mode of life, differing from them only in speech and blood. Wherever the white man went, there would be found a Delaware acting as guide or hunter. They were well armed, and combined the skill of the white hunter with the sure instinct of the red man. The Plains Indians hated them bitterly because they killed the buffalo in their country, and more than once tried to exterminate a band of Delawares who had ventured upon the prairies. But bow and lance could not match those riflemen, and the Plains Indians were badly worsted. The Delawares were cleanly Indians, proud and industrious in their hard profession, and the mountain men freely accepted them on equal terms. This fact is significant, for the mountain men despised the Spaniards, the Mexicans, the French Canadians, the greenhorns from the settlements, even the soldiers of the regular army. Kit knew what he was about when he chose the three Delawares for his band.

"One spring morning the six trappers were riding across the bare prairies, heading south. Not a tree was in sight, not a bush. The mountains far to the west showed dimly, blue and vague in the sunlight. The plains undulated gently away and away, one rolling wave like another, far as they could see. But Bill Mitchell knew his way. He rode steadily forward, his red gee-string flying in the wind, his bare buttocks pounding the Spanish saddle.

"Suddenly Meek reined up, and Kit, looking where he pointed, saw a round black dot on the hilltop ahead. 'Injuns!' It was the season for war parties. The trappers halted and stared at the Indian scout's dark head, waiting to see what it portended. They had not long to wait.

"For the Indians, hidden behind the hill, were at once informed by their scout what had happened. The white men had halted: it was clear that they had seen the Indian scout. The black dot disappeared. Then Meek saw what looked like a flock of blackbirds skimming the ridge toward the right—the heads of Indian warriors. Over the hill they came pell-mell—mounted on their best horses—racing to count their *coups*.

"All at once the skyline sprouted lances, tossing like

grass-blades in the sun, then black-and-white eagle-feather crests, horses' heads, naked, painted warriors. The charge was on. At the same moment the war whoop, like the quick chatter of a machine-gun, pulsated upon Joe's ears. The whole hillside was covered with Indians.

" 'Comanches!' yelled Bill Mitchell, and looked to Kit for orders.

" 'Two hundred of 'em, or I'm a nigger!' said Joe Meek.

"The Comanches were magnificently mounted. They always were. They had more horses and better horses than any Indians on the plains, and they 'ate and slept horseback.' They constantly raided the vast herds of Spanish horses on the *haciendas* to the south of their range—the best animals on the prairies. Kit knew he could not run away from them—and there was no cover within miles. Six to two hundred!

"Meek knew what that meant. He looked at Carson. 'Thar's only one thing to do, Kit.'

" 'Fort, boys!' Kit sang out, and jumped off his mule, jerking out his scalp-knife before his moccasins touched the ground. The mule, with all a mule's instinctive fear of Indians, tried to break away, almost jerking the stocky little man off his feet. But Kit caught the lariat close to the animal's head, and, as it reared back, passed the keen edge of his knife across its taut throat. He jumped clear. While the mule staggered, coughing out its life, drenching the short grass with blood, Kit snatched the cover from his rifle, looking to the priming, glanced round at his men.

"They had followed his example, leading their animals into position first, so that their dead bodies would form a circle. Just then a dead mule was worth a heap more than a live one. The Comanches would kill them anyway. Already three animals were down. Hastily, Kit and his comrades flung themselves prone behind the kicking carcasses, pointing the muzzles of their rifles toward the

KIT CARSON

Meek's fighting partner, and the man with whom he sometimes trapped.

coming warriors. The ground shook with the beat of
eight hundred hooves, the sunlight glittered on the long,
keen lance-points, and lit up the garish war-paint upon
the naked bodies, the flares and blotches of color upon the
spotted ponies. Feathers streamed from lance and war-
bonnet. On they came. It was magnificent, and it was
war. Kit yelled a warning.

" 'Bill, don't shoot yit. Hold on, Joe! Let the Delawares shoot first!' Joe and Bill nodded, grim-lipped,
never taking their eyes off the charging Indians. It was
hard to lie idle, finger crooked on trigger. But they
knew Kit was right: it would never do to empty all their
guns at once. Three shots against two hundred savages!

"Kit was gesturing swiftly to the Delawares. 'You
killum, sabe?' And Tom Hill, muttering a word to his
red companion, grinned knowingly, at the same time
drawing a bead across his dying mule on the foremost
warrior. Tom looked very strong and competent, lying
there, his long body covered to the knees with his
straight, black, unplaited hair.

"Already the horses were so near that Joe could see
the whites of their excited eyes. Ahead rode the chief, his
lance wrapped with shining otter fur, his war-bonnet
streaming behind. Crack! The three long rifles spoke
together. The chief tumbled from his saddle, struck the
ground on his head just in front of the little barricade,
and was dragged away by his frightened horse, having
tied his body to the end of the lariat. The charge split,
and swept by in a thunder of hooves, the rush of crowding
horses, white smoke in clouds from the rifles, a rain of
arrows lancing the dust.

"Immediately the redskins turned and charged again,
and this time Joe and Bill and Kit swung round, faced
the other way to meet them, aimed and fired as steadily
as though they had been armed with repeating rifles or
machine guns. Again the charge was split, and the

Indians dashed by. Two were left on the ground. Bill
let out a war-whoop.

"But now, whirling round in a moment, the Indians
raced back. The white men's guns were empty, they
knew. The Delawares had not had time to reload. Now
they could ride the whites down, lance them with impunity—out of reach of their sharp knives. Back they
came, whooping and laughing with expectation of an
easy victory. One of them recognized Bill Mitchell and
called out, taunting the white man, as he came: 'Lean
Bull, your hair is mine. Now I am going to make the
ground bloody where you lie!' In a flash the Comanches
were upon them.

"But the Indians never reached the whites. They could
not force their ponies to approach the dead mules. The
smell of the blood drove their horses crazy, and the charge
ended in a *melee* of bucking, rearing animals, circling
round the trappers, too unruly to allow their masters to
draw bow and shoot. Their spears, tied for recovery to
the end of a lariat fastened to their belts, could not reach
the whites.

"And now Jonas was taking aim; his rifle blazed, and
the laugh on the face of the taunter changed as he swayed
from his saddle and toppled to the ground. The Comanches saw him fall, saw Manhead aiming, saw Tom
Hill strike the butt of his rifle on the ground, too much
in a hurry to ram down the charge. They turned, they
retreated, and the frightened ponies made the retreat a
rout. The trappers stood and cheered.

"But the Comanches, in spite of their losses, could not
believe that six men could stand off two hundred. Armed
only with bows and lances, they re-formed and charged
bravely, only to split and retire to the hilltop again. All
the while, whenever there was a lull in the fighting, the
trappers were busy with knife and hatchet, deepening
their defenses, and at last they had an adequate fort even

against arrows at short range. And as often as the Indians charged, they kept them off, firing in shifts, so that always three rifles were loaded.

"Again the Comanches charged and retired. Then their medicine man, shaking a big rattle, confident of his power to turn bullets, led them on. Kit dropped him, and the redskins, finding their medicine no good that day, sat and smoked and talked things over on the hill. During the council, the Comanche women came down to carry off the dead and wounded.

"It was scorching hot in the midday sun. The trappers had no shade, no water. Their throats were parched with heat, the fever of excitement, the dust, the reek of the rifles. Flies swarmed about the dead mules, and stung fiercely. And the women cursed and scolded, shaking their fists helplessly at the whites, threatening vengeance: 'Dog-faces, I throw filth at you: Cowards! Women! Wait till the council is over! I shall dance over your scalp!'

"What wonder if Manhead, following the custom of his people, raised his rifle to throw the squaw who screamed out insults? It was an easy shot. And to kill a woman under the eyes of her men was always rated a brave deed—a *coup*—by the Indians.

"Kit saw what Manhead was doing, and commanded him to hold his fire. Many a squaw died at the hands of trappers, and even more fell to the guns of greenhorns and men in uniform. But Kit Carson had only scorn for the skunk who would shoot a woman, red or white. Manhead let the squaw go.

"All day the Indians sat by and the trappers stood them off. The fighting became rather half-hearted—young men galloping round and round in circles, displaying their marvelous horsemanship, shooting from under their ponies' necks, sometimes dashing up close to the dead mules to throw an arrow into them in sheer bravado. The trappers killed a few horses, but could do little damage

to the young men. For every Comanche had a loop of
hair rope braided into his pony's mane, and swinging in
this, with one heel on the animal's back, was able to
screen himself entirely behind his racing horse.

"Come night, the trappers were still waiting, hungry,
dry, anxious, their shoulders sore from the kick of their
guns. They lay low and watched the ragged silhouette
on the skyline. At last it melted away. For some time
they remained in their fort. Then, thinking the redskins
had gone, they got to their feet, stretched arms and legs,
moved about. Most of the charges had come from the
hill to the south. The bodies of the mules on that side
of the fort were so thick with arrows that Joe could not
lay the flat of his hand anywhere upon them without
touching an Indian shaft. Yet not one of the trappers
was seriously hurt. Meek, letting his love of a good yarn
smother his better judgment, estimated forty casualties
on the Indian side.[1]

---

[1] One skeptical historian has doubted that Meek's prairie battle with
Comanche Indians here narrated, and recorded earlier in Chapter IX of
The River of the West by Mrs. Francis Fuller Victor, ever took place. Had
I not had excellent authority for the incident, I should never have included it
in my biography of Kit Carson.

The Cheyenne half-breed, George Bent, (1843-1918) son of Colonel
William Bent, builder of Bent's Old Fort on the Arkansas River in Colorado
and of Owl Woman, daughter of the Keeper of the Cheyenne Medicine
Arrows, was, according to all competent authorities, the best Indian historian of the southern Plains tribes.

Indeed, George Bent was of great assistance to George Bird Grinnell,
author of *The Fighting Cheyennes* and of other books and papers on this
tribe, including the principal monument of Plains Indian ethnology, *The
Cheyenne Indians*. I knew George Bent well for fourteen years, as my stepfather, James Robert Campbell, had known him before I was born. In 1914,
at Colony, Oklahoma, I was present at a conference with George Bent, my
stepfather, and John Homer Seger, later author of *Early Days Among the
Cheyenne and Arapahoe Indians* and once superintendent of the Indian
school at Colony, who had lived among the Southern Cheyennes since the
early '70's.

On that occasion George Bent declared that he had heard Kit Carson
mention such a fight with the Comanches. Kit named Joe Meek and some
Delawares as present in his band when the hostiles attacked.

Bent also declared Carson said that he (Kit) had later talked with
Comanches who were in the fight, at the time of the Intertribal Treaty of
1840 at Bent's Old Fort (when the Kiowas and Comanches made peace with
the Cheyennes and Arapahoes). In this way Kit was able to check his own
impressions and inquire what the actual losses on the Indian side had been.

"The mountain men had to leave their traps, their possible sacks, their costly saddles, their well-filled packs. Slinging their blankets over their shoulders, and carrying only their hatchets, knives, and rifles, they sneaked away through the prairie starlight. After a mile or two they settled down into a steady dog-trot which they maintained all night. Back to the mountains. Back to camp. Bill Mitchell told them it was nearly eighty miles to the nearest water."

That night's endless run was Joe Meek's ruggedest hardship. Thirst was a far worse torment even than the pain of wounds, of utter weariness, of starvation. But at last, half dead, he and his comrades reached a clear running stream.

Bent gave no definite figures for these losses, but said that the Comanches gave him a figure for their losses much smaller than that given by Mrs. Victor in her book *The River of the West*.

It was from George Bent's recollection of Kit Carson's story that I obtained the details which I added to my account of the fight in my *Kit Carson*, quoted here.

No one has ever impugned the veracity of George Bent, who certainly well knew Kit Carson, long a close friend and old employee of his father, the Colonel.

I believe that Mrs. Victor's story as given to her by Meek is essentially correct—*except* for the figures given for Indian losses sustained. But, if Meek exaggerated Indian losses, he was certainly more conservative than the military officers of later days in the West, who generally multiplied Indian losses by from ten to one hundred and fifty times when estimating casualties in the fights in which they took part. (See my *New Sources of Indian History* for figures on comparative casualties, also my *Warpath*, p. 79 ff.)

As a matter of fact a loss of more than 2 per cent was generally enough to cause Indians to retire from a fight. It was only in hand-to-hand combat, where no retirement was possible, that Indian losses mounted. The Sioux (for whom I have compiled exact records of casualties within living memory, taking care to get names of killed and wounded from numbers of informants) tell me that the highest loss in their history in hand-to-hand combat amounted to only 15 per cent. Therefore, if Joe Meek was correct in estimating only two hundred Comanches in the attacking force in this fight, we may assume that his estimate of forty Indians killed is an overestimate. George Bent told me that Kit Carson counted only two certain deaths to his rifle that day and so drove only two brass tacks into its stock.

It must be remembered, however, that the confusion and speed of an Indian attack was very great; powder smoke and dust and the habit the Indian had of throwing himself behind his pony to avoid bullets might easily mislead a busy opponent into imagining that the warrior he fired at had been hit. Also one should remember that Joe Meek's story was narrated to Mrs. Victor more than a full generation after the fight occurred. Of course, there is a possibility that the Comanches minimized their loss in this fight when narrating the story of it to Kit Carson in 1840.

"It was all in the day's work. Trapping was a business —a profitable business at its best—when not interfered with by war. And war—wal, war allus was a pore make-out. You might save yore skin, but whar's yore mule?"[1]

---

[1] Stanley Vestal, *Kit Carson* (Boston, 1928), pp 106-113. (By permission, the Houghton Mifflin Company.)

Rough and Tumble

THAT SUMMER of 1834 was a crucial one for the American fur trade. Things had been going badly with every outfit in the Rocky Mountains. The partners of the Rocky Mountain Fur Company seemed to make no headway. The British operating in Oregon paid no import duties on their blankets, cloth, and other goods (which came from abroad), and so could easily offer far more to an Indian than the American traders could. On top of that the British paid no duty on furs shipped to New York markets, and so were able to undersell their American competitors. In American territory, where ruthless competition was the rule and there was no law, the game was dog eat dog.

When white men first came to the mountains, their guns, steel knives, cloth, and other things which no Indian could manufacture, had given the whites a mighty prestige among the tribesmen. This is well shown by the name applied to white men by the Sioux, *Wasicu*, meaning "Guardian Angel." But cutthroat competition had caused rival traders to belittle their competitors and encourage the Indians to take every mean advantage of them. And the demoralization brought to redskins by liquor not only lowered their morale but made them hate and despise the whites. Soon those who were not actually hostile learned to steal whenever they could do so in safety.

In September 1833, Tom Fitzpatrick, with twenty or thirty men and a hundred horses, rode to Crow camps on Tongue River to ask permission of the chiefs to make his fall hunt in their country. The Crows invited Tom to camp with them. He cautiously declined and pitched his camp three miles off. Then, taking two or three men, he rode over to visit the chief, who received and entertained him cordially. Meanwhile the young braves dashed into Tom's camp, and in spite of the efforts of Captain Sir William Drummond Stewart, drove off all the horses, taking Tom's beaver and everything else they could carry. They met him returning from their camp, and immediately added insult to injury by picking his pockets, taking his watch and even the capote from his back.

These Crows traded forty-three of Tom's prime beaver-skins, each plainly marked "R. M. F. Co.," to the American Fur Company. Fitzpatrick promptly charged that company with instigating the robbery, and both the Indians and the company's agent readily admitted it. In fact, Kenneth McKenzie even offered to sell the furs back to Fitzpatrick at their market value *if* Fitzpatrick would also pay the American Fur Company for its trouble in transporting the stolen skins.

Up to this time (1834) the Rocky Mountain Fur Company had shipped somewhat more than a thousand packs of beaver to the settlements, worth more than $500,000: its losses in property ran to one-fifth that sum; its losses in men, up to seventy. This hard-earned money, however, had nearly all gone into the pockets of Ashley and William Sublette. Sublette, having control of the shipment of supplies for the company (whose note he held) could charge the partners plenty, and he did. The partisans in the field—Bridger, Fitzpatrick, Fraeb, Gervais— were the most expert, enterprising, and experienced leaders in the mountains, and most of the trappers in their brigades were superior to those of other companies. Yet the partners profited little and were steadily falling behind.

And so it was with others. Captain Benjamin Louis Eulalie de Bonneville had now been two years in the mountains. In 1832 his man Montero had been robbed by the Crows of horses, goods and traps. Most of Montero's men deserted. He and the few who were left took refuge at Fort Cass at the mouth of the Big Horn River. But the American Fur Company, owners of the fort, plied his men with liquor and so secured all his furs. Montero made his spring hunt on the Powder. There a Ree war party sent two warriors into his camp to talk, while the rest ran off his horses. Seeing their horses go, the trappers seized the two warriors, threatening to burn them alive if the horses were not returned. But the Ree horse thieves rode off, contenting themselves with wailing for their unlucky comrades, on whom the trappers promptly wreaked the promised punishment. Bonneville's fort, which he had built at great expense on Green River, was in a region so high and cold that nobody could winter there; it earned the name "Fort Nonsense." And his brigade which Walker led to California certainly brought back no furs. Another year must see the end of Bonneville's attempt to make a fortune in the mountains.

Nathaniel Wyeth, the luckless New Englander, a man of vision and enterprise, was also on his way out. Interested in fish as well as furs, he proposed to send a ship around the Horn to Oregon, expecting in that way to supply the trappers more cheaply than could be done by pack train from St. Louis. He clearly saw that the money in the mountain trade went to the man who supplied the goods, and contracted with at least some of the partners of the Rocky Mountain Fur Company to buy their goods at the rendezvous of 1834 from him. Milton Sublette was

in league with Wyeth, who brought his pack train from
St. Louis safely to rendezvous.

But William Sublette never let grass grow under his
feet. He persuaded the partners to abandon Wyeth and
give the business to him. Whether Sublette put pressure
on the partners, or merely appealed to them as old friends,
one thing is sure. On June 20 on Ham's Fork, the
partners dissolved their company. When Wyeth arrived
at the end of the month there was no Rocky Mountain
Fur Company to receive his goods. Worse, rendezvous
was nearly over, and the trappers had already been
supplied by William Sublette. Wyeth was outraged. He
addressed a prophesy—all too true—to Milton Sublette,
then in the settlements: "You will find that you have
only bound yourself over to receive your supplies at such
price as may be inflicted and that all you will ever make
in the country will go to pay for your goods. You will be
kept as you have been, a mere slave to catch beaver for
others."

Wyeth was furious, and furiously he thought—until he
found a way of getting back at the partners, and at no
loss to himself. "Gentlemen," he said, "I will roll a stone
into your garden that you will never be able to get out."

Wyeth was as good as his word. Spang in the middle of
Bridger's favorite beaver country he built Fort Hall, on
the Snake River, proposing to furnish a permanent trading site in opposition to the rendezvous system of the
other American traders. But this was a game that Dr.
McLoughlin, of the Hudson's Bay Company, understood
well. *He* built a fort near the mouth of the Boise. Three
years later, in 1837, Wyeth was squeezed out; Fort Hall
was sold to the British, and the Hudson's Bay Company
took a dominant position in the heart of the fur-trading
empire.

Though Bridger, Milton Sublette, and Fitzpatrick continued to operate as a firm, they knew that the time was

not far off when the men of the old Rocky Mountain Fur Company would have to hire out to their hated competitors, the American Fur Company.

But the American Fur Company had its troubles, too. It had never been profitable, and the management in St. Louis would gladly have abandoned the expeditions to the Rocky Mountains. But they could not afford to leave the mountains to their competitors and so lose face with the very savages with whom they traded at their fixed posts. In trying to hog the mountain trade, they often had to pay more than the furs were worth.

As early as June, 1832, John Jacob Astor had written from London, "I very much fear beaver will not sell very soon unless very fine. It appears that they make hats of silk in place of beaver." Though he already had great wealth and was old enough to retire, being in his seventieth year, Astor was naturally reluctant to let go of the great organization he had created. Yet in the summer of 1833 he had already announced his retirement. On June 1, 1834, he sold his fur business lock, stock, and barrel to some gentlemen in St. Louis: the Northern Department to Ramsay Crooks and his partners; the Western Department to Pratte, Chouteau and Company. Thus the Western trade was once more controlled by the traders in St. Louis.

These gentlemen were not in business for their health. When Astor left the field, there was no likelihood that the high prices paid for furs could long be maintained.

William Sublette and Robert Campbell continued in the trade. On the Platte they built the trading post later called Fort Laramie, and then sold it to the American Fur Company.

All these maneuvers appear to have mattered little to Joe Meek. He had nothing invested in any company, and—thriftless and happy-go-lucky as he was—no hope of becoming a partner, what with his lack of money, or even a company clerk, what with his lack of book-l'arnin' and distaste for any form of paper work. Joe prided himself on being a good mountain man, who could take care of himself, bring home the beaver so long as they lasted, and hold his own at rendezvous and winter quarters. He was never a partisan, and nowhere expressed any desire to be one; it was enough for Joe to be a first-class trapper.

By this time he had learned his skilled trade well. He could set traps to good purpose, wrangle horses, pack a mule, handle a rope, repair a gun, mend and—if necessary —make moccasins, handle an axe, build a fort or corral, run bullets, make a pair of snowshoes or a bullboat, dress hides, kill, butcher, and cook his meat. He could break a horse, doctor it after a fashion, and follow its tracks when it strayed. Like all the mountain men, Joe had formed the habit of keeping in mind the lay of the land along the streams and trails he followed. He could read noises at night, the movements of animals and cries of birds by day—also sign left by animals or men on the surface of the earth.

Though Joe could hardly read, he was not slow at languages. He certainly spoke Shoshone and Nez Percé, and may have had a smattering of other Indian tongues. Certain it is that he was a great mimic, and therefore easily became adept at the Indian sign language, so useful to a hunter and a fighting man while stalking game or lying in wait for an enemy. He rode superbly and was a crack shot.

All this skill and competence made Joe Meek a top hand among the trappers, and he certainly was proud of his rating. But of all the activities of the trapper, it appears that—after b'ar huntin' and Injun-fightin', Joe delighted most in running buffalo—or, as the trappers called it—running meat.

And, since buffalo were larger and more numerous than other game animals, and were generally seen grazing in open country, the trappers killed more of them than of any game in the mountains. "Fat cow" was the choicest food to be had.

Hunting buffalo was hard work, and often dangerous. Says Meek, "One time Kit Carson and myself, and a little Frenchman, named Marteau, went to run buffalo on Powder River. When we came in sight of the band it war agreed that Kit and the Frenchman should do the running, and I should stay with the pack animals. The weather war mighty cold, and I didn't like my part of the duty much.

"The Frenchman's horse couldn't run; so I lent him mine. Kit rode his own—not a good buffalo horse either. In running, my horse fell with the Frenchman, and nearly killed him. Kit, who couldn't make his own horse catch, jumped off, and caught mine, and tried it again. This time he came up with the band, and killed four fat cows.

"When I came up with the pack-animals, I asked Kit how he came by my horse. He explained, and wanted to know if I had seen anything of Marteau: said my horse had fallen with him, and he thought killed him. 'You go over the other side of you hill, and see,' said Kit.

" 'What'll I do with him if he *is* dead?' I asked.

" 'Cain't you pack him to camp?'

" 'Pack hell!' I said, 'I'd ruther pack a load of meat.'

" 'Waal,' said Kit, 'I'll butcher, if you'll go over and see, anyhow.'

"So I went over, and found the dead man leaning his head on his hand, and groaning, for he war pretty bad hurt. I got him on his horse, though, after a while, and took him back to whar Kit war at work. We soon finished the butchering job, and started back to camp with our wounded Frenchman and three loads of fat meat."

CHAPTER SEVENTEEN

The Mountain Lamb

JOE MEEK had now been in the mountains for six years, plenty long enough to acquire a taste for the Indian style of beauty. In all that time nary a white woman had showed up, and, as he put it, the longer he lived in the mountains the whiter the Injun gals looked.

Not but what some of the young squaws were very dressy, fine-pretty girls. When one of these came riding by, Joe gave her the wink. Seeing how gay, daring, prosperous, and handsome he was, he must have had many a glad eye in return.

Yet there was one young woman in camp Joe couldn't get out of his mind.

> Her spotted pony through the ford
>   Waded splash and splash;
> The sleigh bells on her bridle rein
>   At every pace went chink and clash;
>
> Her glossy hair shone rifle-bright,
>   Her face was painted fair to see;
> The fringes over her silver belt
>   Hung down below her knee.[1]

It may be that some one of his comrades already

---

[1] Stanley Vestal, *Fandango: Ballads of the Old West* (Boston, 1927), pp. 27-28. (By permission, the Houghton Mifflin Company.)

married tried to l'arn Joe with just such advice as "Black-foot" Smith once gave Kit Carson:

" '*Valgame Dios!* Your shanty is a pore make-out compared to this hyar Injun lodge. Leaky and cold and open to the weather, and whar's the fire when you come in at night half froze for a hot kettle of soup? And your fingers too cold to strike a light. Why should you freeze all winter like a starvin' coyote? Your rifle shoots plumb-center; she makes 'em come; you kin throw plenty of fat cow, and you know whar to lay hands on a pack of beaver when you want it. It's time you womaned, Kit, and that's a fact.

" 'Maybe you're thinkin' of some sickly gal from the settlements, thin as a rail and pale as a ghost, pretty as a pitcher and so fofurraw she's good for nothin'. Maybeso you've sot yore eyes on some wench to Taos or Santy Fee. Do you hear now? Leave the Spanish slut to her greasers and the pale-face gal to them as knows no better. Put out and trap a squaw, and the sooner the better.

" 'What a mountain man wants is an Injun woman— one who can pack a mule, make meat, dress robes, make moccasins, cook, pitch a lodge, ride all day and then give birth to a likely young 'un after sundown. Look at me, Kit. I'm warm, I'm comfortable, I'm happy as a bear in winter quarters, with the old gal settin' hyar beside me. When I come home at night, froze stiff with cold and starvin', I kin see the big yaller lodge all lit up like a lantern among the pines, and I know when I go in, thar the old gal will be, with a good fire burnin' and the kettle steamin'. And before I kin get out of my wet moccasins and peel off my coat, my woman will have the warm water ready for my feet and a bowl of coffee under my nose. Then I kin set and smoke my pipe and listen to the lonesome wolves a-howlin' on the hills and the wind roarin' through the pine-trees. Do you hear now? My old gal is *some,* she is. I wouldn't swap her for all the beaver in Bent's big lodge. She kin make a home for me wherever grass grows. And you kin lay to that!' "[1]

But Joe Meek needed no such lecture. As Old Milt's right-hand man he had sat around the booshway's snug lodge enough to have a mighty good notion how comfortable an Indian housewife could make a mountain man. A white camp keeper couldn't shine alongside her. Old Milt called his wife "Isabel," and Joe thought her "the most beautiful Indian woman I ever saw."

She was a Shoshone or Snake, in fact the very girl who had helped the "good old man," Bad Left Hand, get Milt and him out of the Snake camp that night.

Even then Joe had admired the girl. But Old Milt was booshway, and so had the jump on Meek, what with his big lodge full of trade goods and dollars galore in his possibles, while young Joe was still scrabblin' along as a hired man.

But now times had changed for both of them. Joe was a free trapper, one of the best in the mountains. The fierce competition of the several companies now trapping in the mountains put the services of such veterans as Joe at a high premium. Every partisan bid for their services. And though Meek preferred working with his friends of the Rocky Mountain Fur Company, he knew what he was worth on the market, and got it.

One day Captain Bonneville was talking with Meek, complaining of the conduct of his own men on the Monterey expedition. Bonneville knew that if he did not pay his men as well as other companies paid their employees, they would desert and leave him flat, taking along their furs and even the supplies for which they owed him.

Bonneville came right out and asked Joe, "How much does your company pay you?"

---

[1] Stanley Vestal, *Kit Carson* (Boston, 1928), pp. 90-91. (By permission, the Houghton Mifflin Company.)

Meek grinned, "Fifteen hundred dollars."

Bitterly Bonneville replied, "Yes, and *I* will give it to you."

Meek could afford to laugh. He was the best-paid trapper in the mountains.

Meek thought it was about time he womaned. Trouble was, the woman Joe found so attractive was the wife of his close friend and booshway, Old Milt.

In the mountains there were two methods of taking an Indian woman to wife. A suitor could make presents to whatever man was her protector—her father, brother or husband—and so, as they called it, "buy" her. But a spunky young warrior scorned such methods, preferring to "steal" his woman—that is, elope with her, thus making sure that she was no mere slave or captive bride. Of course, running off with a woman worth several good ponies was plenty dangerous; it might result in severe punishment for both if they were overtaken. And so a man was pretty sure that a girl who eloped with him really loved him. When the danger of pursuit had blown over and his relatives had squared accounts with the bride's family, the young couple would return to camp.

But "Isabel" looked perfectly content with Milt and her baby, and anyhow Joe was not the man to try to trick Old Milt.

Yet times had changed for Milton Sublette also. He was suffering from an old wound in the leg which had become badly infected and could only be treated in the settlements. He feared—with good cause—that the leg would have to come off. On May 8, 1834, on his way to rendezvous he decided to quit the mountains and head back for Missouri, leaving behind his Indian wife and child. After Old Milt pulled out, he gave Isabel to Joe.[1]

Joe, of course, was aware of certain disadvantages in

1 Statement of Joe Meek's daughter, Olive Branch Riley, quoted in Fred Lockley, *Oregon Folks* (New York, 1927), Chapter II.

mating with a squaw. All his wife's relatives were sure to come for long visits, expecting the rich white man to maintain them. And of course a booshway's ex-wife was bound to expect more fofurraw than a mule could pack. But all that didn't bother Joe. He could afford it, and when he wanted something he was no man to hang back.

An Indian woman couldn't make out alone. Isabel needed a protector, and she was already broken to run in double harness with a white man. And there was Milt's baby. Milt would want the kid protected.

The Indian road to love is short and straight. And Meek was never a laggard. Perhaps Isabel gave him a hint by making him a handsome pair of moccasins or broiling hump-ribs for him. When an Indian woman offered such wifely services it was tantamount to a proposal. Yet, considering Joe's temperament and winning ways, it seems likely he took the first step. Anyhow, he soon swapped his beaver for presents for her.

Joe spent three hundred dollars for her horse, a dappled gray, and proudly declared, "When she was mounted . . . she made a fine show. She wore a skirt of beautiful blue broadcloth, and a bodice and leggins of scarlet cloth, of the very finest make. Her hair was braided and fell over her shoulders; a scarlet silk handkerchief, tied on hood fashion, covered her head; and the finest embroidered moccasins her feet. She rode like all the Indian women, astride, and carried on one side of the saddle the tomahawk for war, and on the other the pipe of peace.

"The name of her horse was 'All Fours.' His accoutrements were as fine as his rider's. The saddle, crupper, and bust girths cost one hundred and fifty dollars; the bridle fifty dollars; and the *musk-a-moots*[1] fifty dollars

---

1 *Musk-a-moots:* apparently Mrs. Victor's spelling of Meek's pronunciation of the Shoshone word *maishoo-moe-goots*, which, according to old Shoshone Indians at the Wind River agency, means "a saddlebag the Indians use for putting Mormon crickets into after gathering them." Meek's daughter, Olive, states that this bridle was covered with Mexican silver dollars. (Lockley, *ibid.*)

more. All these articles were ornamented with fine cut-glass beads, porcupine quills, and hawk's bells, that tinkled at every step. Her blankets were of scarlet and blue, and of the finest quality. Such was the outfit of the trapper's wife, *Umentucken, Tukutsey Undenwatsy,* the Lamb of the Mountains."[1]

Mrs. Victor, who recorded Meek's memoirs, declares that he exhibited "a becoming reticence" on the subject of his "earliest love adventures." It is clear that Meek did not tell Mrs. Victor that Milton Sublette "gave" the Mountain Lamb to him. So Mrs. Victor, with Joe's cooperation—or, at any rate, tacit consent—obviously romanticized this marriage.

This is not to say that Joe Meek was not a good family man, as he abundantly proved in later years.

The date of this marriage given by Meek is 1835. When Milton Sublette left rendezvous June 24, 1833, he was on his way to the Atlantic seaboard where he might hope to find some physician who could heal his bad leg. He certainly planned to return to the mountains the summer of '34, and actually made the start from Missouri, travelling more than a week with Wyeth's pack train. It is not likely that he would have entrusted his Indian family to Meek before he gave up and turned back to the settlements. Probably such action did not occur to him until after his amputation and the operation which followed it had convinced him that there was little chance of an early return to the beaver country.

In that case he could hardly have communicated with Meek prior to the rendezvous of 1835. Perhaps it was at that rendezvous that Joe carried his possibles into the lodge of the Shoshone woman.[2]

---

[1] *Umentucken:* "of the mountain"; *tukutsey:* "bighorn ram, or male mountain sheep"; *undenwatsy:* "his child." Thus the whole means "Lamb of the Mountain," or "Mountain Lamb." The words are from the Shoshone or Snake Tongue.

[2] It would be interesting to know what she—and other Indians—called Meek. He must have had an Indian name or two during his time as a beaver trapper, but no record of it has come to light. S. V.

By Meek's own account they were happy together. He was proud of his handsome Lamb, for she had plenty of spunk.

One summer day, when in camp on the Yellowstone, she and several other women crossed the river to pick cherries. The fruit was to be dried and pounded fine, then mixed with powdered meat and tallow to make pemmican.

While she was busy picking fruit, a Blackfoot war party rushed the women and caught several. But Meek's wife dodged and ran hard for the river. She could hear the yelling warriors tearing through the brush after her. But she reached the bank first, dived off into that gray rushing water, and swam for her life while the bullets of her enemies slapped the water all around her head. She was not hit, and reached cover.

That was not the only time the Mountain Lamb showed a heap of ginger. Once, when Meek was away on a hunt, she found herself in danger.

Camped near by was a big Irish trapper. O'Fallen had bought from the Snakes two of their Indian captives, intending to use them as his slaves. Not liking their new master, the two captives managed to slip out of camp and get away.

Now, it was not an easy thing for a captive to escape from such a camp without help, for trappers as well as Indians had to keep their eyes peeled and were expert at trailing. O'Fallen felt sure that someone in camp had had a hand in the flight of his servants, and for some reason suspected Meek's woman. In a rage he grabbed up his horsewhip and strode to her lodge to punish her.

There are few secrets in an Indian camp. The day was warm, and the covering of her lodge had been raised at the back for coolness. It was easy for her neighbors to give her swift warning of O'Fallen's threats.

When he came blustering to the door of her lodge, she

picked up Joe's pistol, slipped out the back and, hurrying around to the door, took the bully in flank.

"You coward," she said, covering his ribs with the pistol, "you come here to whip the wife of Meek. He is not here to kill you. I will do that for myself." Meanwhile the whole camp came running to see the row.

O'Fallen looked down the black barrel of her weapon, saw her blazing black eyes and steady hand. Quickly he threw his whip down and began to bleat apologies. But she kept him begging for his life in the face of the whole camp until he was thoroughly shamed. Then, relaxing, she lowered her weapon. O'Fallen sneaked away.

She found herself suddenly a popular heroine. All the men looking on gave her a cheer: "Hurrah for the Mountain Lamb!"

Meek tells another story of his wife's adventures. One day on Powder River a party of trappers had gone out to run buffalo. The women followed along with travois and pack mule to bring in the meat. Joe was a good shot, and that day dropped several fat cows. His wife and her helpers had butchered and were on the way back to camp. As always in Indian country, the men rode ahead in the post of danger while the women followed.

Perhaps her pack saddle slipped, or her mule balked. Meek, talking with his fellows, for a time was unaware that his wife had been left behind. Before she could overtake the others, twelve sneaking Crow warriors, who had not dared attack the hunters, ran up and surrounded her.

By that time Meek had missed her, and with six others rode back to see what the trouble was.

When he came over the ridge, there she was in the middle of her enemies. Meek had a good horse, and laid spurs to its ribs. It was a spirited animal. At top speed it carried Meek right in among the Crows.

This bold charge startled the warriors. Meek had a momentary advantage. He lost no time, pulled his trigger, and dropped the nearest Crow. Fired by Meek's example, the other six trappers came charging on his heels.

While the men fought, the woman ran. A minute or two later ten Crows were running, too—but in the other direction.

Unharmed, the trappers headed back for camp, and on the way gave Joe high praise for charging twelve Crows single-handed. Joe kept a straight face. Says he, "I took their compliments quite naturally. I reckoned it warn't worth while to tell them that I couldn't hold my horse!"

Preachin' in Jackson's Hole

THOUGH the old partners of the Rocky Mountain Fur Company had dissolved it, forming a new firm called Fitzpatrick, Sublette and Bridger, the trappers still used the old name as often as not.

On Green River, that summer of 1835, while awaiting the coming of the train from St. Louis, the partners of the old Rocky Mountain Fur Company and the American Fur Company joined forces. The Rocky Mountain Fur Company was in fact absorbed by the American Fur Company, and the new firm was so called. The merger—of men rather than assets—was intended to offer stronger opposition to the British Hudson's Bay Company.

Bridger and Fontenelle were to be booshways in the mountains, and Drips was to bring the goods out from the settlements.

This agreement completed, Drips called for volunteers to help him find the St. Louis company, somewhere, he thought, between Green River and the Black Hills. It was a small party—Drips, Meek, Kit Carson, Doc Newell, Victor (a Flathead chief) and one or two others.

But they soon found sign that Crows, a war party one hundred strong, were on the trail before them.

Kit and Joe, more wary and cautious than the other men, merely loosened their horses' girths at night but did not unsaddle. They tied the lariats of their horses around their own waists. Thus if the horse should be disturbed, its nervousness would be telegraphed at once to its owner, and certainly the horse could never pull up *that* picket pin!

At the earliest dawn Meek and the rest jumped up, deafened by a volley from a hundred fusees and the wild war whoops of the Crows. Away went the horses of all but Joe and Kit. These two, going hand over hand up the lariats to their horses' heads, quickly mounted, dug in their spurs and high-tailed it out of there, leaving the Sandy far behind them.

Once clear of the Crows, they jogged on to the Sweetwater. There they found the Flathead chief who, though afoot, had reached the campsite before them. That night two or three others came in, and soon they went on towards Independence Rock.

Thereabouts the Injuns jumped them again, and again it was every man for himself. This time Kit and Joe turned back, and lost no time getting to camp. Only a few hours' distance from the rendezvous they found Doc Newell, on Horse Creek. Doc was lost and tuckered out, just about ready to give in.

But by good luck, on Horse Creek they also found one of their own stampeded horses which the Crows had so frightened that they could never catch it. The horse was still spooky, but Kit and Joe managed to rope it. So Doc was able to ride.

Two days later all the others turned up in Bridger's camp, tired out, disappointed, afoot, but otherwise none the worse, to sit and wait some more. With them waited large camps of Nez Percés and Flatheads, Utes and Snakes. But it was not till August 12 that Tom Fitzpatrick brought the goods to rendezvous. The train had been delayed by an epidemic of cholera, which might have wiped it out but for the fact that Dr. Marcus Whitman, a Presbyterian medical missionary, was along and nursed the sick.

With Whitman came Samuel Parker, a Congregational minister from Massachusetts and New York. Parker was more than fifty years old, a bookish, unworldly parson, sincere and devoted but without much give-and-take in his disposition.

There is an old saying that the lawyer sees us at our worst, the parson at our best, but the doctor as we are. That saying applies here.

For Whitman, the physician, had learned to face the facts of nature and did not expect of human nature more than it could give.

On the way out the two missionaries had had a difference, because the fastidious parson objected to Whitman's careless, slovenly ways and a habit he had of eating with his knife. But they were both servants of the American Board of Commissioners for Foreign Missions, sent out, as the decamping Jason Lee had been the year before, in answer to the "Macedonian cry" of the Flatheads and Nez Percés for Christian teaching.

When the caravan finally reached the impatient trappers, the usual hell broke loose. The mountain men gambled and raced horses, wrestled and fought, drank and swore, and chased the Indian women. Some traded packs of cards to the redskins for their wives and daughters, declaring playing cards the white man's Bible, and threatening gullible redskins with all the torments of a flaming Hell unless the women were forthcoming.

Here Kit Carson fought and killed the bully Shunar[1] over the Arapahoe girl who was to become his wife.

All this shocked Parker, though he was pleasantly surprised to discover more refined company in the camp, including the British gentleman, sportsman and officer, Captain Sir William Drummond Stewart.

---

1 See *Kit Carson, op. cit.,* Chapter X.

While Parker was digesting his indignation at the irreligion of the mountain men, the more practical and helpful Dr. Whitman extracted from Jim Bridger's back an iron Blackfoot arrowhead. Bridger had safely carried this point in his flesh for nearly three years: for, as he explained to Father De Smet on another occasion, "Meat never spoils in the mountains."

Dr. Whitman's operation and friendly, unpretentious way swiftly won him the liking of Joe Meek and other mountain men, and a vast reputation as a healer among the Indians. They kept the good doctor busy with their ailments, while Parker was busy saving their souls.

The Flatheads and especially the Nez Percés were eager for religious instruction, as the delegation they had sent down to St. Louis in 1831 plainly showed. Nobody was ever more religious than the old-time Indian, and these tribes had had some smatterings of Catholic doctrine from the French Canadians who first inspired them with a desire for Christian salvation.

Indeed, the Nez Percés were Christianized earlier than most Western tribes, and some forty years later, when they made their heroic fight through our troops towards the Canadian border under Chief Joseph, conducted their warfare in a manner to do credit to any Christian soldiers. Already they had adopted a defensive instead of an offensive warfare as being more Christian, and readily submitted to Parker's demands that all divorced Indians must rejoin their abandoned mates. This was a complicated matter, since the parson also held that no man should have more than one wife!

Though Parker was apparently unaware that Indian religion was devoid alike of faith and devotion and was chiefly concerned with gaining supernatural power in order to obtain material blessings, he nevertheless liked Indians. Of course he was shocked, when witnessing their dances, to find "rational men imitating beasts, and old gray-headed men marshaling the dance! And enlightened white men encouraging it by giving them intoxicating spirits as a reward for their good performance!"

Yet he was wise enough to foresee that these people could be Christianized and civilized. This was far more than most missionaries could then understand, much less openly declare.

By the end of the rendezvous both Whitman and Parker were satisfied that missionary work among these Indians was worth while. So Whitman decided to return to the States and bring out more missionaries, while Parker remained in the West to head for Fort Walla Walla and the Columbia River.

Already they had made a number of converts; they had baptized, buried, and married on all hands.

Parker and the Flatheads traveled with Bridger's brigade, heading for Jackson's Hole. On the first Sunday out, with the mighty Tetons looking down on camp, Meek and other trappers rested and turned out in force to listen to preachin'. A ten-prong buck warn't done suckin' when Joe had last sot in a church-house.

The Indians, respecting all religions as sources of power, were eager enough to hear more of the white man's Unknown God, to learn his taboos and so obtain the benefits accruing.

Whatever irreverence some of the trappers may have felt during those religious services held in their camp, Rev. Parker was not made aware of them, and in his journal records, "I did not feel any disposition to upbraid them for their sins, but endeavored affectionately to show them that they were unfit for Heaven and that they could not be happy in the employments of that holy place unless they should first experience a great moral change of heart by the grace of God."

The pleased parson talked on and on to the reverent Indians and the curious, embarrassed trappers, until a sudden interruption enlightened him as to the actual standards of his congregation.

All at once Joe heard a shout. "Buffalo!" Instantly every man jumped up, and without waiting for the benediction, seized his gun, leaped on his horse and was off to kill the meat which had so providentially come to camp. Preachin' was over.

Meek was among the foremost, and killed his share of twenty fat cows. The hunters butchered, loaded their saddles with succulent hump-ribs and tongues, fat fleece and *boudins,* and came romping back to camp to end the day of rest by gorging themselves with the best fixin's on the prairie. For as the Sioux proverb puts it, "When the meat comes to camp, the clouds roll away."

The parson looked on all that noisy revelry with stern disapproval. Still, the odor of the hump ribs roasting by the campfires tantalized him. Mountain air roused hearty appetites. So, after rebuking the Sabbath-breakers severely, the parson sat down to enjoy the abundant hospitality of his hunter hosts.

The Sabbath-breakers silently watched him make a hearty meal of the very meat they had so "sinfully" brought in. But when mastication had ended and pipes were glowing, Meek and his fellows put down Parker's lecture on Sabbath-breaking as no more than pious humbug. The partaker, Joe claimed, was as bad as the thief; he regarded Parker as a hypocritical accessory after the fact. Hell's full of preachers!

To the Indians, however, Dr. Parker's prestige was enormously enhanced by the sudden appearance of the buffalo while he was "making medicine," and on a later occasion their faith in his power was further confirmed when, at their request, he offered prayer for buffalo and "brought" another herd right to their tipi doors.

When Parker left them to go on to Walla Walla, Meek and the rest headed for the Yellowstone country.

"KEEP YOUR DISTANCE!"

Illustrating a tactical maneuver of the early days in the West. From an original painting by A. F. Tait, lithographed by Nathaniel Currier.

Crow Captive

SOON AFTER, Joe ran into trouble—an adventure which called for all his shrewdness, courage, and quick wit. He was alone when it happened; let him tell it:

"I war trapping on the Rocky Fork of the Yellowstone. I had been out from camp five days; and war solitary and alone, when I war discovered by a war party of Crows. They had the prairie, and I war forced to run for the creek bottom; but the beaver had throwed the water out and made dams, so that my mule mired down. While I war struggling in the marsh, the Injuns came after me, with tremendous yells; firing a random shot now and then, as they closed in on me.

"When they war within about two rods of me, I brought old *Sally*, that is my gun, to my face, ready to fire, and then die; for I knew it war death this time, unless Providence interfered to save me: and I didn't think Providence would do it. But the head chief, when he saw the warlike looks of *Sally*, called out to me to put down my gun, and I should live.

"Well, I liked to live—being then in the prime of life; and though it hurt me powerful, I resolved to part with *Sally*. I laid her down. As I did so, the chief picked her up, and one of the braves sprang at me with a spear, and would have run me through, but the chief knocked him down with the butt of my gun. Then they led me forth to the high plain on the south side of the stream. There they called a halt, and I was given in charge of three women, while the warriors formed a ring to smoke and consult. This gave me an opportunity to count them: they numbered one hundred and eighty-seven men, nine boys, and three women.

"After a smoke of three long hours, the chief, who war named 'The Bold,' called me in the ring, and said:

" 'I have known the whites for a long time, and I know them to be great liars, deserving death; but if *you* will tell the truth, you shall live.'

"Then I thought to myself, they will fetch the truth out of me, if thar is any in me. But his highness continued:

" 'Tell me whar are the whites you belong to; and what is your captain's name.'

"I said 'Bridger is my captain's name; or, in the Crow tongue, *Casapy,*[1] the "Blanket Chief." ' At this answer the chief seemed lost in thought. At last he asked me— 'How many men has he?'

"I thought about telling the truth and living; but I said 'forty,' which war a tremendous lie; for thar war two hundred *and* forty. At this answer The Bold laughed:

" 'We will make them poor,' said he; 'and you shall live, but they shall die.'

"I thought to myself, *hardly;* but I said nothing. He then asked me whar I war to meet the camp, and I told him:—and then how many days before the camp would be thar; which I answered truly, for I wanted them to find the camp.

"It war now late in the afternoon, and thar war a great

---

1 Joe Meek, or his amanuensis, was notoriously careless in the spelling of Indian names. The Crows say *Casapy* is derived from the word *bikasopia,* meaning *cloth.* See *Jim Bridger, Mountain Man,* by Stanley Vestal (New York, 1946) , chapter VI, footnote 3.

bustle, getting ready for the march to meet Bridger. Two big Injuns mounted my mule, but the women made me pack moccasins.[1] The spies or scouts started first, and after a while the main party. Seventy warriors traveled ahead of me: I war placed with the women and boys; and after us the balance of the braves. As we traveled along, the women would prod me with sticks, and laugh, and say, 'Masta Sheela' (Yellow Eyes—which means white man) 'Masta Sheela very poor now.' The fair sex war very much amused.

"We traveled that way till midnight, the two big bucks riding my mule, and I packing moccasins. Then we camped; the Injuns in a ring, with me in the centre, to keep me safe. I didn't sleep very well that night I'd a heap rather been in some other place.

"The next morning we started on in the same order as before: and the squaws making fun of me all day; but I kept mighty quiet. When we stopped to cook that evening, I war set to work, and war head cook, and head waiter too. The third and fourth day it war the same. I felt pretty bad when we struck camp on the last day: for I knew we must be coming near to Bridger, and that if anything should go wrong, my life would pay the forfeit.

"On the afternoon of the fourth day, the spies, who war in advance, looking out from a high hill, made a sign to the main party. In a moment all sat down. Directly they got another sign, and then they got up and moved on. I war as well up in Injun signs as they war; and I knew they had discovered white men. What war worse, I knew they would discover that I had been lying to them. All I had to do then war to trust to luck.

"Soon we came to the top of the hill, which overlooked

---

1 On the warpath pemmican was packed in extra pairs of new moccasins. Thus as the men ate the dried meat, they also acquired new moccasins to replace those worn out on the trail.

the Yellowstone, from which I could see the plains below extending as far as the eye could reach, and about three miles off, the camp of my friends. My heart beat double quick about that time; and I once in a while put my hand to my head, to feel if my scalp war thar.

"While I war watching our camp, I discovered that the horse guard had seen us, for I knew the sign he would make if he discovered Injuns.

"I thought the camp a splendid sight that evening. It made a powerful show to me, who did not expect ever to see it after that day. And it *war* a fine sight anyhow, from that hill whar I stood. About two hundred and fifty men, and women and children in great numbers, and about a thousand horses and mules. Then the beautiful plain, and the sinking sun; and a herd of buffalo that could not be numbered; and the cedar hills, covered with elk—I never saw so fine a sight as all that looked to me then!

"When I turned my eyes on that savage Crow band, and saw the chief standing with his hand on his mouth, lost in amazement; and beheld the warrior's tomahawks and spears glittering in the sun, my heart war mighty little. Directly the chief turned to me with a horrible scowl. Said he:

"'I promised that you should live *if* you told the truth; but you have told me a great lie.'

"Then the warriors gathered around, with their tomahawks in their hands; but I war showing off very brave, and kept my eyes fixed on the horse-guard who war approaching the hill to drive in the horses. This drew the attention of the chief, and the warriors too. Seeing that the guard war within about two hundred yards of us, the chief turned to me and ordered me to tell him to come up. I pretended to do what he said; but instead of that I howled out to him to stay off, or he would be killed; and to tell Bridger to try to treat with them, and get me away.

"As quick as he could he ran to camp, and in a few minutes Bridger appeared, on his large white horse. He came up to within three hundred yards of us, and called out to me, asking who the Indians war. I answered 'Crows.' He then told me to say to the chief he wished him to send one of his sub-chiefs to smoke and to talk with him.

"All this time my heart beat terribly hard. I don't know now why they didn't kill me at once; but the head chief seemed overcome with surprise. When I repeated to him what Bridger said, he reflected a moment, and then ordered the second chief, called Little Gun, to go and smoke with Bridger. But they kept on preparing for war; getting on their paint and feathers, arranging their scalp locks, selecting their arrows, and getting their ammunition ready.

"While this war going on, Little Gun had approached to within about a hundred yards of Bridger; when, according to the Crow laws of war, each war forced to strip himself, and proceed the remaining distance stark naked, and kiss and embrace. While this interesting ceremony war being performed, five of Bridger's men had followed him, keeping in a ravine until they got within shooting distance, when they showed themselves, and cut off the return of Little-Gun, thus making a prisoner of him.

"If you think my heart did not jump up when I saw that, you think wrong. I knew it war kill or cure, now. Every Injun snatched a weapon, and fierce threats war howled against me. But all at once about a hundred of our trappers appeared on the scene. At the same time Bridger called to me, to tell me to propose to the chief to exchange me for Little-Gun. I explained to The Bold what Bridger wanted to do, and he sullenly consented: for, he said, he could not afford to give a chief for one white dog's scalp. I war then allowed to go towards my camp, and Little-Gun towards his; and the rescue I hardly hoped for war accomplished.

"In the evening the chief, with forty of his braves, visited Bridger and made a treaty of three months. They said they war formerly at war with the whites; but that they desired to be friendly with them now, so that together they might fight the Blackfeet, who war everybody's enemies. As for me, they returned me my mule, gun, and beaver packs, and said my name should be *Shiam Shaspusia*, for I could out-lie the Crows."[1]

---

[1] On applying to the Crows for the meaning of the Indian name given Meek by The Bold, they explained that the two words are synonymous, the first being English, the second, Crow: *Shiam* being evidently a misspelling of the tribal name, "Cheyenne," and *Shaspusia* a phonetic approximation of the Crow word for that tribe, meaning "His arrow feathers are striped." The name given Joe was no doubt meant as an insult, as well as a face-saving jest, for the Crows were bitter enemies of the Cheyennes. See *Jim Bridger*, *op. cit.*, Chapter XI, footnote 1.

Fighting Fire

BY SEPTEMBER 9, 1835, Jim Bridger was in camp on Henry's Lake. On the ninth, Joe Meek, Kit Carson, and about a dozen other trappers of Jim's brigade saw sign of white men on the Gallatin Fork, about twenty miles north. Following up the trail, they saw smoke rising from the thickets in the narrow valley of a small branch of the Gallatin, and rode noisily in on a high lope in token of peaceful intentions.

They found a small party under Joseph Gale, one of Nathaniel Wyeth's men. As it was near sundown and too late to ride back to Bridger's camp that night, Meek and his friends camped with Gale's men, and around the campfire that night passed the time pleasantly, exchanging news and spinning trapper yarns.

Joe Meek was a mite uneasy. He reckoned Gale and his men were green hands, hardly "up to beaver." Their packs were light, and they were so badly equipped with ammunition and firearms that he doubted they were "up to Blackfeet" either. They were practically destitute of traps, blankets, knives and all the little fixin's that made life worth living in the mountains.

By all accounts Gale's outfit had gone from bad to worse, losing men and animals one way or another. Several, Joe learned, had deserted. And no wonder, the way Gale wrangled with his men. But Joe Meek and his friends wasted no sympathy on the sorry plight of Gale's party; instead Meek tried to raise their spirits by laughing at their misfortunes and rawhiding them to make their hearts strong.

They had built a flimsy pole corral to hold their scanty cavayard of rawboned mules and wringtailed horses at night. Every way that camp was in a mighty poor fix if the cussed Injuns jumped it. The narrow valley was hemmed in between steep bluffs covered with trees not forty rods away, and all the bottoms were deep in a rank growth of dry grass and brush.

Meek told Gale that Bridger had sixty white men and about twenty Flathead Indians in camp, and that they planned to move over to the Madison River.

The night passed without incident, and early in the morning Joe Meek and seven others went off down the creek for the main fork to raise their traps and return to their own camp.

Meek and Liggit were ahead. Suddenly about eighty Blackfeet jumped them. The Indians fired, yelled, and charged. Meek and Liggit whirled and raced back to Gale's camp, zigzagging to spoil the aim of their pursuers, with the Indians so close on their heels that they charged right up to the camp and almost took it before the trappers there could make a stand.

There were less than twenty rifles in working order in that camp, but those were soon at work, their spiteful crack crashing back in mighty echoes from the bluffs on either side. The trappers' volley soon forced the Blackfeet out of the brush.

The Indians took to the bluffs and began firing down into camp, which was within easy range of Kenneth McKenzie's fusees. Meek and his friends dug foxholes, but the poor horses in the corral stood unprotected.

The Blackfeet were surely determined to have those

horses. But Meek knew they could never take them while the trappers squatted round them, cached out of sight in the brush, with ready rifles, holding their fire.

Suddenly Meek sat up, sniffing the wind. Then his heart lay on the ground. Down there out of range two or three Blackfeet were running around, carrying blazing sticks, stopping, then running on, while behind them white columns of smoke mushroomed up, blotting out the valley beyond. Fire! The grass was on fire, and the south wind sucked up the valley straight for the thickets of dry brush where the trappers were making their stand.

"The columns of white smoke spread into curtains, joined, and advanced. Already they could catch the first faint whiffs of burning grass; already the air was glazed with the heat, shutting out all clear vision of the Blackfeet. The black, charred ashes behind the fire grew and widened rapidly, and the little flames danced merrily forward, struck the longer grass in the bottom, swept forward, towering, racing, straight for the dry thicket, now clouded with smoke.

"Behind him, Meek could hear Gale's men cursing the restless horses, and the noise of their plunging and kicking. Some of them would be breaking away soon. He lay and watched the fire advance. Probably the Blackfeet would be following it up, ready to charge through the smoke when the trappers broke cover."[1]

The blaze swept up the narrow valley, filling it from bluff to bluff, and whenever it reached a pine tree shot up in crackling fury, tossing off great sheets of flame.

It was a lively time, with men yelling, guns barking, flames roaring up the trees, squeals of wounded horses, all multiplied in echoes from the bluffs around.

Still that sea of flame washed forward, driven by the wind, crackling through the thicket. Men sprang from

---

[1] Vestal, *Kit Carson*, *op. cit.*, pp. 142-43. (By permission, the Houghton Mifflin Company.)

their foxholes. The smoke choked them, the heat blasted their faces. And the Blackfeet came on behind the smoke screen.

Says Russell, "In a few moments the fire was converted into one circle of flame and smoke which united over our heads."

Gale's men had no more powder and ball. They were no better than camp keepers now. All they could do was to rake and kick everything that would burn away from camp, then set it on fire to combat the conflagration all around them. They prepared to lead the terrified horses and mules into the open up the creek. While Gale's men fought fire, Meek and his comrades stuck to their foxholes and fired through the flames at the Blackfeet.

It was a hard scrape, but the trappers were a game bunch, men whose names have come down to us because of their dauntless courage: Meek, Carson, Hawkins, Gale, Liggit, Rider, Robinson, Anderson, Russell, Larison, Ward, Parmaley, Wade, Michael Head. Not a man showed the white feather. Says Russell, "We did not despair."

Their courage and tactics paid off. All the outer part of the thicket of brush was consumed, but that immediately around the trappers did not burn. Says Kit Carson, "I cannot account for our miraculous escape, unless it was the protecting hand of Providence . . . for the brush where we were was dry and as easily burned as that which had been consumed."

Forted behind their dead and dying animals, they kept up the fight well into the middle of the afternoon. Three men were hit. But after the fire passed around them, it swept up the bluffs and destroyed the cover of their enemies. Then the Blackfeet took a terrible beating. Kit, always conservative, declares that the trappers killed "a large number of them."

Yet ammunition was running low. Joe Meek and the

rest kept wondering when on earth Old Gabe would come to rub those Injuns out. . . .

About three o'clock in the afternoon, says Russell, they saw a tall Indian, whom they supposed a chief, "standing on a high point of rock to signal his warriors. The chief took hold of the opposite corners of his robe, lifting it up and striking it three times on the ground."

After this the firing ceased. The chief shouted to the trappers, "Today we fight no more." Then the Blackfeet disappeared, carrying off their dead and wounded. Their loss had been heavy, but they still outnumbered the trappers by far. Nobody wanted to chase them.

Meek reckoned their scouts had spied Bridger coming with reinforcements.

For when Gabe arrived with his fighters, Bug's Boys had skedaddled. It was too late to do anything except doctor the wounded. Gale no longer had enough animals to transport his men and scanty baggage. He never even bothered to raise his traps. He threw in with Bridger, who had horses to spare, mighty thankful that Meek and his friends had come to visit him and save him and his men from scalping.

They all went back to Bridger's camp on the Madison. Bridger was planning to move into winter quarters.

But first this brigade had to complete their fall hunt. They put out.

Not long after, some Delaware Indian hunters turned up. The Indians said they had found Blackfoot moccasin sign not far off, and asked to borrow some of the white men's horses to use as decoys and so get a shot at the warriors. Meek and his friends gave the eager Indians two head.

Grinning, the Indians rode off, staked the horses out in the open and hid themselves in some tall grass near by.

They had not long to wait. The willows across the clearing moved, as a Blackfoot warrior slipped stealthily through the thicket. It was evening, that time of day when trappers would be setting their traps, and the Blackfoot, probably supposing that the owners of the horses were busy up the creek, walked right out and laid his hand on the bridle of the nearest horse. The two Delawares cracked down on him together and dropped the thief between the horses.

Then they rushed out, snatched the scalp and weapons of their victim, hopped on the horses and rode to camp on a high lope, not hankering for a visit from the Blackfoot war party which would soon come a-running to the sound of their guns.

That was a coup counted upon the Blackfeet. But they would strike back. The whole country was crawling with redskins; almost every day the trappers saw Indian sign. A lone trapper was waylaid and killed; on Stinking Creek Blackfeet drove the trappers back to camp whether they went up or down the stream. Sometimes they were temporarily friendly, as when a band of some forty Piegans came carrying an American flag to smoke the long pipe and talk over the battle of Pierre's Hole in which they had taken part a few moons back. They told Meek the war party which had just tried to burn him out were Blood Indians. Blood, Atsina, Piegan, or Blackfoot, it was all the same to the mountain man—they were all enemies.

But after the trappers fell in with large numbers of friendly Flatheads, and Pend d'Oreilles on the Beaverhead, where the Hudson Bay traders were in camp, they were rid—for a time—of the hostiles.

They trapped the headwaters of the Jefferson, and when snow began to fly went into snug winter quarters on Blackfoot Creek[1] only fifteen miles from Fort Hall. There Bridger's men had only "poor bull" to eat—stringy, tough, lean, and blue!

---

[1] Osborne Russell, *Journal of a Trapper* (Boise, 1921).

Towards the end of March, 1836 Bridger's men went on their spring hunt, afterwards gathering for the summer rendezvous on Green River at the mouth of Horse Creek.

One afternoon an express rode into camp, bringing great news. Tom Fitzpatrick, booshway of the American Fur Company's pack train, had reached Independence Rock, and was pushing on fast. He had along more than seventy men, and about six times as many animals, three wagons. More surprising, the British sportsman, Captain Sir William Drummond Stewart and his party were with Tom. Most surprising, Doctor Marcus Whitman, with another missionary, Henry Harmon Spalding, had brought—their wives! Real white women! Ladies! The first ever seen in the mountains!

Narcissa

IF A WHOLE cavayard of Blackfeet riding grizzly bears had been reported, the camps, both Indian and white, could not have been more excited. Joe Meek, with half a dozen trappers, immediately saddled up. With them rode twice as many Nez Percés, carrying a letter for Dr. Whitman, which had been placed in their hands by the Rev. Mr. Samuel Parker. They rode away, spoiling for a sight of the caravan: the Indians to meet their white teacher, their new healer and medicine man; Meek and the trappers a-rarin' to see the ladies!

A long day's ride towards the Sweetwater gave time for consideration. They all wished to give the newcomers, and especially the ladies, a sure-fire, bang-up, hell-for-leather mountain welcome; that was certain. They would charge on, and "capture" the ladies in the best Indian-mountaineer fashion.

But then, around the fire that night, the boys began to consider. How would the ladies take all that? It might scare the daylights out of them, and wear out the trappers' welcome afore they got thar. To give up the charge was unthinkable, discourteous; but *something* had to be done to reassure the visiting members of the gentler sex. Joe Meek had to roar, but he resolved to roar as gently as any sucking dove! He had a solution: he took a square of white cloth (the scarf he used in scouting, tied over his black head, so that he could not be seen against the sky when peering over a hilltop) , and tied it to his gun barrel. With this white flag snapping in the breeze, the trappers could have their fun without scaring the ladies.

It was the afternoon of the second day when Meek sighted the caravan. There it came, trailing its slow length along across the sagebrush flats. Joe beckoned, they all rode into line, looked to the priming of their guns, and then with the white flag streaming, rode steadily forward, aiming to cut the trail at the very head of the column.

Meek saw the horsemen in the lead halt, the train close up, the loose animals bunched together, driven in. There was Old Tom at the head of the train—which suddenly began to move on again. They had seen his white flag.

At that, Meek let out a whoop, "Yippee!" The trappers and Indians joined in, they drubbed the ribs of their ponies, brandished their weapons, and raced for the train at top speed, yelling and yelping like demons. On they went, like a flash flood, eating up the distance like a prairie fire, swooping down upon the train, veering off, circling it, firing a rattling volley over the heads of their visitors. Then was the time for horsemanship; they sped on along, behind, around the caravan, whooping, putting their horses through all manner of sudden and erratic mazes, riding on the side of the horse, standing in the saddle. Until, finally, in a great cloud of alkali dust, they reined their ponies back on their haunches, and swept off their headgear not ten yards from the wagons beside which the ladies rode. It was all in the good old mountain manner, so often staged in later days by Buffalo Bill in his arena.

One of the ladies was skinny—and scared; but the other, shapely, bright-eyed, with reddish golden hair, riding beside Dr. Whitman, was smiling, eager, pleased. She was some punkins! *Wagh!*

Meek was the man to appreciate a striking, handsome woman; and when she was also a lady of grace and refinement, pleasant and affable, as Narcissa Whitman was, he knew her for his favorite. Eliza Spalding, so far as Meek saw, was second fiddle. During his stay with the caravan, Narcissa filled his eye.

But that stay was not long. After an hour or so of riding with the train, Meek had to be gone, working off his excitement in a dash back to the main camp, there to incite everyone to a grand ceremony of reception, a regular powwow.

An Indian dandy needs at least twenty-four hours notice, if he is to make his toilet with sufficient care: the sweat bath, the brushing of his long hair until it shines like a rifle barrel, the braiding and decoration, all the freshening of all the fine clothes, the fringes to be unbraided, the feathers to be shaken out, the handsome robe, the meticulous face-and-body painting—*and* the decorated, perfumed horse! The Nez Percés dropped everything and went to work to prepare for the grand welcome.

The trappers, in their way, were no less careful to make their best appearance. Out came the fancy coats, the gay calico shirts, the silver horse-jewelry, new beaded moccasins with fringes trailing from the heel, a new shine to that old shootin' iron, maybe even a trim or a shave.

When the scout signalled that the caravan was in sight, the Indians mounted, formed in line, and charged, whooping and firing their guns. This time there was no white flag, no white men. This time the greenhorns with the train were *really* scared. The compliment was appreciated—but not in a way the Indians intended. The missionaries were too busy rounding up their milch cows and spare horses to protect them from the savages, to

have time to admire or enjoy the fun. Their fright set
Captain Stewart and Old Tom a-laughing.

They all rode into the camp together. There the Nez
Percé women, on their very best behavior, kissed the
ladies—as the trappers had always kissed them. And if
the white men did not venture so far, certainly they
showed the ladies every courtesy and attention. In this,
Captain Stewart, Mr. Nathaniel Wyeth, and the bolder
spirits among the trappers had the inside track. Joe Meek
calls the trappers "bashful"—and so they probably were,
like the cowboys who succeeded them—boys who would
have given their right arms to talk with a lady, but instead
lost their tongues, and had to take it out in noise and
horseplay.

But the interest was mutual. While trappers and
Indians stared at the missionaries and their women, the
newcomers from the States were quite as eager to observe
the mountain men and redskins among whom they had
cast their lot. And since Joe Meek was not the man likely
to allow himself to be overlooked, record was made of
the impression he created.

William H. Gray, a layman in the missionary party,
describes Meek as "a tall man, with long black hair,
smooth face, dark eyes (inclining to turn his head a little
to one side, as much as to say, 'I can tell you about it'), a
harum-scarum, don't care sort of man, full of life and
fun in the mountains," as he expressed it. Gray found
Old Joe apt at spinning yarns—and reports that Meek
had taught his half-breed son[1] to say "God damn you!"

---

[1] This must refer to the son of Milton Sublette and his Isabel (the
Mountain Lamb). Meek's first son, Courtney (possibly named after Courtney
M. Walker, a factor of the Hudson's Bay Company) was born at Pierre's
Hole, 1839. See *Oregon Journal*, August 24, 1938. Courtney was the son of
Meek's third wife, (second Nez Percé wife) Virginia, and was followed by
Hiram (1841), Olive (1844) and others. Meek's first child was a girl, Helen
Mar Meek, (born *ca.* 1838) by his second wife. So far as is known, Joe had
no children of his own by his first wife. Mrs. Victor says Virginia bore Meek
seven children; daughter Olive says twelve.

That, of course, was for the benefit of the preachers in
camp!

The portrait has the color of truth.

For Joe Meek was never bashful. He could never be
satisfied merely to dress up in his best trapper's toggery
and parade before a lady's tent. He wanted to talk to
Narcissa, and talk he did as often as she was free to listen.
He was merry, fun-loving, and respectful. She reminded
him of home, of the girls he had seen on his travels before
he left for the frontier—at Pittsburgh, at St. Louis—only
they were faded memories, and Narcissa was real, and
alive. He admired her for her courage in coming to the
mountains, and he had a secret pity for the hardships she
would have to endure. Under her mellowing influence,
Joe actually declared that he wanted to "settle down"
someday—not that he would go back to the settlements—
and give up b'ar fightin' and Injun fightin' and see if he
couldn't find a home somewhere in the Willamette Valley
. . . to which, maybe, Narcissa was going.

When the missionaries pulled out, the camp seemed
mighty lonely to Joe Meek. And there was more than the
loneliness to depress him. Now that Nathaniel Wyeth
had sold Fort Hall and most of his goods to the Hudson's
Bay Company, the redcoats were camped on the preserves
of the Americans. The price of beaver kept falling; traps
would no longer make a profit.

But there was still hope for better times among the
men. The partisans could do nothing but keep on, and if
they could not make a profit, Meek hardly cared—so long
as they paid a fair price for his furs. Probably he neither
knew nor cared that some cussed greenhorn had invented
the silk hat. Though the day of the beaver hat was nearly
over, men like Kit and Joe Meek, free trappers, working
on their own hook or in temporary partnership, could
carry on much as usual.

If only the Indians would allow them to trap in peace!

CHAPTER TWENTY-TWO

Fightin' B'ar and Blackfeet

ONE DAY Meek, with two Shawnee Indians and a white trapper named Dave Crow, rode off to trap in the country of the Crow Indians. Their route was over the pass between the Gallatin Fork of the Missouri and the Great Bend of the Yellowstone, near where Fort Ellis afterwards stood.

As they approached the gap, Meek decided to have a little fun with the boys and rode on ahead. Then, wheeling his horse suddenly, he came tearing back whooping and yelling "Injuns! Injuns!"

To his surprise he heard many answering yells behind him, and saw a party of warriors rush suddenly from the pass on his heels. The four trappers did not wait to count the warriors, but quirted their horses and rode hell-for-leather till they had left the hostile Crows behind.

Meek's joke had backfired; but it had probably saved the trappers. If all four had gone far into the pass, they could hardly have escaped the ambush.

Some time later, according to Meek, the same four men set out again to trap on Pryor's Fork, and this time arrived unmolested. They were successful there. But as winter approached they decided to raise their traps and rejoin the camp. The party split up, the two Shawnees going off together.

On September 7, 1836, Osborne Russell reached the camp of the brigade to which Meek belonged, then on the Rocky Fork, a branch of Clark's Fork of the Yellowstone River. That day he records that a French trapper "named Bodah" (probably Bordeaux) had been ambushed while setting his traps and killed by Blackfeet, and that Blackfoot war parties had been seen in the neighborhood. He continues:

"We had been in camp but a few minutes when two trappers rode up whom we called 'Major Meek' and 'Dave Crow.' The former, a tall Virginian who had been in the mountains some twelve years, was riding a white Indian pony. On dismounting some blood was discovered which had apparently been running down his horse's neck and dried on the hair. He was immediately asked where he had been and what was the news.

" 'News!' exclaimed he, 'I have been, me and Dave, over on to Pryor's Fork to set our traps and found old Benj. Johnson's boys over there, just walking up and down them 'ar streams with their hands on their hips gathering plums. They gave me a tilt, and turned me a somerset or two, shot my horse, "Too Shebit,"[1] in the neck and sent us heels over head in a pile together, but we raised a-runnin'. Gabe, do you know where Pryor leaves the cut bluffs, goin' up it?'

" 'Yes,' replied Bridger.

" 'Well, after you get out of the hills on the right hand fork there is scrubby box elders about three miles along the creek up to where a little right hand spring branch puts in with lots and slivers of plum trees about the mouth of it and some old beaver dams at the mouth of the main creek. Well, sir, we went up there and set yesterday morning. I set two traps right below the mouth of

---

[1] A phonetic approximation to a Crow word *toshe-bit*, meaning "white one," which may be applied to an animal. cf. *shua-shebit*, meaning "dark buckskin" or a "blue horse," and *eshoo-shebit*, meaning "light buckskin."

that little branch and in them old dams, and Dave set his down the creek apiece. So after we had got our traps set we cruised around and eat plums a while. The best plums I ever saw are there. The trees are loaded and breaking down to the ground with the finest kind, as large as pheasant eggs and sweet as sugar. They'll almost melt in yo' mouth; no wonder them rascally savages like that place so well.

" 'Well, sir, after we had what plums we wanted, me and Dave took down the creek and staid all night on a little branch in the hills, and this morning started to our traps. We came up to Dave's traps and in the first there was a four-year-old "spade," the next was false licked, went to the next and it had cut a foot and none of the rest disturbed. We then went up to mine to the mouth of the branch.' "

Meek's own story of that day's adventures adds considerable detail. He had set his traps in the stream about midway between two thickets. As he approached the river, his quick eye saw buffalo running off as though disturbed; suddenly a bear ran out of the willows.

"I told Crow," said Meek, "that I didn't like to go in there. He laughed at me, and called me a coward. All the same, I had no fancy for the place just then—I didn't like the indications. But he kept jeering me, and at last I got mad and started in."

Osborne Russell continues Joe's story: " 'I rode on five or six steps ahead of Dave and just as I got opposite the first trap I heard a rustling in the bushes within about five steps of me. I looked around and pop, pop, pop went the guns, covering me with smoke so close that I could see the blanket wads coming out of the muzzle. Well, sir, I wheeled and a ball hit Too Shebit in the neck and just touched the bone and we pitched heels over head, but Too Shebit raised runnin' and I on his back and the savages jist squattin' and grabbin' at me, but I raised a fog for about half a mile till I overtook Dave.'

"The foregoing story was corroborated by 'Dave,' a small, inoffensive man, who had come to the Rocky Mountains with General Ashley some fifteen years before and remained ever since, an excellent hunter and a good trapper."[1]

Only two days after the Blackfeet attacked Meek and Dave Crow, these Indians ambushed two other trappers of Bridger's camp who were riding along Clark's Fork. Outnumbered and surrounded, Howell and his partner plunged over the riverbank, swimming their horses across, while the Blackfeet fired at them from the bank. Howell caught "two fusee balls through the chest"[2] but clung to his horse and was finally brought to camp. There he died next day. Meanwhile the trappers ran those Blackfeet onto an island and fired at them until it was too dark to take aim. During the night the Blackfeet skipped, taking their dead and wounded. The trappers buried poor Howell.

Meek and the rest kept busy trapping all the streams thereabouts until cold weather iced them over. Camp remained on Clark's Fork until Christmas, 1836, then moved a few miles to the Yellowstone. Buffalo were so plenty that they left no grass for the horses, which had to be fed on bark.

The trappers had little to do but amuse themselves. The men of several messes, seated round a small cozy fire in the snug buffalo-hide tipi, passed the long winter evenings pleasantly in impromptu arguments or set debates, in reciting or improvising verse, in song or jests, or in reading aloud from such books as were on hand—the Bible, Shakespeare, Scott, Byron, *Robinson Crusoe, The Thousand and One Nights, Pilgrim's Progress,* or Mrs. Porter's *Scottish Chiefs.* At other times the trappers

---

1 Russell, *op. cit.,* pp. 52-53. (By permission, the Syms-York Company.)
2 See Osborne Russell, *ibid.* p. 54.

matched coups, swapped yarns, or made fun of the follies and foibles of their comrades.

These good-humored, lively sessions of the tipi literary society were good training. Russell reports, "I for one will cheerfully confess that I have derived no little benefit from . . . what we termed 'The Rocky Mountain College.' "[1]

For Joe Meek, with his meager book l'arnin' and lively mind, the training proved invaluable. In those discussions he learned to think, arrange his ideas, speak, argue, and defend his views—skills he used well in later years.

In debate, as in battle, Joe could not bear to let anybody get the best of him. Once, while the brigade was encamped on the Yellowstone, Meek, Stanberry and six others went off to trap the Musselshell. In camp one day the men got to matching coups, each one bragging of his own warlike exploits and grandstand plays, just like so many Indian warriors. Meek and Stanberry were loudest in their boasting. Brags led to comparisons, comparisons to anger. Meek, tall, fat and sassy, would have it that he was the better man. Stanberry, though a little fellow, was chunky and full of spunk. Neither would give in. That called for a showdown.

"We'll shoot it out," Meek declared. "We'll see who's the bravest!"

Their comrades in camp hardly approved of a duel to settle such a dispute. But now no backing down was possible. The men sat round the campfire, planning a duel at thirty paces with rifles.

Suddenly they heard a shot down the stream, where one of the boys was hunting. Looking in the direction of the sound, they saw a huge grizzly, scared or wounded, tearing straight for their camp. All jumped up and grabbed their weapons.

Quickly one of the men spoke up, "Now let Meek and

---

1 Russell, *ibid.*

Stanberry *prove* which is bravest by fighting the bear!"

That was a fair proposition. Indians counted coups on grizzlies as though they were human enemies. For a big silvertip was a terrible adversary, with his mighty paws able to crush a bison's skull at a blow, steel claws six inches long, a mouth full of sharp fangs, and vitals armored by thick hair, tough hide, four inches of fat, and iron muscles. But both men shouted, "Agreed!" and ran to meet Old Eph, with rifle in one hand and wiping-stick in the other.

Meek's legs were longer than Stanberry's. And after all his brags, it took more than a wounded grizzly to make him show the white feather.

Joe got there first, raised his hickory wiping-stick and whipped the bear quickly over the head—one—two—*three* times, recklessly counting the coup before he up with his rifle and fired—just in time. The huge silvertip slumped at his feet before Stanberry could even set his triggers.

There was no longer any argument in that camp about Meek's courage. He was cock of the walk and the big bull of that lick. There was no more talk of a duel. Instead, the dispute was followed by a feast of fat bear meat amid a great deal of laughter and rawhiding.

CHAPTER TWENTY-THREE

Blood in the Sky

OF COURSE, all Meek's time was not taken up by his studies in the "Rocky Mountain College" or in trapping beaver. Like other mountain men he had to hunt buffalo. Game soon avoided the neighborhood of a large camp, and towards spring the hunters had to make long trips to find meat. While the winter camp remained in the Great Bend of the Yellowstone, Meek and six other hunters went over to Clark's Fork after buffalo.

The weather was cold but clear, and the snow on the level only three or four inches deep. Russell reports that they took seven loose pack animals on which to bring back the meat. After riding up Clark's Fork a dozen miles, a man named Rose killed a cow. There they made camp and butchered.

That night a shuddering, nightmare cry across the fire jerked Meek wide awake and out of his blankets. It was Rose. There he sat, telling them of his fearful dream. Rose said a big white bear walked up to him and insisted on shaking his right hand. Rose said "I warn't willin' to shake hands with no b'ar, even in a dream, but the cussed b'ar made me do it anyhow."

Now Indians, like some modern psychologists, believe that a man's dream contains his destiny, and many of the mountain men shared this faith. Rose was mighty uneasy, wondering what his dream portended.

But Meek, poker faced, laughed inwardly at the troubled man's fears. Said he, "Don't you know what yore dream means? Well, I kin tell you. I'm big medicine when it comes to dreams."

Rose, all unsuspecting, was eager to know what his disturbing vision meant.

Now, among mountain men the Devil was not infrequently referred to as "the Old Black B'ar," a fact which may have suggested Meek's interpretation. At any rate, he did not keep Rose waiting.

"Old coon," he said, "keep your eyes peeled. Unless you're almighty careful of yourself today, you're going to shake hands with Beelzebub afore you sleep again!"

Not much comforted by this assurance, Rose saddled up next morning and rode off with the rest to run meat on Rocky Fork. Keeping his eyes peeled, as Meek had advised, Rose rode in the lead across the snowy plain, heading up towards the hills of the divide along Clark's Fork. In that open country the men rode carelessly, with their rifles lying across their saddles, though Meek and others knew that a large war party was always prowling somewhere around looking for a chance to pick off Bridger's men.

"Suddenly," says Russell, "we came to a deep narrow gulch, made by the water running from the hills in the spring season."

The trappers rode up within fifteen feet of the gulch before they saw their enemies. Meek counted nine, all afoot. An instant later a cloud of powder smoke hid the Indians as they fired a volley from their fusees. Meek heard their bullets whistle by.

Rose, in front, dropped his rifle. He was hit; his right arm dangled, broken at the elbow. A Blackfoot jumped out of the gulch, snatched the rifle up, aimed point-blank at Meek, fired. *Tchow!* The ball jerked his head around, as it tore through his fur cap. That did him no harm. Still, Meek wanted to get out of there before those Blackfeet could reload. Already the others had wheeled and were racing out of range.

Meek's old mule was a stubborn critter, and had to be beaten over the head to make it go. It took some time to thump Meek's notion into its thick skull that speed was wanted. The others were far ahead.

No telling how many Blackfeet were back there. So, seeing that he was going to be left behind, Meek called out lustily, "Hold on, boys! Thar's not many of 'em! Let's stop and fight!"—all the while pounding his old mule over the head without effect.

The Blackfeet saw the fix Joe was in; they ran to grab the mule's bridle. Meek thought his time had come.

But the minute the mule got a whiff of the cussed Injuns up its nose, it high-tailed it out of there in a beeline, racing like a thoroughbred, jumping like a steeplechaser, plunging straight for a ravine. Joe was lucky; the ravine was full of crusted snow strong enough to bear the animal. In no time at all Meek was out in front.

Then the other boys began to yell, "Hold on, Meek! Let's stop and fight!"

But Meek knew that the mule had the bit in its teeth. There was no stopping it. He roared back at them over his shoulder, "Run for your lives, boys! There's ten thousand of 'em! They'll kill every one of you!"

The six trappers headed for Clark's Fork. Russell claims he saw eighty Blackfeet. But Meek's mule had ideas of its own and, carrying Meek, plunged on straight for the Yellowstone. Some of the pack horses took after him, others after the six trappers.

The splitting of the party caused the Indians also to divide. Meek could see three or four of them hot on his trail. There he was all alone, with the ice of the frozen Yellowstone before him, ice on which that spraddle-legged mule could never stand up—in as pretty a fix as a cat in Hell with no claws.

Meek thought fast. He had no time to waste. Jumping from the saddle, he quickly spread his two blankets end to end on the ice, and led the mule out onto the farthest one. Then, taking up the one behind and placing it in front, he led the mule forward again, and so on until he got the animal safely to the other bank.

Just as he got there the Blackfeet reached the river. Their fusees popped, but Joe plunged into the brush. They must have thought him "big medicine" to cross that ice on a mule. Certain it is that they did not try to follow.

But Meek never heard the last of that adventure. Everybody rawhided him for the contradictory advice he had given the others. But Meek laughed and sassed the boys right back. He always enjoyed a good story, even one on himself.

Just what Meek thought of the fulfillment of his interpretation of poor Rose's dream is not of record. But like all the rest he was determined to get even with Bug's Boys. They had wounded Rose and got away unhurt with his rifle. That loss of face had to be made good on the Blackfeet.

That was January 28, 1837. The same month the whites saw twenty warriors crossing the prairie only six miles off. Some forty trappers mounted and chased the Blackfeet onto an island in the Yellowstone.

Russell tells how the Indians found "some old rotten Indian forts, formed of small poles in a conical shape." The trappers surrounded these flimsy shelters, firing into them until cold and darkness put an end to the seige. Two of Meek's party were wounded, one brave Delaware, Manhead, mortally.

Returning next day to examine the battleground, the trappers, Russell reports, "found that three or four at least had been killed and put under the ice in the river."

From the trail made by travoises in the snow, the trappers were sure that seven or eight of the Indians had been wounded badly enough to require such transportation. Others less seriously hurt might have walked. Russell continues, "We found that the old forts were not bullet-proof in any place. Our rifle balls had whistled through them nearly every shot, and blood and brains lay scattered about inside on the shattered fragments of the rotten wood."

The trappers went back to the delights of winter quarters. They passed the time pleasantly, with nothing to do but gather cottonwood bark for their horses, shoot buffalo, and eat what the camp keepers cooked for them.

But Jim Bridger, that careful booshway, warned his brigade. Said he, "Now, boys, the Injuns are not far away, and you can lay to that. Afore long a big war party, maybe five hundred or so, will come hyar to avenge their dead. We'll have to keep a sharp lookout."

They had not long to wait. Old Gabe had a big brass telescope, and every day climbed a high butte near camp— to look out for "squalls," as he humorously put it.

As for Meek, his motto was "Live and let live; but if it comes to one or t'other, I'd ruther live."

Within about two weeks, on February 22, as Russell records, Jim came back early in the afternoon, looking bothered, to report that the plain down river was "alive with savages, coming across the hills to the timber about ten miles below us." They forted on an island, and every day more and more warriors joined their camp, until Kit Carson estimated fifteen hundred Blackfeet were camped there.

Jim put his men to work building breastworks of brush and logs around his camp. According to Russell, they piled these up horizontally six feet high, enclosing a space about 250 feet square, to hold their horses.

Bridger maintained a strong guard, though the night was bitter cold and the trees popped like guns with the frost. The stars shone bright. Says Russell, "At about ten o'clock the northern lights commenced streaming up, darting, flashing, rushing to and fro like the movements of an army. At length the shooting and flashing died away and gradually turned to a deep blood-red, spreading over half the sky. This awful and sublime phenomenon . . . lasted nearly two hours, then gradually disappeared."[1]

All the forenoon following the men spent strengthening their fort, cutting down trees and setting the logs on end inside leaning against the breastwork. Meanwhile Bridger and six spies reconnoitered, then returned to report that there were a heap of Injuns afoot, on the island three miles down river.

There was no attack, but all night Meek and the others could hear the Blackfeet rhythmically thwacking the rawhide parfleches which war parties used instead of drums, hear their wild lilting songs and piercing ululations. They knew that a war dance was going on. Next morning the lookout found the butte occupied and barely escaped by leaping wounded down the slope. A sniper fired on Bridger's cook out gathering wood for his fire, then disappeared.

There were only sixty men in the fort. Yet Kit Carson declares—and Meek and Russell bear him out—"thar was not one of our band but felt anxious for the fight."

Soon after sunrise the warriors, all afoot, moved to the attack. From the top of the breastwork Meek saw dark masses of Indians coming around the bend of the river on the ice. It was the biggest war party any of those men had ever seen—a regular army. Meek reckoned thar war over a thousand. The trappers watched in silence.

---

1 Russell, *ibid.*, p. 57.

On they came steadily—until they had a good view of the trappers' fort. Then they cautiously turned aside, marched into the prairie, and sat in council safely out of rifle range.

Then the mountain men, though outnumbered at least twenty to one, leaped upon their breastworks, yelling, taunting the Blackfeet, insulting them with ugly gestures, hurling polyglot curses at them, daring them to fight. Finally, says Russell, "the chief, who wore a white blanket, came forward a few steps and gave us the signal that he should not fight, but return to his village. Some of them turned and took the northwest trail across the plain toward the three forks of the Missouri. Others headed south into Crow country."

Says Russell, "We came to the conclusion, after numerous conjectures, that the wonderful appearance of the heavens a few nights previous, connected with our strong fortifications, had caused them to abandon the ground without an attack, which is very probable, as all Indians are very superstitious. We supposed, on examining their camp next day, that their numbers must have been about eleven hundred, who had started from their village with the determination of rubbing us from the face of the earth, but that the Great Spirit had shown them that their side of the heavens was bloody, while ours was clear and serene."[1]

Kit Carson declares that there were at least fifteen hundred warriors in that hostile camp on the island, and that they left behind "one hundred and eleven forts." Meek describes these as "forts of cottonwood in the shape of lodges, ten men to each fort." Such war lodges were usually constructed of poles by Indians on the warpath, who never carried tipis with them.

It is clear that Meek, Carson, and other old-timers in Bridger's camp took no stock in Russell's notion that the

---

[1] Russell, *ibid.*, p. 58.

Indians avoided a fight because of fear of the display of
northern lights. Kit says, "Seeing the strength and in-
vincibility of our position . . . they fired a few shots which
did no execution, and finding they could not do us any
harm without charging our breastwork . . . they retired.[1]"

Meek declares ". . . finding there was nothing to be
gained, they departed."[2]

If the Blackfeet had been scared by that blood-red sky,
they would never have fired on, or marched on, the fort
at all. Moreover, red was the Indian color of good luck
and success; it seems probable that since the Indians' half
of the sky was red, that would have encouraged rather than
frightened them. The warriors had had a good long look
at that fort, and their chiefs well knew what a terrible
price they must pay to rub out the warlike mountain men
inside it. The Plains Indians had no weapons, no organization suited to siege warfare or the assault of fortified
positions.

But Jim Bridger knew that such a loss of face would
make the Blackfeet so eager for vengeance that staying in
their country to trap was now out of the question. Giving
the warriors three days' time to be gone, he left the
Yellowstone for the Big Horn. The Crows were insolent
and tricky, but they could be bluffed. They would be far
pleasanter neighbors than the vengeful Blackfeet.

After eight sleeps he reached Bovey's Fork, and every-
body went to work running buffalo, making meat, and
gorging themselves on succulent hump ribs and fat cow.
By the middle of March, according to Russell[3] they met
Long Hair's Crow village of two hundred lodges. Long
Hair's scalp lock trailed the ground at his heels!

According to Meek, it was about this time he met with
trouble—right in Bridger's camp.

---

1 Milo Milton Quaife, editor, *Kit Carson's Autobiography* (Chicago, 1935),
p. 58.

2 Victor, *The River of the West*, p. 196.

3 *Op. cit.*, pp. 58-59.

One day, while Bridger's brigade was camped in the country of the Crows, these Indians came bringing shaggy robes and dressed sheepskins to trade for the ammunition and blankets of the Blanket Chief. Of course, while trading, the Indians behaved as friends. Still, with all those tricky Crows in camp, the trappers were alert.

Meek sat in his lodge, looking out, with his rifle across his knees and his eyes skinned.

One young Crow buck traipsed among the lodges, with his heavy quirt, with double lash, dangling from his wrist. Perhaps to display his superiority to all squaws, and to the wives of trappers in particular, the insolent young man halted and with his whip struck Meek's wife.

Joe never knew why the Crow lashed Umentucken, and didn't have time to find out. Before the Crow could stir, Joe shot him dead.

It was unlawful to fire a gun in camp, unless in defense of it. And to start a fight that way while the camp was full of Indians was rash indeed. No sooner was the shot fired than the Crows, dropping their robes, drew their bows and began to yell and shoot.

Before Bridger could stop the fight and persuade both parties to a truce, two or three of the Indians had been hit, one trapper killed. Bridger had to make presents to cover the dead. But still the Crows rode off sullen and resentful.

Thoroughly exasperated, Bridger went round to Meek's lodge. Old Gabe had come to make Joe see the error of his ways.

"Well, you raised a hell of a row in camp," he said, severely.

Meek never budged. "Very sorry, Bridger; but couldn't help it. No devil of an Injun can whip *my* wife."

"But you got a man killed."

"Sorry for the man; couldn't help it, though, Bridger."

This fracas upset Bridger's plans. He felt in his bones

that the Crows would blame him for the killing and seek revenge. Without delay the brigade packed up and headed out of Crow country.

Meek Womans Again

THAT JUNE of 1837 there was trouble between the Nez Percés and the Bannocks. When the thieving Bannocks found a small party of Nez Percés far from their main camp, they ran off their horses. Outnumbered and left afoot so far from home, the six Nez Percés dared not attempt to recover their animals; they knew the Bannocks could easily run them down.

Accordingly the Nez Percés came to Bridger's camp, told their story, and asked the Blanket Chief if they might take refuge with his trappers when they had recaptured their stolen horses.

The warlike Bannocks were always making trouble, infesting trails and robbing travelers. Bridger and other trappers had been fighting them from time to time since before Meek came to the mountains.

Russell, then in Bridger's camp, reports that they had recently taken horses and traps from some Frenchmen on Bear River. Yet in spite of this they were "impudent enough to come with their village of sixty lodges and encamp within three miles of Bridger's brigade in order to trade, though they still had the stolen property in their possession."[1]

On the other hand, the Nez Percés had always been

---

[1] Russell, *op. cit.*, p. 62ff.

friends of the whites. The trappers could not refuse them protection, even if they had wished to do so.

With Bridger's assurance that they would be safe in his camp, two Nez Percés hit the trail to the Bannock camp, looking for a chance to get their ponies back. According to Russell, four or five white trappers went along.

It was easy for the Bannocks to keep moving. They carried no tents along, making only a miserable little half-shelter about their fires, of sagebrush or willow shoots or any flimsy vegetation found where they happened to stop. What clothing they had was on their backs.

The Bannocks, not expecting any retaliation from such a handful of enemies, were not alert. Most of their men were out hunting. The Nez Percés easily recovered their animals and raced back to Bridger's camp. Afterward they gave the finest horse of all to Bridger. The rest they distributed among the trappers. Thus they saved their faces, increased their war honors, made a grand gesture of friendship, and assured themselves of protection. No doubt they fully expected a fight to follow in which they could win more war honors and get away with enough Bannock horses to mount themselves again.

When the Bannock hunters returned to their camp, their old men soon told them what had happened. The trail of the missing horses led straight to the trappers' camp. The Bannocks painted themselves, took their weapons and mounted their war horses.

About the middle of the afternoon, Meek saw thirty Bannock warriors coming. They galloped into Bridger's camp, right in among the lodges, yelling and making every kind of threatening gesture. It was always the custom to fire and empty one's gun when approaching a friendly camp, as enemies generally sneaked up in silence.

But that day the Bannocks had two hearts.

The trappers were not caught napping. Every man ran from his lodge to catch his best horse and keep it from being stampeded. Those Bannocks might be friendly, but the chances were against it.

Jim Bridger, rifle on arm, stood before his lodge watching and waiting, holding his fine buffalo horse—the very one just given him by the Nez Percés. Near by stood the booshway's Negro cook.[1]

The Bannock chief said they did not wish to fight the whites, but demanded the horses taken from his camp. Finding that Bridger was determined to protect the Nez Percés, some of the Bannocks lost heart and began to drift away.

Says Russell, "One of them as he passed me observed that he did not come to fight the whites; but another, a fierce-looking savage, who still stopped behind, called out to the others, 'We came to get our horses—or blood; let's do it!' "

Luckily Russell understood the Bannock's words; he shouted a warning to the trappers: "Get ready!" By that time every man in camp was standing by fully armed.

But when the Bannock hothead saw Jim Bridger holding that horse which he himself had stolen from the Nez Percé camp, his temper flared again. He laid the quirt on the flanks of his pony, kicking it forward between Jim and Jim's horse, riding over the lariat, seized the bridle, jerking it from Jim's hand "without heeding the cocked rifles that surrounded him any more than if they had been so many reeds in the hands of children."[2]

Bridger, who never liked fighting in camp, might have let that insult pass. But his loyal Negro snatched up a rifle, shot the Bannock dead.

Instantly the Bannocks unlimbered their bows and swiftly loosed their arrows. One of these struck Meek's

---

1 Some say this was Jim Beckwourth.

2 Russell, *op. cit.*, p. 63.

wife, piercing her heart. But the trappers did not waver. Then the Bannocks, without a leader, dashed away. Meek and his friends shot a dozen from their saddle pads before they could ride out of range.

Bridger's men jumped on their horses and rode hard after them—clear to the Bannock camp and into it, driving all the Indians streaming before them—men, women and children—into the river. Splashing frantically through the water, the Bannocks took refuge on an island in the river, finding what cover they could in the scanty willow brush and foxholes which they scooped in the sand.

Day and night the trappers lined the high banks on both sides of the Yellowstone, holding the Bannocks in a heavy cross fire, picking off every person who showed himself by day.

The Bannock warriors soon ran out of powder and ball. With luck an arrow might kill at a range of two hundred yards, but it was good shooting to hit anything at half that distance with a short Indian bow. And with all those crack shots lying around with rifles ready, an Indian who raised up to shoot was a gone beaver.

Even by night Meek and his comrades did not relent. They lay on the high banks, firing down into the island at intervals, preventing any escape from that deathtrap. All night long they heard the continual eerie sound of Indian wailing. Russell says they besieged the Bannocks for three whole days and nights. And of all the trappers, none was more bitterly intent on vengeance than Joe Meek.

When the gray light of dawn revealed the island once more, an old woman came out of the brush holding a long pipe in her hands. She called across to the astonished trappers, "You have killed all our warriors. Do you now want to kill the women? If you wish to smoke with women, I have the pipe."

After that Meek and the others pulled out. The Bannocks had killed his woman, but he had no heart to help kill theirs. He and his friends destroyed and plundered the Bannock camp. The Nez Percés got some horses. The trappers reckoned they had l'arned the Bannocks a hard lesson. There would be no fear of them for a good long spell.

As Russell put it, "the best way to negotiate and settle disputes with hostile Indians is with the rifle, for that is the only pen that can write a treaty which they will not forget."

Doc Newell, coming north from Bent's Fort on the Askansas, arrived in time to join the siege of the Bannocks. Says he, "We joined the sport—but shortly after gave up the contest, as they had been engaged for two days, and the Indians were fortified in the ground, and had plenty of horses for their consumption."[1]

The Bannocks had promised, if Bridger let them go, to be good Indians. Russell tells how, two days after the fight, three white trappers, not knowing of the battle, visited the Bannock camp. The Bannocks explained their wounds and mourning by saying they had been fighting the Blackfeet. The Bannocks treated their guests well and were "good Indians." They kept *that* promise.

Apparently Meek lost no time in finding a new mate to take care of the children in his empty lodge. This time it was a Nez Percé woman, name unknown, who rode at his heels when rendezvous broke up. Before the year was out she was to bear him a baby girl.

That autumn of '37 on the Cross Creeks of the Yellowstone, Meek had his biggest battle with a grizzly. Joe was hunting with Gardner and the Shawnee Indian, Mark Head, when he saw a big she-bear digging roots in the

---

1 Newell's "Memorandum." As quoted in H. E. Tobie's, "Joe Meek, A Conspicuous Personality," Pt. III, *Oregon Historical Quarterly*, XXXIX (June, 1938), pp. 410-424.

bottoms along the creek. They all reined up under the rimrock.

In those days bears often ran in bunches. When disturbed, frightened, or wounded they would sometimes all run together, charging on a hunter. A man on foot stood a slim chance of escape in such a case, particularly if the bears ran uphill after him.[1]

So Joe turned to his friends and handed over his reins. "Hold my horse," he said, "while I throw her."

Joe stalked his game and got within forty yards without being seen. He leveled his rifle and pulled the trigger. The cap popped, but there was no discharge. At that noise the great beast whirled on him with that ferocious growling snarl of an angry bear at close quarters, and immediately charged.

Meek dashed up the hill to his horse, meanwhile trying to put another cap on his gun. The bear was soon close on his heels. Meek made it back by the skin of his teeth. But as the two came tearing up, all three horses took fright, whirled, and ran frantically off, in spite of all Mark Head and Gardner could do. There was Meek at the foot of the rimrock, all alone with the bear. There was no chance to run, no tree to climb.

Just as he got the cap on his gun the bear's teeth met in the tail of his blanket coat, tore off the whole skirt below the belt and whirled Meek round to face her.

She was so close that Joe jammed the muzzle of his rifle into her mouth. But the gun was double-triggered and not set. It failed to go off.

Somehow Joe managed to set the triggers with the gun still in the bear's mouth. But just as he fired, the bear knocked the gun aside. The bullet hit her too far down to hurt her seriously. It only made her mad.

As Joe puts it, "It was then a question of 'Live Meek or live b'ar!'"—and no answer in sight. Then two more bears appeared—half-grown cubs—one coming up on each

---

1 See Stanley Vestal, *Warpath* (Boston, 1934), Chapter XIV.

side. Joe knew that a bear with cubs was always a terror.

The presence of her cubs put the mother in a rage. She made a furious swipe at Joe's empty gun, swept it from his hands and sent it flying end over end down the rocky hillside.

Then in her fury the bear grabbed the nearest cub and boxed its ears soundly. The cub skedaddled. Meanwhile Meek whipped out his knife and struck to stab the bear behind her ear. But she whirled, and quickly knocked the knife from his hand, her sharp claw nearly sending his right forefinger along with it.

Just then the other interfering cub came bouncing up, and had to be spanked like the first one; that gave Meek another free moment. Quickly he jerked his hatchet from his belt, put everything he had into one desperate blow, and struck the bear behind the ear. He felt the blade crash through her skull into the brain. The monster fell dead across his bloody moccasins.

Shaken and hurt, sucking his bleeding finger, Meek climbed the rock behind him. Then, looking down at the dead bear, with its long claws and white fangs, "he came to the conclusion that he was *satisfied* with b'ar fightin'!"

Captain Sir William Drummond Stewart and his artist, Mr. Alfred Jacob Miller, Meek says, appeared soon after. Meek let them have the bear, whose skin was taken and mounted. Miller made a portrait sketch of the "satisfied" slayer and his quarry, and afterward made a picture of the bear fight.[1]

His friends brought back his runaway horse and they all rode to camp, packing in the hide and meat.

---

[1] Stewart brought Miller to rendezvous July 5, 1837. His picture of Meek must have been made after that date, and not in 1836, as Mrs. Victor has it. She is less likely to have been wrong as to the place, near the trappers' camp on the Cross Creeks of the Yellowstone. Russell's group trapped thereabouts in September 1837, but his was not the "main party," with whom, presumably, Stewart and Miller travelled. The picture of the bear and Meek by Miller has not turned up, a fact which may lend some support to Meek's belief that it was "copied in wax" and so adorned a museum in St. Louis for many years. I have followed Mrs. Victor here. But compare Farnham's account quoted in Chapter XXVIII.

Muzzle to Muzzle

J OE MEEK had been close friends with Manhead ever since they and four others had defended "mule fort" against Comanches on the southern plains. So when the Blackfeet killed that brave Delaware, Joe made up his mind to raid the Blackfoot camp. He talked another trapper into joining him.

One night they slipped up and saw the taper lodges, lighted by inside fires, showing like Chinese lanterns on the bench beside the creek.

The high-pitched, lilting songs and yelps told them the Blackfeet were absorbed in a noisy game of Hand. Apparently they had stopped mourning for their warriors killed in the recent fight. Joe could see nobody outside the lodges or walking among the horses staked out there. He and his friend slipped in among the tipis, walked silent as wraiths to the lodges, and peeked in. All was quiet outside. Swiftly the two trappers cut the lariats of nine good horses, led them slowly out of camp, eased them across the creek, mounted and loped away.

As the spring of 1838 came on, Bridger's brigade turned towards the mountains to trap the headwaters of the Missouri. Meek and Mark Head, a Shawnee, one of the best of the trappers, hunted on their own hook and so dropped behind the brigade four or five days' travel.

Following along, they suddenly fell into a broad trail, where many horses and people had passed a few days before. Moccasin sign showed the Indians to be Blackfeet.

On the Madison Fork the trappers found the skeletons of two men, roped to trees. Wolves and buzzards had been busy tearing the flesh from their bones. Meek guessed they were horse thieves of some other tribe, taken in the act by the savage Blackfeet. Those bones were a warning of what might happen to the two of them if they were caught off guard.

After that they lay low daytimes, traveling only by night. Even so, some Indians jumped them. Meek and Mark Head rode hell-for-leather for the river, with the redskins on their tail.

When they came to the river, it was bankfull and roaring. The Blackfeet thought they had them.

But Meek and Mark Head packed their traps on one mule, rode double on the other, and plunged into the wild stream. The rushing water swept them down river out of rifle range and they made it across, leaving their enemies staring from the bank with their hands over their open mouths.

Mark Head laughed. "They took our mule to be a beaver, and us to be great medicine men."

Said Meek, "That's what I call cooning a river."

The two men caught up with Bridger near Henry's Lake.

The Blackfoot camp was ahead of them, and heading in the same direction as the trappers. Meek was now in the advance guard. As they followed warily, they occasionally found the pock-marked body of an Indian dead of smallpox, and once came upon a lone tipi, a death lodge in which nine Blackfeet were laid out.

They judged the Indians were only three or four days ahead. Because of the smallpox epidemic they had had little trouble with this tribe for some time past, since, as the Crows told them, the Blackfeet were moving north of the Missouri to escape the plague, having lost nearly half their number. Meek's former hope was now, he believed, a fact: "Hell's full of Blackfeet!"

On the third of June, according to Russell, Old Gabe Bridger, the booshway, proposed to take into the mountains and so by-pass the Blackfoot village. But after Kit Carson and five others reconnoitered the enemy camp, and learned that the Indians outnumbered them only three to one, all the free trappers objected. Here they had a good chance to throw a lot of Injuns cold, and they didn't aim to turn tail when the hunting was so good.

So Jim turned back towards the Madison Fork and made camp "about two miles from the river on a small spring branch" which "ran through a ridge in a narrow passage of rocks, a hundred feet perpendicular on both sides."

The village was about three miles above on the river.

As Kit Carson puts it, "We were determined to try our strength to discover who had the best right to the country."

The camp moved into the canyon and forted there, while a small party of mounted men took off to attack the village and start the show. Meek, Doc Newell, Cotton Mansfield and Kit Carson were in this party.

Russell reconnoitered with his telescope from a high point. He describes the Indian camp as "on the west bank. . . . About thirty rods behind it arose a bench of land 100 feet high, parallel with the river." This bench sloped to the west towards the mountains two miles off.

When discovered, the Indians were driving in their animals and breaking camp for the day's march.

The attack was a complete surprise. The trappers fired three or four rounds apiece, and dropped ten redskins before the Blackfeet could get onto the bluff above them. For, meanwhile, there was a lot of shooting back and forth in which the trappers had every advantage, with their long-range weapons.

But once the Blackfeet got up above them and ammunition began to run out, the Indians had the edge. The forty trappers fell back to their horses before four times their number.

It was a running fight, and the farther they got from the camp the more savagely the Blackfeet attacked, riding through the trappers' lines to break them up into small parties until every man was fighting alone. It was back and forth, the trappers charging, then retreating, and the Indians doing the same. Among the rocks and brush the trappers had held the advantage. But out in the open, numbers counted heavily. The Blackfeet had the trappers on the run straight back to Bridger's camp.

In this skirmish Joe Meek, on his fine running horse, was in the thick of the fighting. A Blackfoot warrior raced side by side with him, each trying to shoot the other. But the eager warrior drew his arrow so far back that it slipped from his hand. Meek, frantically loading while he rode, was able to fire before the Indian could aim another shaft. He dropped the savage after his arrow.

Kit and Cotton Mansfield happened to be together when Cotton's horse stumbled, fell, and pinned him to the earth. As he went down, Cotton lost his rifle, which fell out of his reach. The dazed horse lay heavy on his leg. Six warriors, eager to count the coup, whipped out their knives and ran to scalp him.

Mansfield thought his time had surely come. He shouted, "Tell Old Gabe that Old Cotton is gone!"

Kit heard his words, turned his horse around, slid from his saddle, upped his rifle and threw the leading Indian cold.

The five remaining scalpers whirled and ran. Cotton got his horse up, snatched up his rifle and was in the fight. By that time other trappers had rallied round, and killed three of the five Blackfeet before they could reach cover. But now Kit's rifle was unloaded. While he was ramming down the charge his frightened horse ran off, leaving him afoot. The Blackfeet, seeing the fix he was in, came charging back, eager to revenge their comrades and count a coup. There was no one to help Kit. Cotton and the others had sped away.

Then Kit saw a fellow named White passing. Kit yelled to him, and White, swerving alongside, clasped Kit's hand and swung him aboard. Away they went, leaving the Indians far behind.

Doc Newell had a desperate hand-to-hand fight. Having dropped an Indian, he got off his horse to take the scalp. He thrust his fingers into the Indian's long hair, which was adorned with gun-screws. But when Doc's sharp Green River blade pricked the Blackfoot's topknot, the "dead man" jumped up and jerked out his own butcher knife.

Doc could not let go. With only one hand free, he found himself fighting an enemy with two. By jerking the Indian about by his hair Doc postponed the stab he felt sure was coming—and he could see other Blackfeet coming, too.

Kit out with his pistol and shot the Indian, bluffed the others. Doc cut off the scalp and so freed his hand.

In this rough-and-tumble skirmish an Indian woman's horse was shot from under her. Meek spurred back to make her prisoner, but was delayed by two or three Indians who rode to help her out. One warrior, galloping by her, shouted something. She grabbed his horse's tail; the animal, on the dead run, soon swung her out of danger.

The fight went on as the trappers gradually fell back, working their way to the upper end of the enclosed part of the valley past the point of danger.

Here Joe Meek turned upon his fine horse to fire a last

shot at an Indian. This incident later became the inspiration for a painting by John Mix Stanley, the celebrated painter of Western life.[1]

But the Indians were not through. Not daring to charge the camp defended by a hundred mountain men, they took cover in a pile of rocks about two hundred yards south of the camp, and poured in a shower of bullets from their fusees for some time. The trappers returned their fire, but were unable to dislodge them.

Russell reports, "Presently one of them called to us in the Flathead tongue, 'You are not men, but women. You had better dress yourselves like women. You began the fight, and now you are hiding in the rocks.'"

Russell goes on, "An old Iroquois trapper . . . an experienced warrior, turned to the whites about him and made a speech. . . . 'My friends, you see dat Injun talk? He no talk good. He talk berry bad. He say you, me all same like squaw. Dat no good. S'pose you go wid me. I make him no talk dat way.'

"On saying this, he stripped himself entirely naked, throwing his powder horn and bullet pouch over his shoulder; and taking his rifle in his hand, began to dance and utter the shrill warcry of his nation."

The trappers cheered and concluded to charge. The Iroquois ran forward. The trappers followed "amid a shower of balls" up the gradual slope to the rocks where the Blackfeet lay.

In spite of the "storm of fusee balls" the trappers held their fire. Reaching the rocks, they stopped to catch their breath, then "mounted over the piles of granite and attacked muzzle to muzzle."

Kit Carson declares, "It was the prettiest fight I ever

---

[1] *The River of the West* is mistaken in asserting that John Mix Stanley witnessed the fight. Stanley, born January 17, 1814, is not known to have gone farther west than Fort Snelling in 1839, one year after this battle. He did not visit Oregon and the Northwest (when he certainly met Meek) until 1847.

saw. The Indians stood their ground. . . . I would often see a white man on one side of a rock, and an Indian on the other side, not ten feet apart, each dodging and trying to get the first shot.''

Though by this time the Blackfeet greatly outnumbered the whites, they gave way, slipping from rock to rock. For now the trappers, having replenished their powder horns and bullet pouches at the camp, pressed close on the Indians' heels, driving them from the rocks and back into the open where they had left their horses. Wailing mournfully, on these they packed off their wounded and dead, except for two or three bodies left on the field. The trappers scalped the dead and counted their own wounded. They had not lost a man!

So, still full of fight, the trappers packed up, followed the Blackfoot trail and insolently made camp within a quarter of a mile of the Indian village.

During the night the Blackfeet moved their camp, but left their mounted warriors to form a rear guard stretching from the river to the timber, watching Bridger's camp pack up. Seeing the Blackfeet so intent, about thirty trappers, Russell tells us, slipped up under cover of a thicket and a ravine to within twenty yards of the Blackfoot line, which was waiting to attack the brigade as it crossed the ravine.

The trappers tightened their girths, made sure their rifles were ready, popped four or five bullets into their mouths and noiselessly mounted. The brave Iroquois who had led the charge the day before charged out of the thicket, yelling.

Taken by surprise, the Blackfeet whirled away to their village "fast as their horses could carry them." The trappers followed, but halted out of range of the village, standing careful guard until their own camp had safely passed the Blackfeet.

That night, appropriately, the brigade camped some

eight miles up the Madison on a battlefield where they had fought the Blackfeet years before.

Near Henry's Lake they soon discovered another Blackfoot camp—fifteen lodges of Piegans under Chief Little Robe. The trappers were all set to rub out the whole band and kill every person in the village. For years they had all suffered cruelly at the hands of those savages, losing horses, blood, and brave comrades—never knowing whether they would live out the day. Their hearts were hot to punish their bitter enemies. But as they advanced to the attack, Little Robe and five others came walking abreast, unarmed and bearing a pipe!

Bridger may have recalled another parley with the Blackfeet, when he got his head broken and two arrows in his back. But Little Robe was so humble and pleaded so hard that Old Gabe and his trappers were ashamed to attack. Those Piegans were all, as Russell puts it, "nearly dwindled to skeletons by the smallpox."

Little Robe invited Bridger into his village to smoke the peace pipe, and complained that all his nation were perishing from this terrible disease thrown upon them by the whites.

But Bridger knew how the smallpox had come up the Missouri, and explained that though the disease may have originated among the white men in the settlements, it had been brought to the Blackfeet by Jim Beckwourth, a Negro and a chief of the Crow Indians, mortal enemies of the Piegans. Beckwourth, Jim explained, had taken two infected blankets from a Mackinaw boat coming up the river from St. Louis and had given these to the Indians. "Blame the Negro, blame the Crows, not the whites!"

Little Robe then agreed to trade horses and peltry, and there was no more talk of fighting. Bridger's brigade moved on.

Next day, while encamped on the trail in advance of

the Blackfeet, the trappers were astonished. A lone Indian, trailed by his wife and daughter, with pack horses and lodge poles and all his plunder, rode calmly in among their tipis, apparently never dreaming that he was setting his feet in a trap.

Probably he took Bridger's camp for Little Robe's, on the trail below. Before he knew it, there he was—right in the middle of his enemies.

The French trappers in camp ran to kill the man and pull the Indian women from their saddles. Their eagerness was all the greater because there was not a plug of tobacco in Bridger's brigade, and they all saw a fat tobacco pouch hanging from the Indian's pipe.

But Joe Meek, Kit Carson, Jim Bridger and other leaders ignored their yells. Meek took the woman's horse by the bridle. Kit led the man's, the daughter following along, and led the luckless party out of camp.

None of the Frenchmen cared to tackle Meek or Kit. Not a shot was fired.

Once out of range of the camp, Meek reined up. He had not had any tobacco to chew or smoke for quite a long while, supplies from the States not having arrived in time. It seemed only fair that the Blackfoot whose life he had saved should make Meek a present of tobacco. Meek demanded it.

Grudgingly the Indian fished out and handed over barely enough for two chaws.

CHAPTER TWENTY - SIX

Squaw Tracks

AT RENDEZVOUS near the mouth of Popo Agie, both trappers and Indians had a wild time. Not that they were so prosperous, for that summer it looked as if there were more preachers than beaver in the mountains. Not that Joe cared for preachers, but some of these had brought their wives along. Four ladies from the States! Big Medicine!

There were high jinks in camp. Shawnees and Delawares danced great war dances before the tents of the missionaries. Joe Meek, mindful of the heroes in *The Scottish Chiefs*, persuaded Captain Stewart to lend him his helmet and cuirass so that he could play the knight in armor, outdoing that wild chivalry under the eyes of the fair.

Well paid, and with little to swap his beaver for, Joe had long since l'arned to pleasure himself like other trappers with raw alcohol. They bragged that they could "swaller fire." By his own account Joe was not infrequently "powerful drunk." In this camp he carried on as usual.

What with his strutting before the strange white women and his over-indulgence in alcohol, his Nez Percé wife came suddenly to the end of her patience.

Eight days before rendezvous broke up she saddled

her Palouse pony, struck her lodge, lashed the lodge poles on either side of one sore-backed mule, piling the rolled lodge cover on the back of a second; packed her parfleches and dubbers, her robes and fofurraw on another. Then, taking her baby daughter, she mounted and hit the trail, leaving Joe's possibles and his kettle of alcohol beside him on the trampled grass where the lodge had stood.

She was homesick, and nobody can be so homesick as a homesick Indian.

The Hudson's Bay Company's brigade, under Francis Ermatinger, were going her way. She traveled with them. That was July 12, 1838.

When Meek sat up and found his lodge and family gone, he tried to recall what he could have said or done to hurt his old woman's feelings. Not being able to recall *anything,* Joe felt it must be her own fault. He prided himself on treating his wives well. Having her walk out on him and leave him flat was a sore blow to his self-esteem.

And when he found out she had carried off his pretty little black-eyed papoose, romantically christened Helen Mar after a heroine in Mrs. Porter's book, he was not only hurt but angry. Who did she think this young'un belonged to, anyhow? Well, to hell with the lousy squaw. Let her go! He still had the kettle.

When the American Fur Company's brigade put out for Wind River, Meek rode along, sore and surly, comforting himself from time to time with a swig from the kettle full of alcohol slung on his saddle horn.

But that first lonely night, Joe's emotions were too much for him. There was no one to talk to, for to confess his trouble would only make the boys laugh. He lay wide-eyed by the ashes of his fire, and his thoughts were blacker than the night around him. While the coyotes yapped and howled, Joe made up his mind.

Next morning he saddled up, filled his kettle with

alcohol, and turned back, determined to find and recover his family. Joe was lonesome. And like many another man who turns to drink for succor, he found it no friend, but a master.

When Joe woke up, he found himself with a head as big as Wind River Mountain, which loomed near by. Wagh! Yet Joe felt lucky. He still had his horse, mules, and all his fixin's.

After taking a hair of the dog that bit him, Joe climbed aboard again and started on, round the mountain and on to the Sweetwater, thence to the Sandy. Northwest from there it was a long dry scrape to Green River, where he hoped to catch up with his family.

It was the twenty-second of July. The endless sage-brush plain, dry as a buffalo skull, stretched away, parched and shimmering under a heaven of brass. The tireless wind was scorching. It was tough on his animals, but Joe himself was burning up with thirst, his head still dizzy whenever the horse stumbled. True mountain man, Joe never carried water on his saddle. But he still had his kettle of Taos Lightnin'. Joe knew the worst of all torments was thirst. So, from time to time, he drank from the kettle. That only burned his raw throat the more.

Halfway across that level purgatory he reined up. Two drooping horses were standing in the trail ahead—and some person with them. Joe rode on. "Wagh!" Of all things, that person was a woman—a *white* woman—Mrs. Smith, the wife of one of the preachers who had been at rendezvous. And there in the shade of one of the horses was Smith himself, flat on the ground, played out.

Joe reined up. Mrs. Smith, with tears running down her nose, ran to him for help. She saw Joe's kettle. "Water!" she begged. "Poor Asa is dying! For God's sake give us water!"

Meek got down to take a look. Asa lay there with his

eyes shut, pale and motionless. Looked like the preacher was gone beaver. But Meek was generous, brought the kettle, propped Asa up and poured a little alcohol down his open mouth.

Sputtering, gasping, the preacher opened his eyes. Meek tried to get him on his feet, but Asa would not stir nor lift a finger.

Meek was damned if he'd carry a greenhorn, and a preacher at that.

He cocked his head on one side and grinned at the limp quitter. If he wouldn't be saved, maybe he could be made to save himself. After several lusty oaths, Joe harangued the weakling.

"You're a damned pretty fellow to be lying on the ground here, lolling your tongue out of your mouth, and trying to die. Die, if you want to, and to hell with you; you'll never be missed. Here's your wife, who you are keeping standing here in the hot sun; why don't *she* die? She's got more pluck than a white-livered chap like you. But I'm not going to leave her waiting here for you to die. Thar's a band of Injuns behind on the trail, and I've been riding like hell to keep out of their way. If you want to stay here and be scalped, you can stay; Mrs. Smith is going with me. Come, madam," continued Meek, leading up her horse, "let me help you to mount. We must get out of this cursed country as fast as possible."

Poor Mrs. Smith did not wish to leave her husband; nor did she relish the notion of staying to be scalped. Despair tugged at her heart-strings. She would have sunk to the ground in a passion of tears, but Meek was too much in earnest to permit precious time to be thus wasted. "Get on your horse," said he, rather roughly. "You can't save your husband by staying here, crying. It is better that one should die than two; and he seems to be a worthless dog anyway. Let the Injuns have him."

Almost lifting her upon the horse, Meek tore the distracted woman away from her husband, who had yet strength enough to gasp out an entreaty not to be left.

"You can follow us if you choose," said the apparently merciless trapper, "or you can stay where you are. Mrs. Smith can find plenty of better men than you. Come, madam!" and he gave the horse a stroke with his quirt which started him into a rapid pace.

The unhappy wife, whose conscience reproached her for leaving her husband to die alone, looked back, and saw him raising his head to gaze after them. Her grief broke out afresh, and she would have gone back even then to remain with him; but Meek was firm, and again started up her horse.

As often as Mrs. Smith reined up her horse, Meek plied his quirt on its hindquarters and kept it moving with the other animals. Had she not been so worried about poor Asa, she might have feared that Meek was kidnaping her. Of course, what Meek was doing with her was just a rehearsal of what he hoped to do with his own wife when he caught up with her. He was in just the mood to boss a woman.

Mrs. Smith protested. But in spite of her tears Joe never even looked back; he kept the animals moving. "Them Injuns'll git you, if you don't watch out!"

Yet, before they were quite out of sight, Joe turned in his saddle. The dead man was sitting up. "Hurrah!" Joe said. "He's all right! He'll catch up in a little while." Mrs. Smith would have waited for Asa, but Meek kept her going, never slowing down

About an hour later Smith came riding up—this time only half dead.

It was long after dark when they reached Green River, and near midnight when they found the camp. When the trappers heard Mrs. Smith's story of her adventures with the unknown trapper, the whole company broke into a laugh.

"That's Meek all over!" said Ermatinger. "He's just the one to kidnap a woman that way!"

When Meek explained that there had been no Indians chasing them the Smiths were grateful; Mrs. Smith expressed her thanks effusively.

This ovation did nothing to mollify Meek's wife. Things were bad enough without having him come riding into camp with another man's woman. The more Joe talked, the harder she set her jaw. She was homesick for her own people, and *she was going home.*

For all that, Meek traveled on with the camp, hoping against hope, heading for Fort Hall.

At Soda Springs, Meek saw the missionary ladies busy about a campfire. They had a big tin reflector, and as he walked up to see what they were doing, the appetizing odor of biscuits baking tantalized his nostrils. For ten years Joe had not tasted bread.

Suddenly Joe was homesick, too. He remembered his mother's hot biscuits in Virginia, the golden butter fresh from the cool springhouse. His mouth began to water. He knew he ought not hang around the missionary camp like that. But he said to himself, "Wagh! I jest cain't he'p it!"

Apparently it did not occur to Mrs. Smith that a biscuit might be a treat to her husband's rescuer.

While Joe hung around, sniffing that delicious odor, he noticed a young man, a Nez Percé convert, whom the missionaries called James. When the biscuits were ready, one of the ladies asked James to sing a hymn they had taught him. Like most Indians, James was a good mimic, and obliged in a very creditable manner. One of the ladies rewarded his pious proficiency by giving him a biscuit. Joe watched the Injun wolf it.

Meek beckoned James over. Though he had lost his Nez Percé wife, he still had her language.

"My friend," Joe said, "go back and sing another song;

and when the ladies give you another biscuit, bring it to me."

James was happy to show off again, and being a meat eater and not craving a second taste of the white man's strange food, willingly brought his prize to Joe. *Mm-mm!* At Fort Hall, finding that his wife would never weaken in her determination to leave him, Meek planned to turn over Helen Mar to Narcissa Whitman to be put to school at their mission in Oregon. Meek loved his little bright-eyed girl. But he could not care for her in the mountains singlehanded. All the trappers had the highest respect for Dr. Marcus Whitman, and by this time Joe had realized—as Jim Bridger and Kit Carson did later— that a tipi was no place to bring up the daughter of a white man. Joe Meek's daughter deserved a better chance in life.

Now rid of domestic responsibilities, Joe turned seriously to trapping. Some old *companeros* were at Fort Hall. They made up a party to trap along the Portneuf River, and Joe came back with 150 prime skins. These he turned over to Joseph Reddeford Walker.

The demoralization of the fur business at this time is shown by the fact that Walker was then working for two fur companies at the same time—one American and one British. But no company was then in a position to discipline him. In fact, half the time he was in business for himself.

Joe took his swing and celebrated with such trappers as he could find at Fort Hall until it was time for the fall hunt.

Wilkins, who had a wife among the Flatheads, was heading for their country. Cotton Mansfield and Meek decided to ride along with him. An old Flathead squaw, wrinkled and tough as rawhide, who dared not travel alone, asked to go with them. Why not? Meek was tired of doing his own cooking.

It was a hot day, with no sign of rain. There had been utter drouth all summer, and most of the creeks were just dry gullies without even a single green-scummed pool of stagnant, stinking water.

Like the heedless Indians, Meek and his friends carried no water on their saddles. For, when traveling in the mountains, men naturally followed up a stream; when riding along a range, they usually crossed some stream at least once a day. Yet, considering his sufferings on the way to Fort Hall, one would think he might have carried the Indian's water bucket—a buffalo paunch—or have used the less common trapper's water bag of beaver skin.

But it was not the custom of the country. Man and horse fared alike, drinking water where they found it— in a spring, in a rushing mountain stream, in a rain-filled buffalo wallow, in a horse track or a hole scooped in the sand of a dried-up prairie river, or in some mudhole.

Of course Meek and his friends had their camp kettles, but most likely had filled them with alcohol before leaving the fort in order to prolong their celebration.

Each member of the little party had a pony and a pack horse. Having no booshway to boss them, they made a late start with the excuse of sparing the horses until these were conditioned to the trail.

Though Meek does not say so, it seems probable that the men were still drinking that first night out. At any rate, though they all must have known that horses after grazing always go in search of water, they carelessly turned their animals loose and posted no guard, forgetful of the trapper's adage—it is better to count a horse's ribs than to count his tracks. In the morning there was not a hoof in sight.

The disgruntled party split up to look for them. Mansfield and Wilkins trailed the animals, Meek and the old Flathead woman went off in another direction. The morning was blistering hot, and none of them had had even a swallow of water in twenty-four hours.

Old as she was, the Flathead woman kept in the lead, jogging along at a dogtrot over that sagebrush desert, losing no time.

Of course, the faster one follows a trail the shorter it is. But Meek and the Flathead woman had a better reason for making haste through that shimmering heat. They knew they would find the horses at the nearest water—if, afoot as they were, they could live long enough to get there. Dried up as she was, the old woman had the advantage of Meek. She had not been on a spree at Fort Hall.

As the sun rose higher and poured its rays down hard and heavy upon them, Meek was more and more tortured by his terrible, consuming thirst. He was hungry too, and feverish, and thoroughly tired of trotting after the old squaw's back—the only thing to be seen in all that waste. He was half out of his head with thirst, and as night came on lay down to die—or dreamed he did—just as Asa Smith had done before.

But it was not of Smith he thought, only of water. He heard it running, splashing, trickling. He heard the old woman lapping it up like a wolf. He struggled on to follow her and find it.

She was always ahead of him, always howling to him to keep him on the trail through the darkness. So he plodded on through the night, little comforted by the cool darkness. In his delirium he was soon possessed with a relentless lust to overtake and kill her, to drink her blood. But he couldn't catch up with her. His strength was failing. It would be too hard. Dropping the notion, he staggered on like an automaton.

And then suddenly his dream was true.

He did hear running water, and there, sure enough, was the old woman, lying prone, lapping it up like a wolf. With a hoarse croak of joy, Joe ran and plunged face down into the shallow water of the narrow stream. He lay on the white pebbly bottom, gulping the clear fluid, thanking God.

Long he lay there in the shallow water, swallowing it, soaking it up through his skin, and then, to prevent surfeit, thrusting his finger down his throat as an emetic before filling his stomach again.

That day on Godin's Fork, Meek and his faithful old guide rested in the shade of the willows. And there Mansfield and Wilkins found them, bringing all the horses.

Next morning they killed a fat cow and feasted. Meek laughed to think that he had ever dreamed of drinking the old woman's blood. It seemed just like a nightmare now.

Having recovered their saddles and other plunder, they camped near water. Crossing over to Salmon River they struck the Nez Percés' trail, leading them to the Beaverhead country, and to the Jefferson Fork of the Missouri, where they found Flatheads and Nez Percés camped together. They traveled with them to the Madison Fork, and on to Missouri Lake to join in the tribal hunt for buffalo.

CHAPTER TWENTY-SEVEN

Preachin' for a Wife

BY THIS time Meek, accustomed to run in double harness and having lost two wives, began to hanker for a third. His experience and observation had convinced him that the Nez Percé women were modest, and good housekeepers. Doc Newell, his lifelong friend, had married a Nez Percé girl, and Meek had his eye on Doc's wife's sister. The girl was fifteen years old, the daughter of the chief.

It would be necessary, Joe reckoned, to buy the woman. And he knew where to lay hand on beaver galore. The Missouri Lake, the Gallatin Fork, Gardner's Hole, he trapped them all.

On his way back, passing through a basin known to the trappers as the Burnt Hole, he happened upon a buffalo skull, smooth and bleached white. A buffalo skull was the mountain signpost. Sure that Bridger's camp would pass that way, Meek, just for the hell of it, marked on the skull with a charred stick the number of beaver he had trapped, adding a postscript to say he was going to Fort Hall to sell them!

Meek rode on, chuckling at his vision of the booshway's face when he read that treasonous message, and hurried, knowing that Old Gabe was sure to send runners after him to persuade him to bring the beaver back. In Pierre's

Hole Joe lay low until Bridger himself passed, heading
for winter quarters. Then Joe boldly rode into camp.

Before he could unsaddle, he was summoned to
Bridger's big lodge. Jim demanded what he meant,
trading furs to the damned Britishers.

Meek swaggered and laughed, confessed nothing and
denied nothing. Old Gabe, who knew Joe of old, was not
entirely taken in. But Drips was furious and threatened
Joe, at which Meek only laughed the more.

Finally Meek pulled out his receipt from Joe Walker,
Bridger's own trader, handed over his new furs, and made
them all join in the laugh.

It was late in the fall, but John Larison and six other
trappers were heading for Salmon River, and Joe went
along. That was a bad venture—bitter cold weather,
poor grass, no fur, and a heavy loss in horses. They all
headed back for the Nez Percé village in the forks of the
Salmon.

It was now nearly two years since Dr. Marcus Whitman
had established his mission at Waiilatpu on the Walla
Walla River, and Mr. and Mrs. Spalding had set up their
own at Lapwai on the Clearwater. They had made a
great many converts among the Flatheads and Nez Percés,
and Joe found the camp humming with stories of the
power of these missionaries.

In particular the old chief, Kowesote,[1] inquired
anxiously if any of Joe's party were preachers. He was
eager to hear more of the white man's gods.

Meek had come there for a wife, and had the beaver
to buy her, but he knew that without the old chief's con-

---

[1] Kowesote is the name given by Mrs. Victor in *The River of the West*,
but (although some Nez Percé names end in the syllable "soote" or "sute,"
I have found no Nez Percé who could translate this one, or recognize it as a
word in his language; Dr. John P. Harrington, linguist on the staff of the
Bureau of American Ethnology, does not believe the name can be translated.
Meek's daughter, in an interview (see Lockley, *Oregon Folks*, Chapter II)
gives the name of the Nez Percé chief (her grandfather) as Tou-u-len-en.
Possibly the chief had more than one name.

sent he could never get the girl he wanted. Always ready to oblige and a born actor, Joe was suddenly struck with an idea.

There was no trapping to be done in winter quarters, and he had not spent his time poring over the Bible in the Rocky Mountain College for nothing. It struck Joe that he might as well receive some benefit from his talents and training. He called his pals around him, made them promise not to give him away and then, after a most unusual display of modesty, informed the chief that he could give instruction in religion.

The chief saw no incongruity in this, being well aware of Meek's rating as a warrior and hunter—in his sight, ample proof of divine favor. The chief pressed Meek to preach, and that night by the campfire, having borrowed a Bible, Meek conducted the services, calling all Indians to the meeting. He had not listened to Dr. Samuel Parker for nothing.

Meek did not know one day of the week from another, but whenever the Injuns had time and urged him to preach, he told them Bible stories and gave them good advice. He kept up his useful missionary work until Christmas, 1838, rolled around.

Then the Nez Percés prepared to break camp for a hunt. Meek thought the iron was hot. There was no time to lose. He suggested to the chief that a wife would be a welcome present.

Kowesote stiffened. The missionaries, he said, had taught the Nez Percés that no man could have two wives and be a Christian, that divorce was bad indeed. Many of the Nez Percés, with several wives, he said, had given up all but one because of this teaching. Everybody knew, the chief went on, that Meek already had one wife still living among the Nez Percés. The white man could not take another without breaking the taboos of his own religion. The chief was unwilling to see his friend risk hell-fire by making such a mistake. Moreover, the new wife would also run that risk—and she was a Nez Percé.

It was all so logical and clear. Meek had to think fast. He began with the truth, explaining how in the white settlements when a man's wife deserted him a divorce was legal and another wife might be taken.

Finding this produced no effect, Meek reckoned he'd have to think of some better argument than the truth if he was to win his case. And now his training in debate in the Rocky Mountain College came swiftly to his aid.

"The white man's holy Book," Meek declared, "tells many stories of its biggest chiefs and best men who had several wives."

Kowesote was not impressed by this argument. If the Bible approved of polygamy, he asked, why should Spalding have insisted that the Indians put away so many wives?

Wagh! Meek knew well enough that you cain't hurry an Injun. But he reckoned that, if Spalding had kept at them until they put away their wives, Joe Meek could keep at them until they let him have one. By the campfire that night he did a lot of boning on the Old Testament, marking texts which mentioned the marital exploits of King Solomon and the patriarchs. Every day he argued and pled and harangued the chief, calling the boys to confirm his stories, defying the converts to refute them, until finally, after some days of hard work, Kowesote weakened.

The chief—rather glad, one may suppose, that the taboos of the white man's religion were not so exacting as he had been led to believe—declared, "You may choose one of my daughters." Joe was not slow to point out the girl he wanted, and the chief gave him the young sister of Doc Newell's wife. Promptly Joe completed his career as a lay preacher by christening his new wife Virginia, after the state where he had first heard those Bible stories.

The camp made a big buffalo hunt in the Beaverhead country. Along in March, 1839, when it was time for the spring beaver hunt, Meek informed the chief that it was the custom among white men to pay their preachers.

The chief stepped out of his lodge and began to shout in the high-pitched, far-carrying voice of a crier, telling his people to bring gifts to the man who had instructed them all winter.

One by one the Indians began to come in, each bringing a good horse, a prime beaverskin, a shaggy buffalo robe, or the soft-tanned hide of a mountain sheep. Altogether Meek received thirteen head of horses, several packs of beaver, and other peltry. Joe reckoned that, what with his pretty young wife and his salary, he had done right smart that winter.

But in such evil times, his prosperity could not endure.

CHAPTER TWENTY-EIGHT

The Last Rendezvous

WHEN JOE parted with the Nez Percés in the spring of 1839, he and an Englishman named Allen trapped the Salmon River, Godin's River, Henry's Fork of the Snake River, Pierre's Fork, Lewis' Fork and the Muddy. They finally set their traps on a little creek running out of the pass which leads to Pierre's Hole.

Next morning when they went to raise their traps they saw Blackfeet coming. The nearest cover was a small thicket just across the creek. Meek reached it without being seen. Allen stumbled and fell in the water, wetting his gun. He jumped up quickly and took cover, but the Blackfeet yelled and Meek knew they had seen Allen.

Still, no Blackfoot was eager to walk up to that thicket and receive the fire of a mountain man concealed among the willows. They held off, and Meek breathed again. He started to dig in.

Unfortunately, Allen, anxious to dry his gun, began snapping caps on it.

When the Blackfeet heard those caps snapping, they knew of the fix he was in. They rushed the thicket, plunged in, shot Allen down and dragged him out into the open.

Allen was not yet dead and Meek, helpless to save him,

lay in the thicket and looked on while the red devils cut the living man to pieces, yelling and abusing their screaming victim with every conceivable gesture of contempt and a hellish delight in their cruelty.

Sick, almost crazy with horror, sympathy, and terror, Meek lay in his sandy foxhole all day long. By sundown, when the Indians left, he was in a high fever.

Some hours later he dared to crawl out to the edge of the prairie, listening intently. He would hear sounds as of the stealthy footsteps of an enemy; then he would realize it was only squirrels running over the dry leaves. Finally he picked up heart enough to crawl into the open and make his slow and cautious way to a pine-clad bluff near by.

Next day he discovered two of his horses not far from camp, and rode off alone for the rendezvous on Green River. For twenty-six days on the trail, he rode alone, frightened, grief-stricken and hungry. But at last he reached Bonneville's old fort.

That was the rendezvous of 1839, the last one held in the mountains by the American Fur Company.

From then on it was a hard scrabble, for there were too many men in the mountains, too few beaver, and the price of fur had dropped out of all reason. Hatters were no longer buying beaver. Most of the mountain men realized that their day was over, their occupation gone. Many went down to Santa Fe or Taos, some west to the Columbia or California.

But Meek and a few others stuck to the mountains. "It ain't human nature not to trap," they said. "Beaver's sure to rise," they told each other. The Hudson's Bay Company would still buy furs at Fort Hall. If that failed there was trade with the Indians, where a man could make a stake somehow and get back to start over in the States.

That summer of 1839, while encamped in Pierre's

Hole, Virginia presented her husband with his first man-child. Joe called the boy Courtney.

Meek left his wife Virginia safe at Fort Hall, and with Big Jim, a Shawnee, rode off in desperation to trap beaver on Salt River, which flows into the Snake. Each night they carefully picketed and hobbled their animals. But one of Big Jim's horses was a slow feeder, so the Indian left it loose all night to graze. When it had eaten all it wanted, the horse came back and lay down behind the others, but for some reason kept throwing its head up at intervals.

Big Jim, alert to danger, awoke, saw the movement beyond the other horses, and poked Meek in the ribs. "My friend," he whispered, "Injun steal our hosses."

"Jump up and shoot," Meek answered.

Big Jim fired, then ran out to see the result. He came back crestfallen; "My friend, I shoot my hoss; break him neck!"

Meek consoled the man—by laughing. That was one on Big Jim! And in those hard, starving times, a man had to laugh whenever he could.

That trip they caught little enough. Back at Fort Hall, Meek learned that his new wife and her sister had gone with Doc Newell and others to Fort Davy Crockett on Green River. Meek set out after them.

On Bear River, late in August, 1839, Joe suddenly saw a party of three men approaching along the trail. One of them rode out, holding up his palm in the sign for peace. Joe made the same sign and rode up, shook the fellow's hand, slapped his shoulder. When the two of them reached the party, Meek was introduced to Thomas Jefferson Farnham. He had come west from the settlements to establish Utopia, but had been abandoned by most of his discouraged followers at Bent's Fort.

"Good morning, how are ye?" Joe said. "Stranger in the mountains, eh?"

Then, before Farnham could reply, Meek went on, "Have you any meat? Come, I've got the shoulder of a goat; let's go back to your camp and cook and eat and talk a while."

Farnham knew "the old swarthy trapper" at once and told Joe he had seen him in waxwork in a museum in St. Louis,[1] grappling with a bear, "with the paws of an immense grizzly upon his shoulders in front, the fingers and thumb of his left hand bitten off, while with the right he holds the hunter's knife, plunged deeply into the animal's jugular vein." Farnham described the figure to Joe. Joe reckoned it might have been made from Alfred Jacob Miller's sketch of his combat with the silver-tip.

But Joe was in no mood to dream of past glory or present fame. He damned the American Fur Company which had made him live in danger, used his talents, paid him a fraction of what he produced and now had turned him off. Joe was "evidently very poor."

Meek told them he was headin' for Brown's Hole to get his squaw and possibles.

Farnham records that Joe's clothes—"scarcely enough to cover his body"—were so worn and thin that on that August morning "the frosty winds which sucked up the valley, made him shiver like an aspen leaf." He also declares that Joe (after eleven years in the mountains) was quite like a redskin, with "the same wild, unsettled, watchful expression of the eye, the same unnatural (*sic*) gesticulation in conversation, the same unwillingness to use words when a sign, a contortion of the face or body or movement of the hand will manifest thought . . . in standing, walking, riding, in all but complexion he was an Indian."

---

[1] "The statue was probably at Koch's Museum, on Market Street, between Second and Third." Thus Bernard DeVoto, in *Across the Wide Missouri* (Boston, 1947), p. 436.

Right! For poor as he was, Joe was Indian enough to be generous. He offered to share the hunk of antelope meat he had on his saddle, and gave them good advice: to get on to Fort Hall and travel from there in safety with the Nez Percés, then in camp on Salmon River one day's ride from the fort, and due to leave in about ten days.

Says Farnham, "Bidding us good morning and wheeling away to the day's ride, he said 'Keep your eye shining for the Blackfeet. They are about Beer Springs; and stay—my white horse tired, one camp down the river; was obliged to cache my pack and leave him: use him if you can, and take him to the fort. And look here, I have told you I am Meek, the bear killer, and so I am. But I think the boys at the museum in St. Louis might have done me up as it really was. The beast only jumped on my back and stript off my blanket; scratched some, but didn't pull my shoulder blade off. Well, after he had robbed me of my blanket, I shoved my rifle against him and blew out his heart. That's all—no fingers bitten off, no knifing; I merely drove a little lead into his palpitator.' So saying he spurred his weary animal to a trot and was soon hidden among the underbrush. . . ."

Within a few miles Joe lost the hammer of his gun. After that he could not hunt, and when his fresh meat gave out he found no jerky in his saddle bags.

Well, there was no use complaining. Joe had been hungry before. He kept going, kept going, carrying empty paunch, until he was plumb tuckered out. It was still fifteen miles to the fort. Joe slid off his horse and lay down to rest beside the trail. He reckoned he'd never get up again.

But by and by Joe Walker and another old-timer named Gordon came along.

"Wagh!" Gordon yelled. "If it ain't old Meek! How are ye, Joe?"

Joe had just one question. He wanted something to eat.

"Sure," Walker replied. He got down from his horse, pulled out some dried buffalo meat, and handed it over.

Joe tied into that jerky like a famished wolf. Seeing how he wolfed it, Walker asked, "How long has it been since you've eaten?"

Between swallows Joe managed to answer, "Five days since I had a bite."

Walker tore the meat from Meek's hands. "Then you don't get any more right now," he warned, and packed the meat away again in his saddle bags.

Joe staggered up, growling, "If my gun had a hammer, I'd shoot and eat *you!*"

Walker soothed Meek, helped him back on his horse, and took him to the fort.

At Fort Davy Crockett they found St. Clair, who owned it, Doc Newell with his wife and Meek's, Farnham's party, Kit Carson, Wilkins and Craig. Everybody was in mighty low spirits.

But when Meek had rested and was fat and sassy again, Newell and he decided to take what furs they had to Fort Hall, trade for goods, come back to their families and trade with the Indians there. It was bitter cold, and there was little game along the way, which lay by Henry's Fork, Black Fork, Bear River and Soda Springs. After a week's rest they set out, with fifteen animals and one camp keeper, a Snake Indian they dubbed Al.

Fort Hall had been too short of meat to supply them for the trip. By the time they reached Ham's Fork, all they had left was a tiny piece of bacon they had been saving to sweeten the stringy, tough meat of "poor bull," if ever they were lucky enough to find any.

Next morning a curious thing happened. It was cold and stormy. Snow filled the air. Yet while Meek and Newell snuggled in their blankets, Snake Al, with a briskness never seen in him before, jumped up and went out to look after the horses.

Said Meek to Newell, "Al has eaten our bacon."

It was all too true. Savagely Meek declared that unless he found game before next-day night he would kill and eat Al to get the bacon back.

As the following afternoon drew on, Al was not too happy. But before night fell, a Frenchman and his wife turned up with plenty of fat antelope meat. Al's bacon was saved.

The snow was deep. But they preferred it that way, for in that bitter February weather and deep snows, Indian war parties were not about; it was safer. Still, they would have starved but for two dogs they bought from a Digger squaw; they were six weeks on the trail.

The goods which Meek and Newell brought back to Fort Crockett were mostly wet goods. Christmas came on, with the usual festivities. Meek and Newell, with the lavish hospitality of trappers, and the appetites of coyotes, made away with more than half the supply they had packed in from Fort Hall with such hardship.

In those hard times a man had to live somehow, and with no buffalo to kill, no beaver to trap, no game to eat, a good many of the mountain men turned horse thief. Thompson and others, Meek reports, went to Snake River to steal horses from the Nez Percés. No luck. So they robbed the Snake Indians of forty head, and ran them off to the Uintah. The outraged friendlies complained that white men had robbed them, and demanded restitution.

Meek knew that it had always been the custom, when one member of a tribe offends, for the others to make amends—or take the consequences. The whites at Fort Crockett knew the Indians held them responsible. Joe Walker organized a party of twenty-five picked men, including Meek, Craig, Doc Newell and Kit Carson, to recover the stolen animals. They found them on an island on Green River. They located the horse thieves in an old abandoned fort at the mouth of the Uintah.

Walker and his men were not eager to spill white blood, and tried to sneak the horses away.

The ice was rubbery, and, while they were crossing, sank under them until the water was knee deep to a horse. In this pretty fix the thieves in the fort saw what was up and came tearing out afoot to get those horses back.

But Joe Walker was no fool. Once across the river, he and his men kicked the horses into a run, led Thompson's force away from the fort, circled the thieves, and so ran the horses into Thompson's own fort, where the thieves could not get at them.

There was a village of Utes not far away. Tricked and furious, Thompson offered the horses to the Utes if the Utes would help recover them. Meek and Walker, on their side, shouted threats of vengeance against the Utes if they dared to interfere.

Now, the Utes had a healthy respect for the trappers' rifles and the arrows of the Snakes. They finally decided to stay out of the fight.

And so, after a day of shouting, threats and arguments, warlike display and anger, Walker and his men rode out of the fort, driving the stolen horses before them back to Fort Crockett, and returned them to the Snakes.

In those bad times men hunted in the most unlikely places. Meek travelled down Green River through the canyon on the ice, and finally got out of it at the mouth of the Uintah.

In March, 1840, Antoine Robidoux brought goods from Santa Fe to trade with Indians. They camped on Ham's Fork and passed the time in running antelope through the deep snow. Once they ran a big herd of hundreds over the Green River ice, drove them into an air hole, and killed them for the fun of it. Robidoux, Meek reports, lost most of his goods playing Hand, and went back to Santa Fe in debt for them.

Joe hung around Fort Hall, trapping and trading for the British until summer. Then he went looking for rendezvous. But the American companies were no longer holding fur fairs in the mountains. On Green River, on Wind River, nowhere could Joe find even one small encampment. There he was, after eleven years in the mountains of risking his hair among the cussed Injuns, freezing and starving, earning thousands of dollars for his employers, far from all law, never sleeping under a roof, scarcely ever seeing a white woman—and whar's the dollars ought to be in his possibles?

The only civilized society he knew in the West was that of the missionaries, and of them Whitman and his wife were the only two he had any use for. He had promised Narcissa that some day he might go into Oregon and settle down. But what could he do there? He was no farmer. Too late he saw that when he came to the mountains he had set his foot in the biggest kind of trap.

To emphasize his plight, he found, on returning to Fort Hall, more missionaries and their wives, heading for the Columbia. He didn't like them, and once more stubbornly turned his moccasin toes to the old trapping grounds. Only one man, a Frenchman named Mattileau, could be induced to go along. The beaver business was played out.

But these two diehards went back to Pierre's Fork, Lewis Lake, Jackson's Hole, Lewis River, and Salt River. They took very few pelts, and on Bear River Meek met a Frenchman who told him that Doc Newell was waiting at Fort Hall with something to tell him. Inasmuch as Newell had been acting as Meek's booshway and trading with the British, while Meek's name does not appear on the books of Fort Hall, it is likely that Meek was in debt to Newell. Well, he reckoned Doc knew he couldn't pay. Maybe Doc had something new up his sleeve.

At the fort Meek found Doc with two wagons which Dr.

Whitman had left behind in his brave effort to find a wagon road from Fort Hall to the Columbia River. Doc proposed to take those wagons to Oregon!

"Come," said Newell to Meek, "We are done with this life in the mountains—done with wading in beaver-dams, and freezing or starving alternately—done with Indian trading and Indian fighting. The fur trade is dead in the Rocky Mountains, and it is no place for us now, if ever it was. We are young yet, and have life before us. We cannot waste it here; we cannot or will not return to the States. Let us go down to the Willamette and take farms. There is already quite a settlement there made by the Methodist Mission and the Hudson's Bay Company's retired servants.

"I have had some talk with the Americans who have gone down there, and the talk is that the country is going to be settled up by our people, and that the Hudson's Bay Company are not going to rule this country much longer. What do you say, Meek? Shall we turn American settlers?"

"I'll go where you do, Newell. What suits you suits me."

"I thought you'd say so, and that's why I sent for you, Meek. In my way of thinking, a white man is a little better than a Canadian Frenchman. I'll be damned if I'll hang 'round a post of the Hudson's Bay Company. So you'll go?"

"I reckon I will! What have you got for me to do? I haven't got anything to begin with but a wife and baby!"

"Well, you can drive one of the wagons, and take your family and traps along. Nicholas will drive the other, and I'll play leader, and look after the train. Craig will go also, so we shall be quite a party, with what strays we shall be sure to pick up."

PART III
PATRIOT

CHAPTER TWENTY-NINE

Oregon or Bust

AFTER ALL his years of wandering in the wilderness, Joe Meek was always ready for the trail, as happy to be moving as any redskin. He and Doc Newell wasted no time, stowed their possibles in the wagons, topped the load off with their Nez Percé wives and children and, with a great cracking of whips, headed for Walla Walla, September 27, 1840.

Meek drove a team of four horses and one mule. Nicholas drove the other team of four horses. But Newell, owner of the outfit, rode horseback with the dignity becoming to the booshway. Another old-timer, Craig, joined the party, and after they got started several others came along, among them Caleb Wilkins.

Opening a wagon road from the Rocky Mountains to the Columbia River was a great undertaking, and though Dr. Whitman was confident it could be done, it was Doc and Joe who had to keep their wheels rolling over the lava, through sand and squelching mud, fording rivers, scaling hills, trailing through canyons where no wheel had ever rolled before.

At Fort Boise Mr. Payette, factor of the Hudson's Bay Company at that post, made them welcome. With typical British regard for social status he invited Newell, the booshway, to share his quarters in the fort. Meek and Craig and the rest were left to camp outside.

The factor, however, for all his regard for protocol, was hospitable enough; he sent out a large sturgeon steak to Meek, with his compliments.

Joe Meek had never let anybody snub him. Andy Jackson, the frontier democrat, was his hero. His faith in human equality had only been strengthened by his years of freedom in the mountains. Joe was as independent as a hog on ice. He and Craig sent the sturgeon back to Payette, with *their* compliments! Maybeso that would l'arn him a thing or two.

Joe had always carried a chip on his shoulder, and now that he was venturing into the unknown world of the settlements, where all his skills and lore might be of no earthly use, he was all the more inclined to insist upon his rights.

In spite of all dangers and difficulties the little party pushed on until they reached the Columbia River, about where the Umatilla comes in. Getting the wagons and stock over was quite a chore, but once across, Newell and his friends headed straight for Dr. Whitman's Presbyterian mission. They were there sometime in November, or a bit earlier.

At Waiilatpu the doctor gave them a hearty welcome. Having no fatted calf, he killed his fattest hog for them. Though Meek had all a mountain man's prejudice against pork and pork-eaters, he joined the feast. For Dr. Whitman, who had heard of Meek's exploits as a preacher to the Nez Percés, told Joe to eat hearty, because "fat pork is good for preachers!"

Mrs. Whitman gave the mountain men a friendly reception, and showed them the Indian children she had in charge, whom she was teaching to read, write, sew, keep house, and garden. All the mountain men greatly admired Narcissa, and Joe asked if he might leave his own little daughter, Helen Mar, with the Whitmans, where she would not be too far away and could get a better education than Virginia, his Nez Percé wife, could then provide.

The nearer Meek got to the settlements, the more he realized how different and how difficult life would be. In the Rockies an Indian woman and a mountain man could live well enough in a tipi on wild meat. But what could they do in the white settlements? For a free trapper to drop from riding fine horses to driving team had been a turrible comedown, and now Joe had a strong feeling that driving a plow would prove a hell of a bigger one.

Joe had most of the traits which those foreigners who, perhaps, understand us best believe characteristic, by and large, of Americans today:

He was exuberant, boisterous, happy-go-lucky, free and easy, generally friendly, rather sentimental, and big-hearted. He prided himself on treating women with consideration and on his way with them. He was also a go-getter, a man in a hurry, impatient for results, a money-maker, tough, hard-boiled, unmannerly, coarse at times, often boastful, cocksure, opinionated, and inclined to throw his weight about.[1]

And as a mountain man, even more than most Americans, he had been a big spender. He chawed tobacco and spoke with a drawl. He was also lazy, and got a heap of fun out of life.

All these qualities had served Meek well in the mountains; they enabled him to cope with most difficulties and to laugh at those he could not handle. So far as character went, he had little to fear in the settlements. His young heart was stout and light and his tall body strong.

Though he could read and write a little, the Rocky Mountain College had not given him any useful book-l'arnin' or any knack with the pen. He knew no trade,

[1] William A. Lydgate, "What the British Think of Us," '47 Magazine of the Year (December, 1947), p. 77 ff. This article is based upon a survey by the British Gallup Poll.

knew nothing of business or public affairs. He was a mountain man, and that only.

The fact that Doc Newell, his old comrade of the beaver stream, was now his booshway in the settlements, because he had what Meek lacked, only made Joe the more conscious of his own handicaps.

And certainly Oregon at that time was not in a promising condition for a man of Joe's gifts. It was a vast region, extending from California to Alaska, from the Rocky Mountains to the Pacific Ocean. Yet there were hardly more than two hundred white settlers, and of these about one in six was attached to some mission or other. North of the Columbia some French Canadian and Scotch settlers had come in, transferred from Red River by Sir George Simpson, governor of the Hudson's Bay Company. These Britishers, not liking the country around Puget Sound, soon settled in the Willamette Valley. About two-thirds of the settlers were Americans.

The two groups were not altogether friendly, inasmuch as the Oregon boundary had never been settled, and by agreement was to be the subject of negotiations at some future date. The missionaries frequently quarreled with each other and with the settlers, both British and American, and particularly with the Frenchmen.

Such authority as existed in Oregon at that time resided in the Hudson's Bay Company and the American Methodist Mission. From them the settlers obtained nearly all their supplies, frequently sought their advice, and when one of them died, allowed one or the other to settle his estate.

The Indians, for their part, were moody and dissatisfied, seeing that the white men were moving into their country without paying them for it. At first they had been interested in following the white man's road in order to enjoy the blessings promised. But, finding that they were expected to labor steadily for these and were treated as social inferiors, they began to repent of setting their feet on the White Man's Road. The white man's prayers had not increased their worldly wealth, and they had strong religious objections to having the breast of their Mother torn and wounded by a plow.

The Nez Percés became so threatening to one of Spalding's men that he—and others as well—left the Willamette Valley. The Walla Walla and Cayuse tribes were, if anything, less friendly than the Nez Percés. And when the new Indian agent, Dr. Elijah White, a rather dictatorial man, came out and talked of filling the country with white settlers, the Indians became more and more alarmed.

In fact Meek was going into a region where small groups, all at odds with each other, formed a most unstable compound which might at any time explode.

To begin with, however, he had to get there. But the weather became so wet, the trail so muddy and greasy that Doc Newell finally despaired of getting those wagons over the Cascades that autumn. They packed their goods on the horses and went over the pass. At The Dalles of the Columbia they found a Methodist mission in charge of Daniel Lee—who was conducting a *revival* for the savages!

Leaving The Dalles, they ran into more missionaries, Waller and Beers, preaching on the Willamette. Meek tried to buy provisions from Waller, but Mr. Waller refused to let Joe have any because it was Sunday. By that time it seemed to Joe that Oregon as well as Hell was full of preachers.

But Joe was a persuasive soul and, having talked Kowesote out of a wife in defiance of mission taboos, finally talked Waller out of a peck of small potatoes.

Fed up with missionaries and their finicky notions, Newell and Joe made tracks for Fort Vancouver, the Hudson's Bay Company post, where they might find fur men with hearts as big as their own. The British gave them rations—dried salmon, tea, sugar, sea biscuit; they filled up. Afterward they threw in with some comrades of the old days, William Doughty, Caleb Wilkins, George Wood "Squire" Ebbert. These, with William Craig, made six mountain men. Clinging together in their strange situation, they pushed out into the Tualatin Plains, looking for land on which to settle, and try their hand at farming.

In those days most American farmers refused prairie-land, holding that, if the prairie were good soil it would have trees growing on it. But to Meek and the mountain men, plowing would be hell enough without clearing the land first. Why swing an ax when you could camp on grass? They reached their new home on Christmas Day, 1840.

That was a hard winter, hard doin's. They had one tiny log cabin and the buffalo-hide lodges of their Indian wives. But in that rainy climate a skin tent was not the cheerful dwelling it had been on the high, dry plains and in the Rockies. Everything was soaked all the time. The lodge skins were always sodden, dripping at every seam. A skin tent leaked the day it rained—and two days afterward. The sinews of their moccasins softened; the soles and uppers parted. Their clammy, clinging buckskins were wet to the waist when they came back from looking after their horses. *And there was no game.*

Meek dreamed of buffalo herds covering the earth like one great robe, of roasting hump ribs running rivers of melting fat beside the campfire, of tasty *boudins* sizzling on the embers, of antelope steaks and mountain mutton, of tender painter meat and roasted beaver tails, and smacked his lips in sleep over fat Injun dog—then woke to eat his scanty daily ration of boiled wheat! *Boiled wheat!* Had it not been for some distant neighbors who gave him dried salmon and sea biscuit, and a few ducks

DR. JOHN McLOUGHLIN
He played a large part in Meek's later life

and swans he traded from the Indians, Meek and his comrades might have starved.

But at any rate, he reckoned, in that country they never would go thirsty! All they could do was to squat in the mud, waiting for spring, in a country made dismal by incessant rain, with every trail impassable and every stream out of its banks.

There were no moneylenders in Oregon in those days, and the ragged trappers, who had always lived on credit, found the going tough. The Hudson's Bay Company lent them seed wheat, farm implements and oxen, or they could never have broken the sod and put in their crop.

All this only confirmed Joe in his conviction: tough as the fur traders and trappers were and scorned as they were by missionaries and other greenhorns, they still had the biggest hearts and could shine in any company.

It isn't likely that Meek would have plowed at all if Newell had not been his booshway. Once the crop was in, there was nothing to do and no way of earning money. But, jaunty, jolly and lighthearted, Joe Meek, all ragged and wet, was still his old reckless self. More and more he hung around Fort Vancouver and there amused himself, plaguing Dr. John McLoughlin by telling tales of gory Indian fights, which of course had never been tolerated by the British in Canada.

Dr. John McLoughlin, chief factor of the Hudson's Bay Company for the Columbia district was an extraordinary man, great alike in character, intelligence, and humanity. His ancestry was Scotch, Irish, and French Canadian. Raised on the farm, he was trained at Quebec in a medical school, and licensed to practice at nineteen. Then for eighteen years he was doctor and later trader to the North West Company, and by 1821 had achieved such leadership that he was sent to London to supervise the merger of the North West Company with the Hudson's

Bay Company. He was a devout Roman Catholic, and
one of the most enterprising and forceful men ever known
on the frontier. When Joe Meek met him, the Doctor
was in his middle fifties.

Joe saw a man fully an inch taller than himself—all of
six feet four, raw-boned, big, strong, energetic. His eyes
were piercing. His brows beetled, his nose was large, his
chin square, his forehead high and broad. But his most
striking feature was a great shock of long hair, pre-
maturely white, hanging to his shoulders. Sometimes
he wore a beard that would "do honor to the chin of
a grizzly bear." What a booshway! Men admired, feared,
and loved him. Moreover, he was a fur man, and the
father of half a dozen half-breed children. Meek liked
the Doctor, but could not refrain from deviling him.
And he soon learned that, of all things, the free-handed
Doctor most abhorred bloodshed. And so Joe kept on
telling him of fights he had taken part in.

But the Doctor was more than a fur man. Fort Vancouver, under his direction, was not merely a fort, but a
small town, with a church, a school, stables, orchards,
and farms. There was a hospital, of course, workshops,
quarters, warehouses, and a wharf on the river. The
Doctor entertained lavishly in his big dining room, and
could serve any kind of meat from his large herds of
sheep and cattle and porkers. But for him, Meek and
other settlers might have starved at first; the Doctor, as
it turned out, went into his own pocket to the tune of
$60,000 helping American settlers. At Fort Vancouver,
Joe noticed, everybody seemed to be in a hurry; there
were mighty few idlers around—except in hospital.

Joe kept on bragging of killing Indians until the good
Doctor would shake his head and rebuke him in his rapid,
clipped accent. "Mr. Joe, Mr. Joe, you must leave off
killing Indians and go to work."

Then Joe would grin winningly at the serious red face,

framed in its shock of white hair, shrug his shoulders and drawl, "But, Doc, I cain't work."

The next year a store was put up, supplied by a ship from Boston. Joe had borrowed a boat, and on the Fourth of July very early rowed out to the vessel in time to hear the salute fired by the ship's guns. They made him welcome, and Joe stayed aboard all day, sharing the grog and enjoying the company. Among the guests were some missionaries, whose highfalutin airs annoyed his democratic soul. They coolly took possession of Joe's borrowed boat to row home. At that Joe, in spite of their protestations, made them all get out of his little craft and find some other way to get ashore. He preferred food to missionaries in his boat and, having stowed provisions there, drank the captain's health with a flourish under the long noses of those indignant preachers. Then he shoved off.

If only all the missionaries had been like Dr. Whitman and Narcissa!

When winter came, the mountain men were in need of an ax. Joe always restless, rode and rowed some fifty miles to the nearest mission to get one. He was also in need of a cow, for the Hudson's Bay Company would not part with its own stock. At Champoeg Joe found the superintendent of the mission farm.

Mr. Whitcom was a very pious man, and when Joe asked for a cow—on credit of course—Mr. Whitcom saw an opportunity to do a little missionary work on a sinful mountain man. He advised Joe to *pray* for a cow.

Meek grinned back at him cheerfully and said, "I cain't pray; that's your business, not mine."

Mr. Whitcom stiffened. "It is every man's business to pray for himself."

At the moment this general rule seemed a bit irrelevant to Joe. Said he, "Sure; but some other time will do for that. What I want now is a cow."

Sternly Whitcom inquired, "How can you expect to get what you want, if you won't ask for it?"

Joe laughed, "I reckon I *have* asked. I asked *you*. But I don't see nary cow yit."

"You must ask God, my friend," Whitcom explained. "But first you must pray to be forgiven for your sins."

Joe considered. After all, he was an old trader. "Tell you what I'll do. If you will furnish the cow, I'll agree to pray for half an hour right here on this spot," said the merry reprobate.

Whitcom's eyes gleamed. "Down on your knees, then."

"You'll sure furnish that cow?"

Cornered, Whitcom could only say, "Yes."

Joe Meek had always paid his debts. Without a moment's delay he dropped to his knees and prayed loudly until the half hour was up. Then Whitcom was satisfied, and Joe went home driving his cow before him.

With what little Joe could earn, the wheat he had saved and the milk from the cow, he managed to survive another winter.

Yet for all his pranks and amused resentment towards the missionaries, Joe was serious in his intention to make the best of things. The missionaries often impressed upon him what a grievous fault he committed in living in sin with his Indian wife and her two children. And so finally Joe led her to the altar, gave her a church wedding. Though he had lost his first wife and had bad luck with his second, and was not much of a provider after he left the mountains, no one could say that Joe Meek was not a good family man.

Joe's daughter, Olive, bears witness to this. It is recorded that she said, "Very few Indian women who lived with white men lived to be very old. When the settlers came, the white men were ashamed of their Indian wives and abandoned them and took white girls for wives, but my father loved my mother and always lived with her.

She died on March 5, 1900. She was eighty years old when she died."[1]

Of course, when there was any work suitable for a mountain man, Meek was in demand and never hid his light under a bushel. In the summer of 1841, when the United States Exploring Expedition commanded by Lieutenant Charles Wilkes, U.S.N. reached Oregon, Meek was employed as guide in that region. The British officials entertained the Lieutenant with due formality; but Wilkes reports that he found them rather stiff for his taste. In those days, Americans had not forgotten the War of 1812.

Wilkes had had bad luck at the mouth of the Columbia, where the sloop-of-war *Peacock* had run hard aground on the bar and been beaten to pieces by heavy seas, though all on board were saved.

At Fort Vancouver, when Dr. McLoughlin and other Britishers paid an official visit to the squadron, Wilkes showed them all the honor due to representatives of a friendly foreign power, and entertained them at dinner. The Britishers politely regretted the loss of the *Peacock*.

Now Joe Meek had not studied history at the Rocky Mountain College for nothing. Like most American patriots of those days, Joe proudly remembered the engagement on February 22, 1813 in the Caribbean, when Captain Lawrence of the U.S.S. *Hornet,* off the mouth of the Demerara River, had, in a fight lasting only fifteen minutes, taken the British sloop-of-war *Peacock,* of twenty guns, two swivels, and 130 men. It was this action which had caused Captain Lawrence to be promoted to command of the frigate *Chesapeake.* So now, with a laugh Joe spoke up, interrupting the condolences, "No loss at all, gentlemen. Uncle Sam can get another *Peacock* the way he got that one!"

Wilkes very properly ignored Joe's remark at the

---

[1] Lockley, *op. cit.,* Chapter II, pp. 15-16.

time; but when the Britons had departed, he looked at
Joe with a twinkle and said, "Meek, go down to my cabin.
There you'll find some first-rate brandy."

Meek's problems were not individual ones. They were
common to most of the settlers. All were ill-equipped;
society was not organized. Though the Hudson's Bay
Company had authority over its employees and the
Indians in its domain, the Americans had no government
whatever. As Doc Newell wrote, "As there is no laws in
this country, we do the best we can."

On most frontiers American pioneers got along among
themselves pretty well without laws, yet after a time have
usually felt that they should have them as standard equipment. But in Oregon, they had the British interest to
combat; the international boundary had never been
settled by treaty.

As early as 1840, the year Meek came to Oregon to
settle, the handful of Americans there had sent their first
petition to Congress begging for "the blessings of free
institutions, and the protection of its arms," pleading for
"a territorial government," and ignoring the fact that
the treaty of joint occupancy between the British and
Americans was still in force. The next year, Ewing
Young, that enterprising mountain man who, at Taos,
gave Kit Carson his first chance to join a trapping brigade,
died in Oregon. There was no law of inheritance, and a
meeting to talk this over and arrange for the settlement
of Ewing's estate was called after his funeral.

In February, a committee was formed to "draft a code
of laws"—a group comprising both Protestant Americans
and Canadian Catholics who were, of course, British subjects. They agreed upon a judge and a constable, but
could not agree on a governor. No laws were passed. The
Canadians withdrew.

Meanwhile, Charles Wilkes,[1] commanding the United

---

[1] In the account of his expedition set forth in his voluminous report,
Lieutenant Wilkes makes no mention of Joseph L. Meek, his guide in Oregon.

States surveying squadron anchored in the Columbia River, advised settlers that no organization was needed, as the United States would soon take Oregon over. All the settlers could do was to try to get Congress to understand what Oregon needed. By 1842 there were perhaps 250 Americans in Oregon; the British brought in a new quota too. Dr. McLoughlin kept the restive Indians quiet through the Company's system of trade at fixed prices (possible only under its now-endangered monopoly), and swift, sure punishment for depredations. But the new American Indian agent stirred them up again, the settlers complained of McLoughlin, and Dr. Whitman went to Washington, leaving his mission and wife to the tender mercies of the Cayuses.

The Cayuses promptly destroyed Whitman's mill and granary; Narcissa managed to escape them. The American agent had to appeal to McLoughlin for goods to pacify the redskins, and the Hudson's Bay Company had to enforce a truce. The next year, 1843, real immigration into Oregon from the States began. An abortive bill was even introduced in Congress to grant free land to settlers in Oregon. Meek and his fellows felt that the time was approaching for action.

Many of the Hudson's Bay Company men were educated, and cheered their rather lonely lives by reading voraciously. Accordingly, the Americans proposed that all combine their personal libraries to form a "circulating library." It was set up. Shares sold for $5.00 and a hundred were taken. Several hundred books were gathered, and others ordered. Here was something upon which everyone could agree. Reading led to discussion, and from the library soon developed a "literary society" or discussion group. Inevitably there was talk of creating an independent government. But it was *only* talk. Something more purposeful, more practical, was required. And it was provided.

American government in Oregon began in a very simple, but devious way. Though the country was comparatively lacking in edible large game animals, there were plenty of bears, wolves, and panthers. These soon made heavy inroads on the settlers' scanty herds of cattle and swine.

Some of the settlers therefore announced a meeting to consider how best to prevent the destruction of their stock. All interested persons were invited to attend. The meeting convened on February 2, 1843, and was well attended. A second meeting on March 4 was arranged, at which an organization was perfected, to be known as the "Wolf Association."

The Association provided bounties on predators as follows: fifty cents for a small wolf; $3.00 for a large wolf; $1.50 for a lynx; $2.00 for a bear; $5.00 for a panther. Indians were to be paid only half the bounties paid to white hunters. To pay the bounties they proposed to raise money by subscription. Each member of the Association was assessed $5.00

At that time the only currency in the country were drafts on the missions, the milling company or on Fort Vancouver; much of the business done was necessarily by barter.

Under cover of this Wolf Association a resolution was soon passed "that a committee be appointed to take into consideration the propriety of taking measures for the civil and military protection of this colony."

Some wished to form an independent government, some merely to establish law and order in the country, others hoped that the British or the United States government might take over. Dr. McLoughlin, so Meek heard, favored an independent government. Meek discovered that some of the French Canadians favored a provisional government under the protection of the United States.

There was much debating and talk about these matters,

in which Joe Meek played no small part. The real question was whether Oregon should go British or American. Now Joe Meek was a patriot—and no two ways about it. He kept after his friends, going from one settlement to another, to argue men into attending the meeting.

In May a committee was to meet at Champoeg, originally a settlement of French Canadians. So (according to his wife, Virginia) Joe made repeated trips to see Caleb Wilkins, Charles McKay and George W. Ebbert, urging them to attend the meeting.

"Ebbert, I was born in Washington County, Virginia, and I'm now living in the Tualatin Valley. I want to say to you that I am now 33 years of age—and I have lived two years in experience for every year of age—and for a week I've had but two wishes, and I want them granted. I want to live long enough to see Oregon securely American, and then I want this section, where I expect to die, to be named Washington County, so I can say that I was born in Washington County, United States, and died in Washington County, United States."[1]

Champoeg had been named as the place of meeting, probably because it was the only place along the river, where there was any open prairie. The meeting was to be held at a small house on this prairie.

Joe's three friends reached Champoeg on the eve of the meeting, May 1, 1843. Joe used all his charm, his quick wit and keen intelligence, arguing particularly with the French Canadians. These British subjects naturally distrusted the Americans. It was not only that they were Catholics and the Americans Protestants; nor that they looked to Britain for their protection. They nearly all believed that American laws were tyrannical and unjust, that taxes under an American government would be excessive—that, in the United States, there was

---

[1] As quoted by Virginia Meek. See *The Sunday Oregonian* Sept. 17, 1905, p. 38.

even a tax on windows! Some of them were rebellious
already against British government in Canada; bad as
they found British rule, they were not going to jump from
the frying pan into the fire! And more than half the
voters who turned up for the meeting were French
Canadians.

However, there was one of them who was better informed. This man, F. X. Matthieu, was a refugee from
Canada; he had taken part in the rebellion of 1837-38.
And he was still bitter against the British. His liberal
views, his resentment, had made him study the American
way after he found refuge on the Willamette in the home
of Etienne Lucier. There, all winter, the two men had
observed the American settlers, and learned something
of life and law in the United States. Result: Matthieu
resolved to join with the men from the States; Lucier held
out, though his faith in the prejudices of his French Canadian neighbors was shaken.

Moreover, not all the Americans were agreed that a
new government was needed.

Joe Meek saw that it would be a hotly contested
decision. But there was nothing Joe loved more than a
fight. There was a great deal of talk and politicking
before the meeting, and at first the Americans were sure
of a victory. The chairman called the meeting to order.
George W. LeBreton was secretary. Meek grinned: Le-
Breton was a good man, popular with both parties, but
certain to back the proposed government.

The Committee, originally chosen to propose a plan,
was asked to report. Among them was Meek's old *com-
panero* of the beaver streams, Dr. Robert Newell, Etienne
Lucier, and the carpenter-teacher-politician William H.
Gray. The Committee reported, outlining its plan. A
motion was made to adopt the report, seconded—and
immediately put to a vote. The Canadian faction voted
"Nay"; the motion was lost. Meek learned that they

had all agreed beforehand to vote down every motion proposed at the meeting! Their veto was as disconcerting as it was unexpected. The official minutes record that, after this vote was taken, "considerable confusion" existed. To the Americans it looked as though all was lost. The Canadians gloated.

Even the chairman was nonplused.

But Joe Meek did not give up. He saw it was necessary to make every man stand up and be counted. He felt in his bones that there were enough independent, on-the-fence voters to swing the decision his way, if every man were compelled to vote. He whispered to LeBreton.

LeBreton took advantage of the crowd's confusion to make a new motion, quickly seconded by Gray, "that the meeting divide, preparatory to being counted." This motion was carried by acclamation, each side being certain of advantage. The Canadians were sure of victory; the Americans eager to have a second chance. Joe saw that the moment for leadership, for action had come—and action came easy to Joe. Boldly he pushed to the front and turned to face the crowd.

Before the voters could move to right or left to be counted, Joe Meek, that big American full of life, with head high and eyes flashing, yelled: "Who's for a divide! All in favor of the Report, and for an Organization, follow me!" Joe waved his arm and stepped off to the right of the chairman. Those opposed, like sheep without a shepherd, straggled to the left.

When the count was made, fifty-two voted with Meek, fifty against. The chairman announced the result. Joyously Meek sang out, "Three cheers for our side!"

His enthusiasm set them on fire. The mountain men let go with a mighty yell; others followed their lead. Loud rang the shouts for Freedom!

Joe turned to his friends, grasped their hands. "Ebbert, by God, we are living in the United States. And if I had not kept after you until you came, we'd now be living in England!"

And so the die was cast that eventually brought Oregon into the United States.

Massacre

THE PROVISIONAL Government of Oregon was set up forthwith, to have a judge and clerk of the court and a staff of magistrates, constables, and a military establishment consisting of two officers under instructions to organize companies of mounted riflemen. Nine men, among them "Doc" Newell and Doughty, were elected to form a legislative committee. Meek got Ebbert appointed Constable, and McKay a captain of Volunteers.

The Canadians had withdrawn from the meetings and prepared an address protesting against the measures taken by the American majority. But eventually compromises were worked out, and in the long run the Hudson's Bay Company co-operated, and most of the objectors finally became naturalized citizens of the United States. Meanwhile, the new government, based upon American principles, guaranteed "until such time as the United States of America extend their jurisdiction over us" the old American "freedom of worship, trial by jury, habeas corpus and the sanctity of private contracts."

Meek's known courage, popularity and good humor had made him the ideal candidate for Sheriff. He was elected, and in this capacity was enabled to be of more service to the needy settlers than ever before.

Sheriff Joe Meek, however, found it a problem to perform the duties of his new office. The settlers, for the most part old mountain men, retired employees of the British company, or independent mission folk, required a little time to get used to the notion that they had a government and had better obey the laws. There were no taxes, no jails. When in a good humor, men accepted the Provisional Government as something harmless and novel; when in trouble, they didn't care shucks for it.

One day a carpenter—or rather, the carpenter—a fellow named Dawson, got into a fist fight, and the Sheriff was called for. Joe probably had no badge, certainly had no salary; but he had been elected, and so he went to arrest Dawson. When he announced his mission, Dawson was scornful, picked up his ax, and defied the law.

Unluckily for Dawson, the law was Joe Meek. And it was dangerous to defy Joe. He pitched into the carpenter, disarmed him, and made him say "Uncle" to the law. It dawned on the fellow that Oregon really had a government. He gave in, saying, "I reckon, if I have to submit, so must every other man."

But the settlers were nearly all in the same boat. They were a ragged lot of men, short of rations most of the time, without money, lacking nearly everything. With supplies so scanty, they had to help each other, with food, with everything. But Meek, after his long education in mountain generosity, was never satisfied merely to provide for the physical man. He went about things in his own way.

One day one of Meek's neighbors, so poor that he had only one boot and went with one foot bare, was driving his wagon to Willamette Falls. Meek begged a ride.

"Come along," said his neighbor. "But bring something to eat, for I've got nothin'."

Meek agreed, and brought along a bundle, so big it made his neighbor stare and lick his hungry lips. When they made camp that night the fellow waited impatiently for Meek to produce his food. "Bring it out, man. I'm starving!"

Meek went to the tail gate and came back lugging his great round bundle, wrapped in his blanket, and deposited it beside the fire. His neighbor leaned eagerly down to watch. It was big enough to be a haunch of venison, or, as Meek would have called that, "deer meat."

Gravely Meek removed the wrapping, and displayed an immense pumpkin. The disappointed neighbor straightened up. "Hell!" he protested. "Is that all we've got for supper?"

Meek looked up and laughed. "Roast punkin's not so bad. I've et worse in the mountains. I tell you, roast punkin is buffalo tongue compared to ants or moccasin soles!"

His neighbor joined in the laugh, and in cutting up and roasting their pumpkin. They found it "not so bad" —since there was nothing better. Thus Meek provided his neighbor not only with a full belly but a strong heart.

In the beginning, Oregon had been under the thumb of the Hudson's Bay Company. With the coming of the American missionaries, the missions—and especially the Methodist mission—gained great influence, and when the Provisional Government was set up, were still powerful, politically, economically, and socially. The coming of the mountain men altered the balance somewhat, and these men, young, ambitious, accustomed to act bravely and decisively, were soon dominant in political affairs, since they were wise enough to consider the wishes of the other factions and interests, realizing that the strength of a government depends upon the number of interests it represents.

But with the coming of caravan after caravan of settlers, year by year, the missions and the British lost ground, and the American farming population prevailed. Though

Meek had a patriotic distrust of the British, he liked Dr. McLoughlin, and had an ingrained preference for the fur men, American or French Canadian. For the missionaries, who had held themselves so high, he had an ancient dislike, and an eagle eye for anything like hypocrisy. But now that his family was increasing, and he had been elected by the community to high office, Joe mellowed a little. A second son, Hiram, had been born to him in 1841; and now in '44, a daughter, Olive. It may be that his wife, Virginia, had been converted by Joe's own preaching in the Nez Percé camp, when he was bringing Chief Kowesote round to letting him marry her; it would be natural that she should listen to the sermons of her suitor. But whatever his motives, Joe became less hostile to the missionaries.

Then, one Sunday, Joe Meek went to meeting. The annual report of the Methodist Mission, dated May 13, 1844, relates what happened:

"On Sabbath, the number present on the ground was about 60, 19 of whom was not professors of religion, but before the exercises of that day had closed, 16 of this number were rejoicing in a sense of sins forgiven and praising God for salvation through faith. Among these were several who had been Rocky Mountain trappers and rangers. One of them, who was well known and almost proverbial for his boldness, joyfully exclaimed, 'Tell everybody you see that Joseph Meek, that old Rocky Mountain sinner, has turned to the Lord!' "

Having become a Christian, Meek had his Indian wife christened Virginia, after his native state, and married her.

That same month, Sheriff Joseph L. Meek came up for re-election; of the 146 votes cast, Meek received 143. The election was held May 14, the day after the Methodists made note of Meek's redemption. On June 2, Joe was sworn in. His was the hardest job in the government, and his hard work won him staunch support. There were court orders, subpoenas and summonses to serve, and an occasional arrest to make.

But the hardest work of all was collecting taxes; the settlers were not helpful. Said Joe Gale, mountain man, "Darn my soul if I pay!" By the end of the year an "Act of Relief of Joseph L. Meek" was passed, extending the date for paying taxes for another five months. Later he had a census to make, and served as auctioneer. In appreciation of his great services, the Legislative Committee provided that he should be paid *first* out of any money that might be in the treasury.

At that, he was not always able to collect his fees and wages. The tax record shows that his own property was assessed at less than $900. The harder he worked, the less he seemed to acquire. But there is no doubt that Joe enjoyed being Sheriff. He was on the move, he was important, he was meeting people all the time. He saw no reason why he might not climb to the top in Oregon; and in fact, he advanced faster than any of them in those days. He might be poor, like everybody in Oregon; but he was in the saddle, packing a rifle, ranging the country, feared and looked up to. It was almost like old days in the mountains.

No mail reached Oregon unless by way of the Hudson's Bay Company's annual express to western Canada, or by ship from the Sandwich Islands. And as for the scanty goods in the new store, the rare settler who was able to buy anything had to content himself with anything there was to buy.

The Hudson's Bay Company had prevented the importation or manufacture of liquor in that region, and the Methodist mission had co-operated, in the most effective way. Ewing Young, the New Mexican trader, had been induced to give up making Taos Lightning, though there was no dry law in Oregon at that time.

With so many disgruntled Indians about, the sale of
liquor would have been a great danger to the scattered
settlers. A drunken warrior was apt to turn homicidal.

Dr. Elijah White, surgeon to one of the missions, announced that he had received from the United States a
commission as Indian agent for Oregon. This was hardly
consistent with the terms of the treaty of joint occupation.
Not that the American settlers were unwilling to have
the authority of the United States extended over them.
But it seemed to them that Dr. White acted as if his commission conferred on him the authority of governor of
the colony, since no one else there had any public post
under the United States government.

He was full of zeal, and when he learned that a distillery was being built by one of the settlers, felt it to be
a time for action. Some of the settlers, in fact, appealed to
him to act. And so, in the summer of 1844, Dr. White
handed Joe Meek, the sheriff, a writ with orders to
destroy the distillery.

Meek proceeded to Willamette Falls—now Oregon City
—frightened the distiller into submission, pulled the
worm from the still and, putting his lips to one end of it,
waggishly blew it like a bugle as a signal to Dr. White
of his success. Then Joe threw the thing into the river
and went home.

But a ship from Australia soon came into the river, and
one Madam Cooper disembarked, bringing with her a
barrel of whisky.

Dr. White went personally to her cabin, accompanied
by two witnesses. He spoke blandly, "You have a barrel
of whisky, I believe."

His hostess, supposing he had come to buy, frankly
confessed that she had, and pointed to the barrel in the
corner. Dr. White then stepped sternly forward, placed
his foot on the offending barrel and declared sonorously,
"In the name of the United States I levy execution on it."

For the moment the woman was too amazed to speak. Then she snatched up the poker from the chimney corner, swung it over White's head and answered, "In the name of Great Britain, Ireland and Scotland I levy execution on *you!*"

The Doctor ducked out of the house before she could hit him.

Next day Sheriff Meek and his political friend Le-Breton called upon Madam Cooper, and soon spied the barrel.

Madame Cooper was now on guard. Said she, "Have you come to levy on my whisky?"

"Yes," said Meek with a grin. "I have come to levy on it. But as I am not quite so high in authority as Dr. White, I don't intend to levy on all of it at once. I think about a quart will do me."

The lady of the house hurriedly seated her visitors at table, produced a bottle and a tin cup. Meek spent the rest of the afternoon regaling the pair with his adventures, and himself with the lady's imported whisky. It had been a long, long time since he had taken a horn.

But Meek's days of Indian fighting were not entirely over. Dr. White and his Indians did not get along, and the aggrieved Indians took out their spite in small thefts and depredations, smashing windows, frightening women and so on until settlers began to leave their claims and huddle at the falls of the Willamette. Dr. White tried to induce the more friendly tribes to take the responsibility of punishing the depredators, but without success.

One day when a number of Indians came to town and got drunk, and Meek happened to come riding in on his fine horse, the citizens begged him to "settle those Indians."

"I reckon it won't take me long," Joe answered. Taking his rawhide lariat from his saddle, he charged the Indian lodges, laying the rawhide on bare shoulders right and left. In twenty minutes every Indian had left town, running into the woods or swimming the river. All had a deep respect for Meek, whom they called *tyee,* chief.

Finally, when a trouble-making Wasco Indian named Cockstock brought a party of Molalla Indians to the settlement, a real collision occurred, with some shooting, and two settlers fell, and Cockstock was beaten to death by a Negro. Meek's friend LeBreton died of his wounds after the Indians had been driven off.

Meek, then employed in rafting timber for Dr. John McLoughlin, was appealed to and, following his usual method, laughed the settlers out of their fright. There was already talk of an appeal to Washington for protection from the savages.

In that sparsely settled country, where the only legal tender was wheat at sixty cents a bushel, it was quite a chore to collect taxes. Naturally the Britishers objected to paying taxes to support American officials; but on the advice of the patient Dr. McLoughlin they yielded the point, since it was no longer possible to maintain the provisional government by subscription. Meek retained a commission of 10 per cent on the taxes he collected.

One day Joe Meek called on McLoughlin, who was then in conference with some American friends. McLoughlin made the Sheriff welcome, and inquired what his business might be.

Joe grinned a little and announced blandly, "I have come to tax you, Doctor."

McLoughlin showed astonishment. "To tax me, Mr. Joe? I really was not aware. I believed I had paid my tax, Mr. Joe," the honest doctor stammered. Joe could see he was not only greatly astonished, but actually somewhat annoyed at this fresh demand.

"Doctor, thar is an old ox out in my neighborhood, said to belong to you. Thar is a tax of twenty-five cents on him."

"I do not understand you, Mr. Joe. I have no cattle in your neighborhood."

Joe shook his head. "I couldn't say how that might be, Doctor. This is all I know about it. I went to old man G—— to collect the tax on his stock—and he's got a powerful lot of cattle—and while we war a-countin' 'em over, he left out that old ox and said it belonged to you!"

The doctor grew red in the face. "Oh, oh! I see, Mr. Joe. Yes, yes, I see. So it was Mr. G——! I do remember now, since you bring it to my mind, that I *lent* Mr. G—— that steer *six years ago*. Here is your twenty-five cents, Mr. Joe."

Meek went off laughing, but he was tired of that job. He had his eye on the legislature.

For politics, as an occupation, was picking up. Settlers came pouring in by the hundreds. President Polk had served notice required by the joint-occupation treaty on the British government that the Oregon boundary question must be settled. The question was where the line should run. The British hoped the Columbia River would be the boundary, but thousands of Americans, full of patriotic spirit, called "Warhawks" by their opponents, held that our government must have every square inch of territory possible under the Florida treaty. Their slogan was "Fifty-four forty or fight!" They were convinced that the Yankees could lick England, and Mexico and California to boot. Both England and the United States would be sending fleets of armed vessels to the Pacific. Meantime, the inhabitants of Oregon, taking a hand in their destiny, broadened the bases of the provisional government to include the British and Canadians. Dr. McLoughlin became a member of the body politic. For this action, interpreted as the culmination of his policy of assistance and forbearance to American settlers, he was forced to resign from the Hudson's Bay Company.

In July, 1845, a special election was held, which confirmed the provisional government and Governor Abernethy. On August 9, Sheriff Meek was continued in office, although the office was not created, officially, until ten days later. The settlers preferred to vote when it was convenient; they could not go running to the polls every day in the week. And, of course, the legislature would never ignore the evidence of votes already cast and counted.

Joe, however, found it much easier to get elected than to get paid. Getting the hard-pressed settlers to vote was one thing; getting them to pay taxes, fees, and salaries quite another. Early in 1846 Joe found it necessary to resign, and he made no bones about announcing lack of income as his reason.

On February 5, 1846, the Oregon Printing Association was formed, with the object of publishing a newspaper, in addition to other printing ventures, which paper was known as the *Oregon Spectator*. Betimes Joe found opportunity to act as collector for this company—having acquired experience in the collection line—taking as his commission somewhat less than 3 per cent of what he collected.

Upon his announcement of his resignation an anonymous letter was circulated, attacking Joe, alleging that he had been paid in full. William H. Gray, who represented, more or less, the mission element, had fallen out with Joe. They exchanged opinions in letters published in the *Spectator*. They disagreed on what should be legal tender, and on the liquor question.

Well, Joe had always believed in carrying the war to the enemy. In the elections of 1846 he ran for the legislature, polled ninety votes, and won a seat.

That December, when the legislature convened, Meek found only one other old mountain man in the House—Doc Newell. However, there were two men from the Hudson's Bay Company, making four fur men out of fifteen members. Meek was one of the three men nominated to be Speaker of the House, but he was not elected.

Nothing very pressing came before the legislature in that session. Considerable agitation marked the passage of a bill to regulate the manufacture and sale of spirituous liquors; but the bill was passed, and passed again over Governor Abernethy's veto. Meek voted to regulate, although he was described as "a notorious drinker."

Being entirely familiar with the situation, he sponsored a bill to provide for the inspection of the wheat in which taxes were paid—too often frauds were worked on the young government.

There was no law providing for divorce in Oregon; those who wished to be free of their marital bonds had to secure the passage of a bill specifically authorizing the division; a separate bill for each separation. Generally the appellants were men. But Joe was approached to sponsor such a bill, in this session, by a woman who wished to be free of her husband. With his own experience in Kowesote's camp in mind, Joe was sympathetic. He prepared a bill, but held it back until the last day of the session, when it was passed hastily, after a certain amount of hemming and hawing by his colleagues.

Election time came around soon again, in 1847. Joe stumped the country and was re-elected handily, whereupon he swam out to a ship anchored near the mouth of the Willamette to get liquor to treat his constituents.

The international border having been settled too late in '46 for a proper combination of celebrations, the Fourth-of-July celebration in 1847 was a spectacular event for Oregonians. All day at regular intervals a cannon boomed in triumph. At the time an American vessel, the *Brutus*, was lying at anchor in the Willamette River; the officer in command had issued a general invitation to the public to come aboard during the day. Half a hundred people gathered, among them Meek and Newell, and rowed out in boats. But the captain allowed only one boatload of people—all of them from the mission—to come aboard. Others he ordered off.

This was the day of liberty, the holiday of free men, and no time for favoritism, prejudice, or protocol! Meek was furious. He and Newell ran off to fetch the cannon, a twelve-pounder, which had been banging way all morning. They brought it to bear on the *Brutus*.

They had no cannonballs, but rammed in some powder, loaded her up with rocks, and prepared to put fire to the touchhole. With true frontier democracy, they resented the captain's actions, despising a host who would stoop to *pick* his guests. They were not going to stand for any such discrimination that day.

But before the first blast could be fired, Dr. McLoughlin came running, his white hair streaming, protesting, "Oh! Oh! Mr. Joe, Mr. Joe, you must not do this! Indeed you must not do this foolish thing. Come now, come now! You will injure your country, Mr. Joe. How can you expect ships to come here if they are fired upon? Come away, come away!"

Meek, even in his wrath, loved the good Doctor. He settled for a quip: "Doctor, it's not that I love the *Brutus* less, but my own dignity more."

That year of '47 was a sad one for the pioneers. The bill providing for a territorial government for Oregon failed in Congress. The Southerners objected, because the Organic Law of the territory excluded slavery forever.

That fall Joe made speeches about the country, in favor of temperance! When the Washington Temperance Society was organized, favoring total abstinence, a list of members was recorded: and lo, Joe Meek's name led all the rest! His oratory was so effective that it led many to sign the pledge, and brought him many warm testimonials.

On December 7, 1847, when the new legislature assembled in Oregon City, Robert Newell was chosen Speaker of the House; Meek missed being named sergeant at arms by a single vote. He was named to serve on several important committees.

But his service as a lawmaker was about to end abruptly. On December 8 came news of the massacre at Waiilatpu. The legislature received letters from the governor announcing "the horrid murder of Dr. Marcus Whitman's family and others," and urging the House to take immediate action.

Envoy Extraordinary

THE NEWS was a cruel blow to Joe Meek. The Whitmans were his good friends, whom he admired above all other missionaries. Narcissa Whitman was the finest woman Joe had known since his mother died, the beautiful lady to whom he had entrusted his daughter, Helen Mar. And now they were murdered—and probably his own child with them. Joe was on his feet in a moment, moving that the governor's letters be referred to a committee of the whole.

The first thing to be done was to pass a resolution requiring the governor to raise a company of riflemen and send them to occupy the mission at The Dalles. It was obvious that representations would have to be made to Washington. But the Legislature was short of paper, and Meek was named on a committee to secure some stationery.

At Jesse Applegate's urgent appeal that they must send a "special messenger to the United States," the House referred the matter to the committee, of which Meek was one; the Chairman, Nesmith, offered a resolution, referring to the existing state of "actual hostilities" and declaring it the duty of the House to send a messenger to Washington to solicit "the immediate influence and protection of the U.S. Government in our internal affairs." As soon as possible, the House set about providing for that mission.

Nobody seems to have doubted that Joseph L. Meek was the man to go to Washington. For Joe represented that large and growing body of settlers who were neither connected with the missions nor with the Hudson's Bay Company. He was a popular, vigorous figure in the legislature, which of course preferred to send one of themselves. He was a mountain man, hardy and bold enough to travel through snowbound passes, and able to live off the country as he went. More, he claimed to be related by marriage to the family of the President, James K. Polk.[1]

The Legislature naturally resented Governor Abernethy's independent action in sending a private representative—J. Quinn Thornton—to Washington, to represent Oregon, the Governor—and the Mission.

In due course, the bill passed—a document much too important in Meek's life to be omitted here. I quote:

Section first. Be it enacted by the Legislature of Oregon Territory that Joseph L. Meek is hereby authorized, and appointed, a Messenger, to proceed with all possible dispatch, by way of California, to Washington City, and lay before the Executive of the United States, such official Communications, as he may be charged with, by the Executive, or legislature department, of the Government of Oregon.

Section second. Said Messenger, before entering upon the discharge of his duties, shall take an oath, faithfully to discharge his duties to the best of his abilities.

Section third. Said Messenger shall receive as full compensation for his services, such sum or sums, as the Government of the United States shall think proper to bestow.

Section fourth. That said Messenger be and hereby is authorized,

---

[1] The mother of Joseph L. Meek was born a Walker, sister of James Walker, who, in 1813, married Jane Maria Polk (1798-1876), sister of James Knox Polk, who later became President of the United States. James Knox Polk (1795-1849), married on January 1, 1824, Sarah Childress (1803-1891). Meek's mother was aunt to Sarah Childress.

to negotiate a loan, not to exceed five hundred dollars, and to pledge the faith of the Government, for the payment of such amount, as may be negotiated for by said Messenger, for the purpose of carrying into effect this act.

Section fifth. And be it further enacted that the said Messenger be required to enter into bond, and surety, with the Executive of Oregon Territory, in the amount of one thousand dollars, for the faithful performance of his duty.

Section sixth. This act to take effect from and after its passage.[1]

Immediately, Meek resigned his seat in the House; his resignation was accepted on December 17, and on January 4, 1848 he saddled up, packed his plunder on pack horses, and with his papers hit the trail in company with George Ebbert, John Owens, and a few others, heading for Washington, D.C.

Of course, Meek had no money; nobody in Oregon had any. He was faced then, not only with an arduous and dangerous trip through snowy mountain passes and freezing, starving plains, but, once he reached the settlements in Missouri, with an equally long and tedious journey through towns and cities without one cent in his pocket. True, the Mission had given him a draft on the treasurer of the Methodist Church—in New York. He had a letter from Dr. John McLoughlin of the Hudson's Bay Company, and some messages (to be delivered en route!) to the governor of California and the officer in command of a squadron of the Pacific fleet. The bill authorizing Meek's journey had provided, and the governor of Oregon intended, that he should go by way of California.

But Meek headed for the Rockies. The California mountains were unknown to him, and he had no time to waste making mistakes. Besides, California was the long way around. It may be too, that Joe was a bit nostalgic for the Rockies; certainly he could count upon some help from old companions, if any were left in the mountains.

---

[1] *Provisional and Territorial Papers,* Nos. 1312, 1564; *Archives,* 231; *Laws,* 1843-49, 9.

In this decision, Meek was wise—and as it turned out, quite right. Jesse Applegate, one of the ablest men in Oregon, who was sent for help to California about that time, found the snows on the Siskiyous too deep for his party, and had to turn back.

Joe's little party reached The Dalles towards the end of January, and was still in Oregon at the end of February, at Fort Walla Walla, waiting for the troops to gather and clear his path of Cayuse hostiles. Colonel Cornelius Gilliam, in command of Volunteers, together with an unpopular Peace Commission (which included Meek's old friend "Doc" Newell) were anxiously trying to obtain the surrender of the murderers of Dr. Whitman. It does not appear that Meek played any conspicuous part in the engagements of the campaign, in the chief of which, at Sand Hollow, the troops killed the Cayuse chief Gray Eagle, and severely wounded Chief Five Crows. The shooting of these two supposedly "bullet-proof" chiefs caused the Cayuses to give way. The command reached Waiilatpu March 2, 1848.

The mission was a scene of desolation, houses abandoned, looted, burned, bodies and goods lying at random.

Whitman had been repeatedly warned against the Cayuses. These Indians had welcomed white men, expecting the new religion would bring them all the blessings of white men's civilization, as they were promised. But, as time passed, they found that the wealth, power, and prestige, which they looked for and which white men enjoyed, did not reach them. They found, at the mission, instead of wealth, work; instead of power, domination; instead of prestige, social inferiority. They saw more and more white men coming into their country year after year, and Indians from the east told them how they had been deprived of their country. When an epidemic of measles—for which they had no immunity—struck the mission and decimated their families, killing many children, they blamed the good Doctor for the deaths. It is claimed, too, that it was ancient Cayuse custom to kill any doctor who failed to effect a cure. A malicious half-breed encouraged their fears and hate.

The Cayuses had already found that Whitman would offer only passive resistance to insults and abuse. It was easy for a few of them to enter the Whitman house, engage the Doctor in talk, and strike him down from behind. That done, others rushed in to kill and rob and burn. Of some seventy-two persons then at or near the mission, the Indians killed fourteen. Of the fifty-three captives, most of them women and children, nearly all were terribly abused, starved, and terrorized, until Peter Skene Ogden, of the Hudson's Bay Company, manned an expedition and, on December 29, ransomed the wretched prisoners with goods worth four hundred dollars.

Helen Mar Meek had been bedfast with measles and under Narcissa's care at the time of the massacre. Meek found her little body dug up by the wolves, and sadly buried it again. He also interred what the Indians and wolves had left of Narcissa Whitman, except for a few locks of her fair hair, which he cut off and kept as memorials for her friends. Then Joe was ready for the trail.

Colonel Gilliam provided an escort. A number of emigrants, eager to return to the States, joined Joe's party, along with a few Volunteers whose term of enlistment was up. At that, there were hardly a dozen of them.

It was still winter, 1848, when Joseph L. Meek, George Wood Ebbert, John Owens and several others set out for Washington carrying the Oregon settlers' appeal for help. A company of the Oregon Volunteers traveled with them.[1]

---

[1] We have not only Meek's account of this journey—in *The River of the West*—but that of Ebbert also. See, George Wood Ebbert, "Autobiographical Sketch of George Wood Ebbert," *Oregon Historical Quarterly*, XIX (September, 1918), pp. 263-67.

At the Blue Mountains the soldiers turned back. Next morning Joe and his comrades pushed on through snow five to eight feet deep, sometimes making as much as ten miles a day while their horses lasted. Under such conditions they would not last long.

Some of the party, who had no official status but were traveling with Meek merely to get back to the States, lost heart and remained at Fort Boise.

Three days beyond, Meek ran into a camp of Bannock Indians. When they saw his small party coming, they gave every sign of hostility. But Meek knew his redskins, and had a trick or two up his own sleeve. He was then wearing the red belt and Canadian cap used by employees of the Hudson's Bay Company, with whom few Indians cared to tangle.

So Joe went boldly forward, and shook hands with the chief. He told the Bannocks that he was going to Fort Hall on business for the Company, and that Thomas McKay was following, one day's march behind with a large party, bringing goods to trade.

The chief, delighted by this news, prevented hostilities, and Meek and his friends proceeded. But once out of sight of the Bannock camp they wasted no time, traveling night and day, hoping to reach Fort Hall before the Bannocks discovered how they had been fooled.

At Fort Hall Meek found that the factor, Captain Grant, was absent. Though Mrs. Grant admitted them to the fort and fed them, she had no authority to lend them supplies. After a few hours rest they pushed on through falling snow, their horses struggling and floundering through the soft drifts. The deep snow made it almost impossible to find feed for the animals. They soon played out and had to be abandoned.

Starving as they were, Meek and Ebbert killed a horse. Meat's meat. They butchered the animal, and the two of them feasted by the campfire. The other men, never having roughed it in the mountains, could not stomach horseflesh.

They made snowshoes of willow sticks and rawhide and pushed on, carrying only their rifles and blankets. They made their next meal on a couple of polecats, which Meek delighted in shooting and dressing and offering for supper. Said Meek, "Since you don't like the pork, try the peppersass!" By that time his squeamish comrades probably wished they had eaten their share of the horse.

In the valley of Thomas' Fork, where the tall grass rose above the snow, Meek found a party of ten men herding cattle. Their booshway was none other than Peg-leg Smith, the celebrated mountain man, who was said to have amputated his own leg. He had a horse trained to lie down so that he could mount and dismount in comfort.

Here at last was mountain hospitality. Peg-leg shot the fattest cow in his herd and threw a grand party. He and his men had Indian wives, and after the feast they all turned to and danced, pounding the dirt floor half the night till the dust rose up to the ceiling. Joe Meek was not the man to forego his fun merely because he had important business on hand.

Carrying rations for two days, they plodded on next morning, still on snowshoes, up Bear River to the head-waters of Green River, crossing from the Muddy Fork to Fort Bridger. They covered the distance in less than four traveling days, though on the way Meek met with misfortune. Crossing the Little Muddy he got his papers all wet. They had to stay in camp two days drying these out.

At the fort it was Meek's hard duty to inform his old booshway that Mary Ann Bridger, like Helen Mar Meek, had been lost in the massacre at Waiilatpu. Bridger and Meek had one more bitter experience in common. But it was not the way of mountain men to prate of loss and sorrow.

That night they talked of old times over a hearty meal, and next morning Bridger gave Meek four good mules and supplies for a week. The five men, furred with hoarfrost, took turns riding the four mules, so that they got on much faster as far as South Pass. There they encountered deep snow again, and lost two of their mules in it. In that country covered with drifts they found scarcely any game, and often rolled up in their blankets under a cut bank and slept without their suppers.

When they reached Independence Rock, they found sign of hostiles near by. They lay low in the brush, taking no chances.

Their food was utterly exhausted. But at Red Buttes Meek was lucky enough to find a lone buffalo. He shot it, and the famished men filled up again. Once they reached the Platte, they found the going easier, game more plentiful, and made rapid time to Fort Laramie.

Papillion gave them a hearty welcome, supplied them with fresh mules, and gave Meek unsolicited advice.

"There is a village of Sioux, about six hundred lodges, a hundred miles from here, square on your trail at Ash Hollow. Keep your eyes skinned."

Just how Meek felt on being told how to look out for himself by a trader who, as the trappers scornfully put it, "slept inside," is not of record. But, as it turned out, the advice was good.

Meek planned to pass Ash Hollow during the hours of darkness, but snow was falling so heavily along the Platte that he rode right into the Sioux camp before he knew it, all in broad daylight. When he found himself among the lodges he reined up; and consulted Ebberts and the rest.

It was as dangerous to go back as to go on. Meek believed that boldness usually paid off, and in such a blizzard he thought it unlikely the Sioux would be stirring out of their lodges. If they did, the thick snowfall was all on his side.

Kicking his mule through the drifts as fast as the poor gaunt wringtail could make it, he led on. The snow, he hoped, would cushion the beat of the animals' hoofs, but in this he was disappointed. Suddenly a head poked out from a lodge door and shouted, "Allo, Major!"

The fat was in the fire. The five reined up. The French trader invited them in, and after giving them food and tobacco, offered to ride with them a few miles.

So they all rode on again, until night fell and the village lay safely behind them. LeBean defended his courtesy, saying, "The Sioux are bad people; I thought it best to see you safe out of the village." Then he turned back.

But Meek and his comrades rode all night, turning aside from the Oregon Trail so that they could not be overtaken. They knew the falling snow would soon cover their tracks leading from the main trail.

Later they went back to the Platte, following the Oregon Trail until it left the Platte for the Big Blue. In that country, far east of the buffalo range, they nearly starved to death. Within a few days' ride of civilization, they had to cook and eat their parfleches!

Meek was just about to kill his mule, when a wagon train heading west came rolling along. Instead of mule, he had ham and eggs. Other trains followed soon after to keep them in supply.

Though there were no provisions at the Kaw agency, they met a man beyond it who shared his bread—and whisky! The settlements could not be far off.

But the nearer Meek got to them and the more he thought of having to deal with high society, the more scairt he felt. Here he war, ragged and dirty, with nary a cent to his name, and only mountain manners, with nothing to depend on but the dispatches in his pouch and his own wits. For two cents he would have turned back into the snowdrifts, where there war nothin' to bother a man but a parcel of screeching Injuns. Was he putting his foot into another trap?

The question was, how to behave up thar to Washington?

"Finally," says Meek, "I concluded that as I had never tried to act like anybody but myself, I would not make myself a fool by beginning to ape other folks now. So I said to myself, 'Joe Meek you always have been, and Joe Meek you shall remain; go ahead, Joe Meek!' "

On the morning of May 4 they reached St. Joseph, Missouri. There Meek led his friends into a good hotel, and explained to the landlord that they had come to order a meal for which they could not pay. Anywhere west of the Mississippi any man, white or red, would have been happy to entertain Joe Meek and his friends as long as he cared to stay.

But the landlord, possibly fearing that these tattered, bearded men would frighten away his guests, refused to serve them. Meek led his party out of town and made camp. It was not until then that he remembered the credentials he carried. Documents had played little part in his life.

Joe had a letter to the father of two Oregon Volunteers. He looked up the gentlemen who, learning of the fix Joe and his friends were in, took them in, fed them and offered to provide for their trip East.

Some of the boys voted to stay in St. Joe. Meek and the rest rode with their host in his carriage to Independence. There Meek was astonished to meet one of his sisters.

His host arranged for his passage on a steamboat going down to St. Louis, and introduced him to the captain. At St. Louis, Joe's luck still held. Robert Campbell, the Indian trader, who had fought with Joe at the battle of Pierre's Hole, happened to meet the boat at the wharf, entertained him in St. Louis overnight and, having heard Meek's story of affairs in Oregon, called in the press.

Meek woke up next morning to find himself famous. He telegraphed the President and received orders to hurry on to Washington. There was only one difficulty. He had no money to pay his way.

At the levee that morning he found two steamers side by side, both up for Pittsburgh and each with runners striving to secure passengers. It occurred to Joe that he could earn his passage by outdoing the runners at their own game. He looked the boats over and made his choice. Boarding it, he climbed up to the hurricane deck and harangued the crowd.

"This way, gentlemen, if you please. Come right on board the *Declaration*. I am the man from Oregon, with dispatches to the President of these United States, that you all read about in this morning's paper. Come on board, ladies and gentlemen, if you want to hear the news from Oregon. I've just come across the plains, two months from the Columbia River, where the Injuns are killing your missionaries. Those passengers who come aboard the *Declaration* shall hear all about it before they get to Pittsburgh. Don't stop thar, looking at my old wolf-skin cap, but just come aboard, and hear what I've got to tell!"

The novelty of this sort of solicitation operated capitally. Many persons crowded on board the *Declaration* only to get a closer look at this picturesque personage who invited them, and many more because they were really interested to know the news from the far-off young territory which had fallen into trouble. So it chanced that the *Declaration* was inconveniently crowded on this particular morning.

After the boat got under way, the captain approached his roughest looking cabin passenger and inquired in a low tone of voice if he were really and truly the messenger from Oregon.

"Thar's what I've got to show for it," answered Meek,

producing his papers. The captain looked them over. "Well, all I have to say is, Mr. Meek, that you are the best runner this boat ever had; and you are welcome to your passage ticket, and anything you desire besides."

On the boat Joe was a lion, holding the passengers spellbound with his stories of mountain life, Injun fights and Oregon politics. Each man to whom he presented a letter gave him letters to others farther along his route.

At Wheeling, Joe found the stage had already departed for Cumberland, where people caught the train for Washington. Undaunted, Meek swaggered into the stage office and demanded, "I would like to have a stage for Cumberland."

Joe's request amazed the neat little old man at the desk, who sat motionless and silent, staring through his spectacles. Then, as if unable to believe what he saw through them, he raised them so that they rested on his forehead and took another look. Meek endured his scrutiny until he spoke.

"Who are you?"

Meek now had an attentive audience, and he could never resist one. Drawing himself up to his full six feet two inches, he replied with superb self-confidence, shouting out his mission.

The dazed man with the spectacles asked to see Joe's credentials. But when he found these genuine, he quickly yanked the bell rope, and in a few minutes a coach and driver stood at the door.

By that time other passengers waiting for the next stage began to stare at Meek. In the close quarters of the stage, their curious glances stimulated him afresh. Just as the horses started off, Joe stuck his head from the window and let out a war whoop in the best mountain style, setting the team off at a gallop. The rest of the journey he spent entertaining eager listeners.

And so all along the route Joe divided his time between

grave pomposity and fits of mountain manners, amusing everybody—including himself.

On the train Joe had no ticket—and no money to pay his way. When the conductor came through calling, "Tickets, please!" Meek sat wrapped in his greasy, smutted blanket, silent and poker-faced as any Indian.

"Ticket, please," the conductor said, halting beside the bearded stranger. Meek, pretending he knew no English, never budged.

The conductor tapped him on the shoulder, "Ticket, sir!" he demanded.

Meek started up, towering above the conductor. *"Ha ko any me ca, hanch?"* he said, using the Snake tongue.

Staring up at the wild, bearded stranger, the conductor repeated his demand: "Ticket, sir!"

But Joe, staring down at the man with a puzzled frown, declared, *"Ka hum pa, hanch."* His acquaintances of the stage ride, now seated about him, had a hard time hiding their mirth.

Unable to make himself understood, the conductor finally passed on—only to return and make another demand.[1]

Still Meek never faltered in his new role, until at last the laughter of the other passengers let the conductor in on the joke. One of them explained to him in a whisper who Meek was. There was no more talk of a ticket.

So Meek joked his way to Washington.

But when the train halted at the station there, Joe's bluff was wearing thin. His heart felt mighty small.

Yet his mission as representative of Oregon must not fail. Its importance, he felt, demanded dignity and conformity to protocol and precedents—of which he knew

---

[1] The meaning of the Snake or Shoshone phrases used by Joe Meek on the train are as follows: *Ha ko any me ca, hanch* (More phonetically, *Huggapah-mia, hintz*), "Where are you going, friend?"; *Ka hum pa, hanch* (properly *kah-hey-wah, hintz*) "All gone, friend"—meaning that Joe had no ticket.

nothing. How to be dignified, dressed in dirty blankets and a wolfskin cap, was the big problem.

But Joe clung to his slogan, *"Joe Meek I must remain."*

He stepped off the train, boldly inquired the name of the most fashionable hotel, and said doggedly to himself, "To Coleman's I will go!"

The Man From Oregon

WHEN MEEK arrived at Coleman's it was the dinner hour, and, following the crowd to the dining saloon, he took the first seat he came to, not without being very much stared at. He had taken his cue and the staring was not unexpected, consequently not so embarrassing as it might otherwise have been. A bill of fare was laid beside his plate. Turning to the colored waiter who placed it there, he startled him first by inquiring in a low growling voice—

"What's that, boy?"

"Bill of fare, sah," replied the "boy," who recognized a Southerner in the use of that one word.

"Read!" growled Meek again. "The people in *my* country cain't read."

Though taken by surprise, the waiter, politely obedient, proceeded to enumerate the courses on the bill of fare. When he came to game—

"Stop thar, boy!" commanded Meek, "What kind of game?"

"Small game, sah."

"Fetch me a piece of antelope," Meek ordered, leaning back in his chair with a look of satisfaction on his face.

"Got none of that, sah; don't know what that are, sah."

"Don't know!" with a look of pretended surprise. "In

my country antelope and deer are small game; bear and buffalo are large game. I reckon if you haven't got one, you haven't got the other, either. In that case you may fetch me some beef."

The waiter disappeared grinning, and soon returned with the customary thin and small cut, which Meek eyed at first contemptuously, and then—accepting it in the light of a sample—swallowed it at two mouthfuls, returning his plate to the waiter with an approving smile, and saying loud enough to be overheard by a score of people—

"Boy, that will do. Fetch me about four pounds of the same kind."

By this time the blanketed beefeater was the recipient of general attention, and the "boy" who served him, comprehending, with that quickness which distinguishes servants, that he had no ordinary backwoodsman to deal with, was all the time on the alert to make himself useful. People stared, then smiled, then asked each other "Who is it?" loud enough for the stranger to hear. Meek looked neither to the right nor to the left, pretending not to hear the whispering. When he had finished his beef, he turned from the table and again addressed himself to the attentive "boy."

"That's better meat than the old mule I eat in the mountains."

Upon this remark the whispering became more general, and louder, and smiles more frequent.

"What have you got to drink, boy?" continued Meek, still unconscious. "Isn't there a sort of wine called—some kind of *pain?*"

"Champagne, sah?"

While Meek drank his champagne, with an occasional aside to his faithful attendant, people laughed and wondered "Who the devil it was." At length, having finished his wine, and overhearing many open inquiries as to his identity, the hero of many bear fights slowly arose, and addressing the company through the before-mentioned "boy," said:

"You want to know who I am?"

"If you please, sah; yes, if you please, sah, for the sake of these gentlemen present," replied the "boy," answering for the company.

"Well then," proclaimed Meek with a grandiloquent air quite at variance with his blanket coat and unkempt hair, yet which displayed his fine person to advantage, "I am Envoy Extraordinary and Minister Plenipotentiary from the Republic of Oregon to the Court of the United States!"

With that, Joe turned and strode from the room. He knew that his antics had served their purpose.

Meek, of course, was expected in Washington. As he left Coleman's, Senator Underwood, of Kentucky, introduced himself. Meek said he must see the President. As tactfully as possible the Senator asked whether Meek did not wish to make his toilet before visiting the White House. Joe answered, "Business first; toilet afterwards."

"But," said Underwood, "even *your* business can wait long enough for that."

"No, that's your mistake, Senator, and I'll tell you why: I can't dress for two reasons, both good ones. I have not got a cent of money or a second suit of clothes."

Though the Senator offered to supply Meek's needs, Joe declined. "I'll see the President first and hear what he has to say about my mission."

He hopped into a carriage while the Senator and others watched. The driver asked where Joe wished to go.

"Whar should a man of *my* style want to go? The White House, of course!"

The driver cracked his whip and Meek rolled away, leaving the Senator laughing under the portico of the hotel.

The doorman at the White House was a mulatto with

whom Meek had played when a boy, and soon directed him to the office of the President's private secretary, Knox Walker. The President's family was related to the Meeks; the secretary himself was one of Joe's relatives.

The waiting room was filled with important-looking gentlemen and office-seekers waiting their turns. The secretary glanced at Meek over the papers he was reading and asked him to be seated. But after his long trip Meek was in no humor to be kept waiting. He walked up and down, then declared, "I should like to see the President immediately. Just tell him, if you please, that there is a gentleman from Oregon waiting to see him on very important business."

The secretary jumped up, dropped his papers and shouted, "Uncle Joe!" at the same time stretching out both hands to greet his long-lost relative.

Meek stepped back. "Take care, Knox. Don't come too close! I am ragged, dirty, and—lousy." But that did not stop Knox.[1]

After a cordial greeting, the secretary soon arranged an interview. President Polk made Joe welcome and invited him to stay in the White House.

Now that Meek had done his errand he felt his courage failing, and tried to beg off. But the President would not have it so, and sent for his wife and another lady to make Joe welcome. Long afterward Meek said, "When I heard the silks rustling in the passage, I felt more frightened than if a hundred Blackfeet had whooped in my ear. A mist came over my eyes, and when Mrs. Polk spoke to me I couldn't think of anything to say in return."

But the ladies were kind. The President supplied all

---

[1] This was Joseph Knox Walker (1818-1863) then private secretary to President James Knox Polk. He was the third child of Samuel Polk Walker (1814-1870), and Eleanor T. Wormley. In 1841 he married Augusta T. Tabb, and was later colonel of the Second Tennessee Infantry, C.S.A. His grandmother, Jane Maria Polk Walker, was sister-in-law to the mother of Joseph L. Meek.

his wants and called in a gentleman on his staff to see that Meek was "got up" in a style creditable to himself and his relations.

After the barber and the tailor were through with Joe, they led him up before a full-length mirror. When Old Joe, who still had the familiar feeling of being in buckskins and blankets, saw that handsome, well-dressed stranger, he r'ared back, unable to face such a gentleman. Everybody laughed—and then Joe recognized himself!

The addition of Oregon to the territory of the United States had been one of the principal planks of Polk's platform, and he made the most of the presence of his relative from Oregon. Meek met Senator Thomas Hart Benton of Missouri, the indefatigable champion of Manifest Destiny; the president of the Senate; General John Charles Frémont, General Sam Houston, Stephen A. Douglas, and every important man who approved the Westward Movement. Meek was mightily impressed with Douglas, and later named one of his sons for him.

Luckily Meek did not have to sit as delegate for Oregon in the Congress, since Mr. J. Quinn Thornton, sent by sea around Cape Horn, was already on hand. Thornton was identified with the influential missions in Oregon. But Meek had all the advantages of a delegate without any immediate responsibility. While Thornton sat, Meek circulated, meeting everybody, and often talking in private with the President.

In fact he was the lion of the day in Washington, and of Baltimore as well. He was so constantly in attendance on his cousins and other ladies at the White House, while riding and driving, that some of their admirers resented his priority, and when Meek passed with a lady on either arm and someone asked "Who is that?" he heard the jealous grumblers reply, "It is that damned Rocky Mountain man!"

Once bathed, shaved and tailored to the mode, it is

hardly surprising that Meek, the man of the moment, tall, vital, handsome, good-humored, responsive—and shy —should be a favorite of the ladies there. But not all of them understood his background.

On one occasion a lady with whom he was promenading through a drawing-room at some Senator's reception, admiring his handsome physique perhaps, and wondering if any woman owned it, finally ventured the question— "Are you married?"

"Yes, indeed," answered Meek, with emphasis, "I have a wife and several children."

"Oh dear," exclaimed the lady, "I should think your wife would be so afraid of the Indians!"

"Afraid of the Indians!" exclaimed Meek in his turn; "Why, madam, she is an Indian herself!"

Kit Carson was with Frémont at the house of Senator Benton, and was as hard up as Meek himself had been, neither having any aptitude for thrift or caution. Whenever they met, the talk was likely to take this turn:

CARSON: "Meek, let me have some money, cain't you?"

MEEK: "I haven't got any money, Kit."

CARSON: "Go and git some!"

MEEK: "Damn it, whar am I to get money from?"

CARSON: "Try the 'Contingent Fund,'[1] cain't you?"

All who had known Meek in the mountains sought him out. Charles Wilkes,[2] now a commander, who had employed him as guide in Oregon and was then ill in Washington, sent for Joe: "Meek, come and tell me some more of those damned Oregon lies of yours!"

---

[1] Contingent Fund. A fund available to the President for emergencies.

[2] Wilkes, in command of the celebrated Surveying and Exploring Expedition, under Act of May 14, 1836, sailed from Norfolk August 18, 1838. He was the Admiral Byrd of his day. He discovered the continent of Antarctica, and explored 1500 miles of its coastline, thus establishing the fact that it was a continent. After exploring the South Seas, he explored Oregon, where, as we have seen, Joe Meek was his guide in 1841. Wilkes was commissioned lieutenant, U.S.N. 28 April, 1826; commander, July 13, 1843; captain, 14 September 1855; retired list, 21 Dec. 1861; commodore retired list, 16 July, 1862.

Of course Meek obliged, outdoing himself to please his old friend.

On the Fourth of July, 1848 President Polk went to witness the laying of the cornerstone of the Washington Monument. There was a great military display and much oratory, and fireworks after sunset. In the parade, General Winfield Scott and his staff rode on one side of the President's carriage, Colonel May and Joe Meek on the other. Such an opportunity was not to be dismissed. Joe made a fine showing as a horseman, having lived in the saddle for a dozen years, and outdid all the paper-collar soldiers.[1]

Joe was taken on a tour of the principal cities in the north, traveling with Congressmen who were stumping the country, and had a good time generally. But he found that he was not "up to society" as a steady business. In the mountains his gaiety had been limited to a few hectic days at rendezvous or winter quarters. But here the daily round of social life soon grew tiresome.

One day the President, laughing, asked, "Well, Meek, what do you want now?"

"I want to be franked."

"How long will five hundred dollars last you?"

"About as many days as there are hundreds, I reckon."

"You are shockingly extravagant, Meek. Where do you think all this money is to come from?"

"It is not my business to know, Mr. President," replied Meek, laughing, "but it is the business of these United States to pay the expenses of the messenger from Oregon, ain't it?"

"I think I will send you to the Secretary of War to be franked, Meek; his frank is better than mine. But no, stay; I will speak to Knox about it this time. And you

---

[1] The President's diary, now published, edited by Allan Nevins, makes no reference to Meek during this time in Washington, though it devotes two hundred words to the ceremony of July 4, and a good deal of space to the problems of Oregon.

must not spend your money so recklessly, Meek; it will not do—it will not do."

Meek thanked the President both for the money and the advice, but gave a champagne supper the next night, and in a week's time was as empty-handed as ever. Washington manners were in some respects too much like mountain manners for five hundred dollars to go a great ways.

Meanwhile Thornton sat and negotiated. There is no point in going into all the maneuvers which finally brought about the passage of the bill authorizing a territorial government for Oregon. It was a struggle of such intensity that Senator Butler of South Carolina accused Senator Benton of Missouri of dishonorable conduct. Benton sprang to his feet, throwing the lie in Butler's teeth, and a duel might have followed but for the arrest of the two Senators.[1]

Meek and Polk both became very anxious. For Congress was to adjourn on Monday, August 16, and late Saturday night the Senator from Mississippi began a filibuster. He kept at it until well into Sunday morning, cannily limiting his remarks to Bible stories, lest anyone call him a Sabbath-breaker. But at length he and Butler and the rest agreed to let the bill come to a vote. It passed,

---

[1] The curious may consult: *Senate Executive Document No. 47*. 30th Congress, 1st session, which contains the message of the President concerning Indian difficulties in Oregon, May 29, 1848, the memorial of the legislature of Oregon, and other pertinent documents; the remarks of Senator Benton, May 31, 1848, concerning the establishment of a territorial government in Oregon may be found on page 804 of the *Congressional Globe*, Part I, 30th Congress, 1st Session; those of Senators Benton and Butler on the same subject, August 12, 1848, in the same volume, pages 1074-1075. A letter from Joseph L. Meek, dated August 16, 1848, is on file among the records of the State Department; it gives Meek's opinion concerning the value of the Hudson's Bay Company's property on Vancouver Island. Records of the United States Senate in the National Archives show that the President nominated Joseph L. Meek on August 14, 1848, to be Marshal of the United States for the District of Oregon and that the nomination was confirmed by the Senate the same day, the very day on which the President approved the act to establish the territorial government of Oregon. See *United States Statutes at Large*, Vol. IX, page 323.

and Meek felt that his mission was accomplished. Joe
let out a whoop.

President Polk appropriately appointed Meek U.S.
Marshal for Oregon, which suited Joe perfectly. General
Joseph Lane of Indiana was appointed Governor of
Oregon and Indian agent. At the time, Meek was with
the President at his summer residence[1] outside Washington. Meek was instructed to deliver the General's commission to him in person as quickly as possible and get
him to Oregon with all haste. When Meek brought his
papers to be signed, he found the President at dinner.
Polk explained that he had made reservations for Joe on
the train by telegraph. Joe immediately requested the
orchestra to play "Home, Sweet Home!" That was sentimental, but it raised a laugh; Joe could have asked for
nothing better.

Polk was most anxious to have the new territorial
government set up during his term of office. He had in-
curred severe criticism because he had accepted the
British compromise (it had actually been proposed by
the Americans earlier) as to the Oregon boundary. Said
he, "God bless you, Meek. Tell Lane to have a territorial
government organized during my administration."

Joe readily promised. He did not know what a slow
fellow General Lane could be. When he met Lane, Joe
asked, "How soon can you be ready to start?"

"In fifteen minutes," Lane declared. That was to
Meek's mind; he began to like the man, until he found
that, to the General, fifteen minutes actually meant three
days! Early in September, they were on their way.

---

[1] Polk was at Bedford Springs, Pennsylvania, for a rest after Congress
adjourned, leaving Washington Friday, August 18 with his nephew Samuel
P. Walker of Tennessee and Dr. Foltz, a Naval surgeon; Mrs. Polk remained
in the White House. The President passed the night at Cumberland,
Maryland, and reached Bedford Springs August 19. Sunday he devoted to
walks and a sermon in the evening in his parlor. Tuesday he rode, with a
party of friends to Bedford Village, received visitors, supped and went early
to bed. On Friday, August 25th he returned to Washington. His diary makes
no mention of Meek.

Meek and Lane, and Lane's young son Nat, reached St. Louis after some delay, planning to follow the Santa Fe Trail, the Gila River, and on to San Pedro, California. An escort of riflemen, with a surgeon, and a number of hangers-on, made up the party, totalling fifty-five persons.

In St. Louis, young Lane wanted a pocketknife. They met a peddler who had a whole trayful. But Nat, son of his careful father, haggled so long that Meek became disgusted, and promptly bought the lot, just to keep Nat from getting any and so teach him a lesson. True mountain man, Joe had no use for thrift, which he regarded, Indian fashion, as simply a species of cowardice.

While he was buying wholesale, Joe also invested in three bolts of silk, paying $1.50 a yard.

Puzzled, Lane asked, "What on earth do you expect to do with that stuff?"

"Caint tell yit," Meek said. "But I reckon it's worth the money."

"Better save your money," Lane warned.

Vain advice! Meek was feeling his oats. The President had paid to Joe the lion's share—three-fourths—of the $10,000 appropriated by Congress for "services and expenses" of the messengers from Oregon, and for "purchase of presents for such Indian tribes as the peace and quiet of the country required." Thornton got what was left, and the Indians nothing. Meek and the other pioneers knew better ways of keeping Indians quiet. Meek could afford to spend.

Near Santa Fe, Meek was riding ahead of his party, when he had a most unexpected encounter. Seeing a covered traveling carriage drawn up under the shade of some trees growing beside a small stream, not far from the trail, he resolved, with his usual love of adventure, to discover for himself the character of the proprietor. But as he drew nearer, he discovered no one, although a camp table stood under the trees, spread with refresh-

ments, not only of a solid, but a fluid nature. The sight
of a bottle of cognac induced him to dismount, and he
was helping himself to a liberal glass, when a head was
protruded from a covering of blankets inside the carriage,
and a heavy bass voice was heard in a polite protest:

"Seems to me, stranger, you are making free with my
property!"

"Here's to you, sir," rejoined the purloiner; "it isn't
often I find as good brandy as that"—holding out the
glass admiringly—"but when I do, I make it a point of
honor not to pass it."

"May I inquire your name, sir?" asked the owner of
the brandy, forced to smile at the good-humored audacity
of his guest.

"I couldn't refuse to give my name after that"—re-
placing the glass on the table—"and I now introduce myself as Joseph L. Meek, Esq., marshal of Oregon, on my
way from Washington to assist General Lane in establishing a territorial government west of the Rocky Mountains."

"Meek!—what, not the Joe Meek I have heard my
brothers tell so much about?"

"Joe Meek is my name; but whar did your brothers
know me?" inquired our hero, mystified in his turn.

"I think you must have known Captain William
Sublette and his brother Milton, ten or twelve years ago,
in the Rocky Mountains," said the gentleman, getting
out of the carriage, and approaching Meek with extended
hand.

The stranger was Solomon Sublette. His wife was
with him. When Meek's friends rode up, they joined
the party, and all had a most agreeable evening.

At Santa Fe, pack mules took the place of wagons, for
the long dry scrape across the deserts. The Yuma Indians,
who needed meat, managed to drown some of the government mules at the crossing of the Colorado. But Meek

hardly cared, as mules were dying every day from lack of forage and water, anyhow. Thirst continually cursed the party. Hastening on to Cook's Wells, they found, to their dismay, the only water polluted by a dead mule. But drink they must. So they boiled it, Lane remarking that "maggots are more easily swallowed cooked than raw!"

Finally there were no animals left to ride, only a few mules to carry indispensable packs, and Meek once more endured the same feverish torments of an endless dry march which he had suffered on the parching sagebrush flats along Snake River. Weary, footsore, famished, fevered, and dirty the little party reached California at last.

In Washington, Meek had acquired a fine pair of new Colt's revolvers, weapons fit for a United States marshal. But when Lieutenant Hawkins ordered two men to pursue some deserters, Meek, always ready to oblige, lent his weapons to one of the men. The deserters killed them both, and Meek never saw his revolvers again.

By the time they reached the coast, the party had lost so many men through desertions that there were only seven left. All the rest had slipped off to the gold mines.

It had been a hard trip, but at Williams' ranch on the Santa Ana River they were made comfortable. When Meek unpacked his knives and silks, the Spanish ladies were fascinated. They persuaded Williams to offer to buy them.

Meek shrewdly declared he had bought the goods for his own wife, but the ladies kept after Williams. Finally Meek parted with the silks at the rate of $10.00 a yard.

The miners were eager to pay an ounce of gold dust for a pocketknife, so that Meek's little speculation netted him some five hundred dollars. Meek did not fail to remind Lane that he had objected to the original purchase.

Lane laughed, shaking his head ruefully. "Well, Meek," he said, "you were drunk when you bought them, and I think you must have been drunk when you sold them; but drunk or sober, I will own that you can beat me at a bargain."

In San Francisco, Joe was surprised to find some two hundred Oregonians, who had abandoned their homes and joined the gold rush to California. Probably Meek was not tempted to take up the shovel and pick himself; but he grubstaked two miners he knew, and in due time received from Nat Lane two pickle jars filled with gold dust as his share of the takings. Many of the Oregonians had had no such luck, and were trekking back home, sadder and perhaps wiser men.

Meek, whose self-importance had been greatly inflated by his appointment as U.S. Marshal, demanded that the Governor and he should sail swiftly, grandly home on the U.S. sloop of war, the *St. Mary's;* they could do no less, he declared, for the dignity of Oregon. Meek was damned if he'd travel in less style than Thornton, who had no official status really, either in the States or in Oregon. But Governor Lane would not agree; he saw no sense in spending so heavily, when they might take passage on the slow *Jeanette,* then about to set sail, packed with miners, for the Columbia River.

All the time, Meek had been trying to hurry the Governor along, so that President Polk's desire might be fulfilled. Now, frustrated by Lane's dilatory ways, Joe had to take it out on somebody. Finding a smuggler who had gentlemen's clothing for sale, Joe let the fellow think him a U.S. Customs officer, terrified him by threatening to confiscate his entire stock, but finally compromised, accepting a suit of clothes for himself as a peace offering. Joe let the poor wretch agonize over this extortion for a whole day, then went back, lectured him on the wickedness of smuggling, and paid him for the suit.

Such pranks, though they could not hurry the Governor, did relieve Joe's feelings.

By this time, Governor Lane was beginning to find Joe's high spirits somewhat wearing. And this was just to Joe's taste; he loved nothing better than to "get a rise" out of Lane. And in this, when their ship dropped down the Bay, and the *St. Mary's* fired a salute for Governor Lane, was eminently successful; for he pretended that the salute was fired in his sole honor. Meek knew that, if Lane had consented to ship on the naval vessel, no such thing could have happened. Lane needed a burr under his saddle to keep him moving. Day by day, Polk's administration was running out.

At last the *Jeanette* dropped anchor at the mouth of the Columbia. The Governor's party—now dwindled to Lane, Meek, Hawkins, Hayden the surgeon, and the soldiers—took to small boats, for the trip to Oregon City —another hundred and twenty miles. By the time the impatient Meek reached Oregon City, it was already March 2, 1849. Next day was the very last day of Polk's administration!

But for once, the Governor lost no time. On March 3 he proclaimed the new territorial government. Joseph L. Meek was sworn into office. Joe had made good his promise to the President.

But his mission—to secure military aid—had failed. He had brought back only *two* soldiers!

CHAPTER THIRTY-THREE

U. S. Marshal

"COLONEL" JOSEPH L. MEEK came back from Washington "a-r'arin' to go." In all the world there was no job he would have preferred to that he held. All his past experience, training, his temperament as well, had fitted him to perform the duties of that office justly, skilfully, and—in the main—magnanimously. He was head man in his field now, an important figure, with a good salary, and the respect of all around him. The Colonel, as he had been called in Washington, could afford to dress well, and was well acquainted with the Governor and all other men of importance in the Territory. His authority came direct from Uncle Sam. Best of all, he was no outsider, but an early settler, a local boy who had made a success of himself. Not yet forty, Joe was young enough to rejoice in all that.

True, his mission—seeking military aid for Oregon—was so far fruitless; the troops intended for Oregon had been diverted to the Mexican War: the Regulars did not reach Oregon until the fall of '49. But the Cayuse War was well in hand; the Oregon riflemen had equipped themselves and put the Indians on the defensive. By the time the Regulars arrived, the hostiles were thoroughly cowed.

President Polk had appointed Meek U.S. Marshal "for

the term of four years from the date (August 14, 1848) of his commission," with the usual proviso that he should remain in office "unless the President of the United States for the time being should be pleased sooner to revoke and determine this commission." Though appointed by a Democrat, Meek threw in with the Whigs, whose candidate, Zachary Taylor, became President within a few hours after the new territorial government was proclaimed.

One of the Marshal's first important duties was to receive and hold for trial the Indians who had been accused of killing Dr. Marcus Whitman and his wife, Narcissa.

The Cayuse Indians had been given an ultimatum. They must deliver up five chiefs to be tried for murder, to wit: *Te-lou-i-kite,* "Victorious Home-coming Warrior"; *Tam-a-has,* "Pierced by Throwing"; *Klok-a-mas,* "Battle Gourd"; *Ki-am-a-sump-kin,* "Dressed in Cougar Skin"; *I-sa-i-a-cha-lak-is,* (*Giaa-shetuc-teas*) "Wet Coyote."[1] Otherwise, there would be war.

Of course, those Indians had no machinery for turning members of their tribe over to aliens. Such a thing was unheard of. Had the five chiefs cared to run away they might easily have done so and left their people to take the consequences. But the terms of the ultimatum made that a matter of honor for them. Their standing as chiefs and braves was at stake. They scorned to fly, and came in voluntarily, knowing very well they were going to their death. One of them maintained to the last that he was innocent. However, he—as well as his judges—considered that irrelevant.

These Indians freely explained their motives for killing Dr. Whitman. They saw that the white men intended to take their country from them. They saw their children die while being treated with strange medicines by the

---

[1] For the translations of these names I am indebted to Superintendent Henry Roe Cloud, Umatilla Indian Agency, Pendleton, Oregon.

missionaries, and they were told by a half-breed—who, they thought, certainly must know the whites better than they did—that Dr. Whitman had poisoned them.

With such ideas they were scornful of the Christians for seeking revenge on them. When asked why he had surrendered, one chief replied, "Did not your missionaries tell us that Christ died to save his people? So die we to save our people!"

Another one of the captives, on being offered some dainties on his way down the river, refused them and lectured his would-be benefactor. Said he, "What sort of heart have you, that you offer food to me whose hands are red with your brothers' blood?"

When the five Indians were brought to Oregon City, they were turned over to Meek. There, on learning that they were to be tried in court and would be defended by lawyers, the Indians offered fifty head of horses to the counsel for the defense. Probably they had no notion that the fee would be claimed if the chiefs were found guilty.

The grand jury found true bills against the five chiefs and they were arraigned for trial. Joe Meek, as quoted by Mrs. Victor, described the scene as follows: "Captain Claiborne led off for the defence. He foamed and ranted like he war acting a play in some theatre. He knew about as much law as one of the Indians he war defending; and his gestures were so powerful that he smashed two tumblers that the Judge had ordered to be filled with cold water for him. After a time he gave out mentally and physically. Then came Major Runnels, who made a very good defence." But Joe thought that they would have to do a heap better than that, for "they would never ride fifty head of horses with them speeches."

The defense held that the court had no jurisdiction, inasmuch as, at the time of the murder, the laws of the United States were not in force in Oregon.

The chief counsel for the defense was the secretary of the territory, Kintzing Pritchett. Judge Orville C. Pratt was on the bench.

In Meek's own words: "Mr. Pritchett closed for the defense with a very able argument; for he war a man of brains. But then followed Mr. Amory Holbrook, for the prosecution, and he laid down the case so plain that the jury were convinced before they left the jury-box. When the Judge passed sentence of death on them, two of the chief's showed no terror; but the other three were filled with horror and consternation that they could not conceal."

After court had adjourned, and Governor Lane had resigned (June 18, 1850), Secretary Pritchett came to the Marshal, and said, "I am now acting governor of Oregon, and I mean to reprieve those Indians. Now, Meek, I want you to liberate those Indians, when you receive my order."

Pritchett may have resented losing their case in court, or perhaps he had been carried away by his own argument, and now believed the Indians should go free. He waited for Joe's reply.

"Pritchett," Meek said, "so far as Meek is concerned, he would do anything for you."

Pritchett's face lighted up; he relaxed. "I'm glad to hear that, Meek; I'll go right off now and write the reprieve."

"Hold on thar," Meek objected. "Pritchett, let's now talk like men. I have got in my pocket the death warrant of them Injuns, signed by Governor Lane. The Marshal will execute them men as certain as the day arrives."

Pritchett looked surprised, annoyed. He remarked, "That was not what you just said, that you would do anything for me."

Meek grinned. "You were talking then to Meek—not to the marshal, who always does his duty."

At that Pritchett lost his temper and strode off. Joe laughed.

When the third of June, 1850, the day of execution arrived, Oregon City was thronged with people come to witness it.

Says Meek, "I brought out the five prisoners and placed them on the drop. Then the chief, Ki-am-sump-kin, who always had declared his innocence, begged me to kill him with my knife—for an Indian fears to be hanged. But I soon put an end to his entreaties by cutting the rope which held the drop with my tomahawk. As I said, 'The Lord have mercy on your souls,' the trap fell, and the five Cayuses hung in the air. Three of them died instantly. The other two struggled for several minutes—the little chief, Tam-a-has, the longest. It was he who was cruel to my little girl at the time of the massacre; so I just put my foot on the knot to tighten it, and he got quiet. After thirty-five minutes they were taken down and buried."

At this same term of court, after the conviction of the Cayuse chiefs, there was a case before Judge Pratt, in which a man was charged with selling liquor to the Indians. In these cases Indian evidence was allowed, but the jury room being upstairs, caused a good deal of annoyance in court; because when an Indian witness was wanted upstairs, a dozen or more who were not wanted would follow. This happened so often that the Judge began to get a little restive. The Judge's bench was so placed that it commanded a full view of the staircase and everyone passing up or down it.

A call for some witness to go before the jury was followed on this occasion, as on all others, by a general rush of the Indians, who were curious to witness the proceedings. One fat old squaw had got part way up the stairs, when the Marshal, full of wrath, seized her by a leg and dragged her down flat, at the same time holding the fat member so that it was pointed directly toward the Judge.

A general explosion of laughter followed this *pointed* action, and the Judge grew very red in the face.

"Mr. Marshal, come within the bar!" thundered the Judge.

Meek complied, with a very dubious expression of countenance.

"I must fine you fifty dollars," continued the Judge; "the dignity of the Court must be maintained." He looked severely at Joe.

When court had adjourned that evening, the Judge and the Marshal were walking toward their respective lodgings. Said Meek to His Honor:

"Why did you fine me so heavily to-day?"

"I *must* do it," returned the Judge. "I *must* keep up the dignity of the Court; I *must* do it, if I pay the fines myself."

"And you must pay all the fines you lay on the marshal, of course," asked Meek.

"Very well," said the Judge; "I shall do so."

"All right, Judge. As I am the proper disbursing officer, you can pay that fifty dollars to me—and I'll take it *now*."

At this view of the case, His Honor was staggered for one moment, and could only swing his cane and laugh faintly. After a little reflection, he said:

"Marshal, when court is called to-morrow, I shall remit your fine; but don't you let me have occasion to fine you again!"

After the removal of the capital to Salem, in 1852, court was held in a new building, on which the carpenters were still at work. Judge Nelson, then presiding, was much put out by the noise of hammers, and sent the Marshal more than once, to request the men to suspend their work during those hours when court was in session, but all to no purpose. Finally, when his forbearance was quite exhausted, he appealed to the Marshal for advice.

"What shall I do, Meek," said he, "to stop that infernal noise?"

"Put the workmen on the grand jury," replied Meek.

"Summon them instantly!" returned the judge. They were summoned, and quiet secured for that term.

At this same term of court, a great many of the foreign-born settlers appeared, to file their intention of becoming American citizens, in order to secure the benefits of the Donation Law.[1] Meek was retained as a witness, to swear to their qualifications, one of which was, that they were possessed of good moral characters. The first day there were about two hundred who made declarations, Meek witnessing for most of them. On the day following, he declined to serve any longer.

"What now?" inquired the judge; "you made no objections yesterday."

"Very true," replied Meek; "but two hundred lies are enough for me. I swore that all those mountain men were of 'good moral character,' and I never knew a mountain man of that description in my life! Let Newell take the job for today."

Not all of the Marshal's duties were so pleasant. When a white man was killed by some Indians on Puget Sound, the court found two of them guilty of murder in the first

---

[1] The Donation Land Law, enacted September 27, 1850, granted 320 acres to every male settler or occupant of the land, above the age of eighteen, being a citizen of the United States, or who should declare his intention of becoming one on or before December 1, 1850, while if he were then married or should marry within one year from December 1, 1850, the law granted him 640 acres, "one-half to himself and one-half to his wife, to be held by her in her own right." To all above the age of twenty-one who should settle in Oregon between December 1, 1850 and December 1, 1853, a similar grant of half as much land (married or unmarried) was provided for. After 1843, the first year of considerable immigration, numbers mounted until 1852, the newcomers being for the most part homemakers. The Donation Law greatly stimulated immigration from the States, early marriages, and short courtships. Many sought American citizenship in order to benefit by this enactment. The census of 1850 showed 13,294 in the territory. The Donation Land Law, "made no exception predicated on the extinguishment of Indian land titles, and the effect of this omission was to foster settlement in advance of treaty making." See C. H. Carey, *General History of Oregon Prior to 1861* (Portland, 1935-36), pp. 564, 565, and 508.

degree. Meek had transported the whole court, jury and all, to the remote point where the trial was held; and now he had to improvise some gallows and find a rope, which was finally obtained from a ship at anchor in the Sound. So many Indians attended the execution that the gallows had to be guarded by a company of artillery from the fort.

While Meek went about his duties, the wife of one of the condemned came to beg and plead for her husband's life. Meek, of course, had no power to reprieve or pardon, but she kept on begging. Finally she promised Joe that if he would spare her man she would divorce him and marry the Marshal himself!

When she had been quieted, the hanging took place. After the bodies had been taken down, Meek personally went to the poor woman and said she might take her husband's body. Sullenly she replied, "You killed him, and you can bury him."

Meek was out of pocket to the tune of a thousand dollars as a result of this judicial expedition, and was never able to recover any part of the money he had spent to transport the court. "Colonel" Meek, while exhibiting those qualities of "integrity, ability, and diligence" mentioned in his commission as marshal sometimes found duties more agreeable than supervising a hanging.

An ardent patriot, and a thorough believer in pioneer democracy and the equality of men, Joe did not suffer snobs gladly. He seldom missed a chance to exhibit his official dignity and use his authority to discomfit anybody who was "stuck-up" or had "put on airs" and had snubbed him while he was just a trapper or an impoverished settler.

One day Meek was sent aboard ship to arrest a captain and mate who had ignored a writ of the District Court. Five of their sailors had been summoned as witnesses, but had been held aboard ship.

Once on deck, Meek marched to the forecastle and called out the names of the five men. Every man came up. Meek ordered a boat lowered to take the witnesses to Oregon City.

The Captain interfered, "You can't take that boat for such a purpose. It belongs to me."

The Marshal smiled. "That is of no consequence at all. It is a very good boat and will suit our purpose very well. Lower away, men."

Once the witnesses had manned the oars, Meek invited the mate to enter the boat. The mate somewhat hesitantly obeyed. Then Meek turned on the blustering Captain and extended the same invitation. The Captain chose to remain aboard his ship.

Cool and smiling, Joe pulled out his revolver. "I don't like to have to urge a gentleman too hard," he said, "but *thar* is an argument few men will ever resist. Take a seat, Captain!"

The story goes that both officers were heavily fined, while the men, once ashore, promptly deserted.

News was received that a British vessel was unloading goods for the Hudson's Bay Company, somewhere on Puget Sound. Under the new order of affairs in Oregon, this was smuggling. Delighted with an opportunity of doing the United States a service, and the British traders an ill turn, Marshal Meek immediately summoned a posse and started for the Sound. On his way he learned the name of the vessel and captain, and recognized them as having been in the Columbia River some years before. On that occasion the Captain had ordered Meek ashore, when, led by his curiosity and general love of novelty, he had paid a visit to this vessel. This information was "nuts" to the Marshal, who believed that a "turn about is fair play."

With great dispatch and secrecy he arrived entirely unexpected at the point where the vessel was lying, and proceeded to board her without loss of time. The captain and officers were taken by surprise and were all aghast at this unlooked-for appearance. But after the first moment of agitation was over, the captain recognized Meek, a man not likely to be forgotten. Thinking to turn this circumstance to advantage, the captain approached Joe with the blandest of smiles and the most cordial manner, saying with forced frankness—

"I am sure I have had the pleasure of meeting you before. You must have been at Vancouver when my vessel was in the river, seven or eight years ago. I am very happy to have met with you again."

"Thar is some truth in that remark of yours, Captain," replied Meek, eyeing him with lofty scorn. "You did meet me at Vancouver several years ago. But I was nothing but 'Joe Meek' at that time, and you ordered me ashore. Circumstances are changed since then. I am now Colonel Joseph L. Meek, United States Marshal for Oregon Territory; and you sir, are only a damned smuggler! Go ashore, sir!"

The captain saw Joe's point, but obeyed with just as bad a grace as Joe had obeyed him on that former occasion, years before.

This vessel was confiscated and sold; netting, above expenses, about $40,000 for the government. But somehow or other, this money was never accounted for. Probably nobody believed the Marshal at fault, but some may have thought he placed too much confidence in certain others, according to Mrs. Victor. One day, someone asked Meek what had become of all that money obtained from the sale of the smuggler.

At that question, Joe looked plain astonished. "Why," he said, "thar was *bar'ly enough* for the officers of the court!"

People never stopped laughing at that remark. Neither did Joe; it was his most successful witticism.

Wholly without experience or aptitude for handling money or keeping records, Meek was nevertheless held accountable by the government for the funds he collected and disbursed. And so he soon found that his office, instead of bettering his financial position in the world, simply kept him poor. Still, though he did not like the cards he held, he liked the game, and never dreamed of quitting. His lack of book l'arnin' and indifference to paper work stood in the way of his progress as Oregon became more settled.

Even in the fur trade, it is doubtful whether Joe Meek could ever have saved enough, or managed his investments wisely enough to have become a partner or a partisan, master though he was of all the tricks of that tricky trade. None could outdo him in a fight, a debate, in anything that called for immediate action or talk to the point. But routine in an office, the keeping of records and books—it seemed Joe could never get right down to things as picayunish as that. So less capable, though more methodical, men grew up with the country. Though just entering his forties, Joe was as high as he seemed likely to go.

President Zachary Taylor died; Vice-President Fillmore took his place in the White House, and still Meek performed the duties of his office. The new Territory of Washington was carved out of Oregon, reducing Joe's field of operations; settlers came thronging in by the thousands. Congress authorized the survey of a railroad to the Pacific. Fighting Indians was no longer a part of Meek's duties, yet he was not unaware that, even in eastern Oregon, still empty of settlers, the redskins were growing restive. Joe witnessed many changes. And at length Fillmore's term of office expired, and Franklin Pierce was elected President of the United States.

Pierce was a Democrat, and promptly appointed a new slate of officials for the Territory of Oregon. James K.

JOSEPH L. MEEK WITH D. V. SMITH, ENGINEER OF
THE RIVER STEAMER "COLUMBIA"

Smith is listening to one of Meek's stories. Possibly the picture
was taken about 1865, when Meek was fifty-five. The illustration
is copied from *Lewis and Dryden's Marine History of the Pacific
Northwest* (1895), edited by E. W. Wright.

Polk was dead; Meek had no connections in Washington who could save him. Suddenly he found himself plain "Colonel" Meek, no longer U.S. Marshal of Oregon.

It was 1852; Joe was bar'ly forty-two years old.

Soldier

ONCE MORE, Joe found his occupation gone—
once more his farm on the Tualatin Plains was
his only recourse. Joe was "an indifferent tiller
of the earth," to put it gently. Nothing in his training or
experience qualified him to practice or take the slightest
interest in agriculture. As a boy in Virginia, his father's
slaves had done all such work; among the trappers, he
had been attended by camp keepers or squaws, who left
to him only the care of his private mounts and his
weapons; temperamentally, at any rate, he shared the
Indians' conviction that digging in the ground is characteristic of the lower animals. The Plains Indians, who
passed the time pleasantly, hunting, fighting, gambling,
and chasing the women, were—as the Jesuit put it—"all
gentlemen"; Joe understood them: moreover, the reading he had done in the Rocky Mountain College had
idealized the aristocratic hero and his way of life.

Everything in Joe's life turned him away from farming.
Farming was lonely work, and Joe was sociable; farming
was menial work, and Joe loved to cut a figure; farming
did not pay well, and Joe was extravagant in his tastes.
In short, the farm offered him none of those opportunities
for which he lusted, and to which he had become accustomed. Life to Joe, as to any mountain man or old-time

Indian was a series of exploits, and the farm seemed to offer no platform for exploits whatever. No reservation Indian was ever more reluctant to plow than was Colonel Joseph L. Meek, and for precisely the same reasons. "The farm cain't shine with this child, anyways you fix it!"

Nothing short of an Indian war could give scope to his talents again.

That war was not long in coming. For the emigrants who streamed westward from the States to Oregon with their horses and cattle, their knives and hatchets and guns —and their scalps—offered constant temptations to Indians along the trails. There were outrages on both sides. Finally the Yakimas killed A. J. Bolon, a subagent, on his way home from a council. Then the fat was in the fire. Of a sudden, it seemed that all the Indians in Oregon were hostile.

Governor George Law Curry called for eight companies of Volunteers, on October 11, 1855. In this crisis, Joe Meek did not hold back. For a mountain man not yet fifty, fighting was better than farming any day. Joe was one of the first to offer himself, and enlisted as a private in Company A. At The Dalles he was detailed for special service as messenger and scout, but was soon commissioned a major on the staff of Colonel J. W. Nesmith. The two were old friends and colleagues of the Provisional Government's legislature. More recently, Nesmith had succeeded Joe as U.S. Marshal. Joe respected Nesmith; they got on well together.

The Federal troops in the Territory co-operated, but their commanders had no authority to equip volunteers, or muster them into the U.S. Army; nor, in fact, did the volunteers want that. They managed to equip themselves after a fashion, but had great difficulty in obtaining supplies and rations. It was difficult for the territorial government to swap the wheat collected as taxes for other supplies and there were long delays. Still Nesmith led five companies into the Yakima country on November 1. There his command and the regulars fought shoulder to shoulder, whipped an Indian party, and returned to The Dalles.

Winter came early. The Volunteers, with few tents, few blankets, and little food, suffered severely. Their command had to discharge 125 of them for lack of rations and mounts. Those who remained, having no flour or beef, had to forage for subsistence. They dared not disband, for the Indians had already defeated Haller's men, and it looked like a long war.

One day Meek spied a stray cow. Poor thing! It might be pulled down by wolves or killed by hostile Indians any day. Joe reckoned he ought to do something about that; it would never do to let that cow go to feed the hostiles—more especially as the cow was fat!

Joe dropped the animal, and then, in mountain-man fashion, handily butchered it on the ground. That evening at his campfire he proceeded to roast twenty pounds of marbled beef for supper. The scent of that fresh beef roasting was wafted about the camp; very shortly a number of his brother officers gathered round. Of course Meek knew, as well as they did, that he could never eat such a quantity of meat at one sitting.

"Major Meek," said they, "we'll sup with you tonight."

Joe turned to them with a look of innocent amazement on his face. "I am very sorry, gentlemen, to decline the honor," he said. "But I am very hungry, and thar is *bar'ly enough* beef for one man!"

Some of the officers looked glum at that, but those who had heard that "bar'ly enough" story before retained their good humor and hung around.

Major Meek went solemnly on with his roasting. When the beef was done to a turn, he suddenly laughed and invited his anxious visitors to share the feast. They spent a jolly evening together.

All went well with Meek's military service until a new commanding officer replaced Nesmith. The newly elected Colonel meant to be obeyed. He had issued an order prohibiting the firing of guns in camp—an order which had always been in force during Meek's years in the fur brigades. Certainly it was nothing to which Joe could have objected.

But when the Colonel ordered Major Meek to ride through enemy country to Salem bearing dispatches, Joe thoughtlessly fired his rifle to make sure it was in working order before he set out. While he was saddling up to put out, he was told to report to the Colonel at his tent. There they had breakfast together. Afterward the Colonel inquired whether Major Meek was aware of the order against firing guns in camp.

"Sure," Meek admitted.

"Then," said the new Colonel, "I fear I shall be obliged to make an example of you."

A guard appeared at the door of the tent and the commanding officer told him what Meek's punishment was to be: "Mark time for twenty minutes in the presence of the whole regiment."

Says Meek, "When the command 'Forward' was given, you might have seen somebody step off lively, the officer counting it off 'Left, Left,' but some of the regiment grumbled about it more than I did. I just got my horse and my dispatches and left for the lower country. When I returned, I asked for my discharge and got it."

CHAPTER THIRTY-FIVE

"Uncle Joe"

DOWN ON the farm, Colonel Meek had to content himself with watching from afar the squabbles, between Oregon politicians and their Volunteers, with General John E. Wool of the Regular Army. Wool, then in command of the Department of the Pacific, refused to budge from Fort Vancouver, or to aid the territorial troops in any way. He declared them inefficient and needlessly expensive, and loudly proclaimed that the war was wholly unnecessary, thus arousing bitter attackers East and West. Meek was inclined to think the general was probably right. Ringed round by enemies as he was, Wool reminded Meek of a b'ar fight he had seen once in the Rocky Mountains. "A big old grizzly war surrounded by a pack of ten or twelve dogs, all snapping at him and worrying him. It made him powerful mad, and every now and then he would make a claw at one of them that shut him up quick!"

Joe loved company, liked to entertain his visitors right along until supplies ran low; then, Indian-fashion, Joe would go visiting in his turn. Like the Indian who was asked why he did not work hard, save his wages and invest them, so that he could take it easy in his old age, Joe might have answered, "I'm taking it easy now!"

For Joe had his critics. His neighbors, pious and in-

JOE MEEK WHEN HE WAS NEAR SIXTY (ABOUT 1870)

dustrious farmers, found the Colonel "full of levity, too good-natured to amount to much—outside of being a good fellow in general." They said he was "too free-handed, excessively liberal," so that he was often a victim of imposition; but Joe would always laugh such matters off as a good joke played on him. He showed no animosity, but passed by the petty spite of his enemies in silence—or, if he did fight it out, afterwards considered the business closed and settled once and for all. No wonder then that, as years passed, the Colonel came to be known as "Uncle Joe."

Yet Meek never lost his strong convictions or his courage. Though the son of a slaveholder and powerful proud of his native state, Joe had no heart at all for secession. He had suffered too many hardships in bringing Oregon into the Union to have any hand in trying to shatter it. He was staunchly loyal throughout the Civil War.

His daughter Olive reports, "Father was intensely interested in the Civil War. I used to put in hours every day reading books of history to him and newspaper accounts about the war."[1]

When that was over, Oregon rapidly filled up with strangers, most of whom knew and cared nothing for Uncle Joe's heroism in the winning of the West. They saw his extravagances and ignored his solid worth. Few took much stock in "trapper tales," as they called his stories.

His daughter says of Joe, "Father was not naturally a stern man. I never saw him strike one of us children. At the same time I don't remember of ever disobeying him nor do I remember of any of my brothers or sisters doing so. When Father said a thing, he said it in a low, easy voice, and we children obeyed instantly." She adds, "As long as I knew him he was always perfectly willing

---

1 Lockley, *Oregon Folks*, p. 18.

to let someone else do the work around the place. When it came to fighting Indians, or hunting, trapping, or making long, dangerous trips, there were few men as willing and good as Father was, but he had no liking for manual labor. He was a great hand to make friends. You couldn't know him without liking him. . . . He was very indifferent about his dress. He didn't believe that fine feathers made fine birds."[1]

Then one day Mrs. Frances Fuller Victor came along to take down the story of his life. And she was not long in talking him into that. Joe was ready to relate his exploits in the good old days, how he lifted topknots, made a raise of Injun ponies, sparked the Snake gals, and threw the buffalo cold.

Joe was then in his late fifties, still tall and erect, with a round, jovial, bearded face, twinkling dark eyes, and a pleasant voice, still talking trapper slang. He looked bold, hardy, fearless and direct, but she found him always behaving with "an inborn grace and courtesy."

The lady "wished that her memory had permitted her to clothe his personal adventures in his own peculiar language" and convey . . . "the tones of his voice, both rich and soft, and deep too, or suddenly changing with a versatile power quite remarkable, as he gave with natural dramatic ability the perfect imitation of another's voice and manner." Uncle Joe was a great mimic, and still accompanied his remarks with all the rich pantomime of the Indian sign language.

Mrs. Victor aptly reports that Meek had the look of "a good-humored, quiet, and not undignified citizen of the [Tualatin] 'Plains,' and no one would attribute to him any very bad or dangerous practices." But she adds, "when recalling the scenes of his early exploits in mountain life, the smouldering fire of his still fine eyes brightens up with something suggestive of the daredevil spirit

---

[1] Lockley, *ibid*, pp. 17, 18.

which characterized those exploits and made him famous even among his compeers."

She vouches for her conviction that Uncle Joe was telling the truth. And it was a disappointment to her, after *The River of the West* (in which she included Joe's memoirs) appeared, to discover how many readers considered Joe's stories a pack of lies. So many people were unable to distinguish between the legitimate exaggerations of a fish story or a b'ar story, and the sober statements of an eyewitness to historical events. They could not see how a man could joke and tell the truth at one and the same time; in their eyes, any man who spins a yarn is unable to tell the truth, as if an author who writes fiction must be incapable of history! Such witless readers discredited Meek's story as so much romantic yarning.

Of course, as every lawyer and historian knows, even honest men seldom tell the truth, the whole truth, and nothing but the truth.

In nature everything appears distinct, so that nothing stands out; but art—like every other product of man's mind—is a matter of values. Now Meek was no mean storyteller: he was histrionic, loved a striking effect, and within his limits knew well enough how to produce one. He loved a good story, and understood, as well as Dr. Samuel Johnson, how seldom is any splendid story wholly true.

Yet Meek had splendid materials ready to his hand, events which required little arrangement to make them amusing. Though no scholar, and therefore careless of dates, numbers, and minor details, his recollections (as recorded by Mrs. Victor) rarely violate the truth of the events he witnessed. Modern research has amply demonstrated that. And if, sometimes, they are not strictly history, they are perfectly suited to biography. For Joe Meek told his life story as Joe Meek had lived and felt it, and so gave himself away. And we must not forget that a man's aspirations and pretensions are just as real an expression of his personality as any other. And heaven knows Joe Meek had them both in plenty!

His life, like an Indian's, had consisted of long periods of dull, dirty drudgery, alternating with brief spells of thrilling adventure and wild excesses; and so, like an Indian, he inevitably saw his life as a series of personal exploits. How lucky we are in the careless prodigality with which he poured out his casual story—the good and the bad alike—and so gave us all the joyous privilege of knowing Joe himself!

In those days, Mrs. Victor was not the skillful historian she became later. She took down Joe's stories as he told them, and he told them, naturally, as they occurred to him, without much regard for exact chronology. Though she made some effort to arrange his adventures in order of time, she—or he—was not able to straighten them out. And now, only the recording angel can tell when and where some of his adventures took place!

But at length her book was published, and Joe Meek, though alive and kicking, found himself half-buried in a sprawling history of Oregon. That book made all Oregon aware of Uncle Joe's past prowess and achievements, and they loved him for the dangers he had passed, and the hardships he had endured in helping build their state. All but the preachers!

These, determined to save him from "the pit" and hell-fire, would preach earnestly at him as often as he got around to attending church. For, now that Whitman was dead, Joe found few clergymen who had any use for a mountain man.

Now Uncle Joe prided himself most of all on having been a mountain man. He never let on that he was any better than the rest of them. His code was practical: he loved courage, loyalty, generosity, justice and mercy. But he was, as Mrs. Victor reports, "indifferent to some of the commandments." And his habit of treating everything as a joke was extremely painful to some of the local preachers. Baiting the bigots became Uncle Joe's indoor sport. Many a skirmish he had with them, for they always returned to the attack. He shocked them—he seemed to take his sins so easy-like.

He could take their sermons with a grin. But if the attack became too personal, Colonel Meek, like General Wool and the grizzly, would "hit one a claw that shut him up."

Here our last glimpse of Uncle Joe is on a Sunday morning of his fifty-eighth year—in a church. He had come to hear a new preacher, had done the stranger that honor. The fellow pitched into Joe. Outraged by his "stupid" and "vulgar" remarks, Meek got up, marched deliberately up to the preacher's desk, took the terrified man under his mighty arm. Then to the amazement, horror—and final amusement—of the congregation, Joe carried the preacher out of the church, and set him down.

Seven years later, on another Sunday morning, Uncle Joe died at his home four miles north of Hillsboro, Oregon, June 20, 1875.

Two days later, nearly four hundred people came to see him laid away under a lone tree at the northwest corner of his farm. He was buried in Washington County, Oregon, as he had wished to be, having been born in another Washington County, in Virginia.

Joe Meek has a place in the heart of every lover of the West; yet somehow people do not make pilgrimages to his grave, or build monuments to his memory.

For the plain fact is that nobody who knows his story can possibly think of Joe Meek as dead. He was always so magnificently alive!

Bibliography

BOOKS

ALTER, J. CECIL. *James Bridger.* Salt Lake City: Shepard Book Company, 1925.

BANCROFT, H.H. *History of Oregon.* San Francisco: The History Company, 1886.

BONNER, T. D., editor. *The Life and Adventures of James P. Beckwourth.* New York: Harper and Brothers, 1856.

BUSHNELL, DAVID I., JR. "John Mix Stanley, Artist-Explorer." *Annual Report of the Smithsonian Institution.* Washington, D.C.: The Smithsonian Institution, 1924.

CANNON, MILES. *Waiilatpu, Its Rise and Fall, 1836-47.* Boise, Idaho: Capital News Publishing Company, 1915.

CAREY, CHARLES H. *General History of Oregon Prior to 1861.* In two volumes. Portland: Metropolitan Press (Binfords and Mort), 1935-36.

CARSON, CHRISTOPHER. *Autobiography;* edited by Milo Milton Quaife. Chicago: The Lakeside Press. R.R. Donnelley and Sons Company, 1935.

CHITTENDEN, H. M. *The American Fur Trade of the Far West.* (New York: F. P. Harper, 1902) Elmira, New York: Press of the Pioneers, 1935.

——. *The Yellowstone Park.* Cincinnati: The Robert Clarke Company, 1903.

——., and A. T. RICHARDSON. *Life, Letters, and Travels of Father Pierre-Jean DeSmet, S.J., 1801-1873.* New York: F. P. Harper, 1905.

CLARK, W. P. *The Indian Sign Language.* Philadelphia: L. R. Hamersly and Company, 1885.

DALE, HARRISON C. *The Ashley-Smith Explorations.* Cleveland: The Arthur H. Clark Company, 1918.

DEVOTO, BERNARD. *Across the Wide Missouri.* Boston: Houghton, Mifflin Company, 1947.

DRURY, C. M. *Marcus Whitman, M.D.* Caldwell, Idaho: The Caxton Printers, Ltd., 1937.

ELLISON, WILLIAM H., editor. *The Life and Adventures of George Nidever.* Berkeley: University of California Press, 1937.

FARNHAM, T. J. *Travels in the Great Western Prairies.* Poughkeepsie: Rilley and Lossing, Printers, 1841.

FERRIS, W. A. *Life in the Rocky Mountains.* (Edited by P. C. Phillips.) Denver: Old West Publishing Company, 1940.

GARRARD, L. H. *Wah-To-Yah and the Taos Trail.* New York: A. S. Barnes Company, 1850.

GHENT, W. J. *The Road to Oregon.* New York: Longmans, Green and Company, 1929.

GREGG, JOSIAH. *Commerce of the Prairies.* New York: H. G. Langley Company, 1844.

HAFEN, LEROY R., and W. J. GHENT. *Broken Hand.* Denver: Old West Publishing Company, 1931.

HODGE, FREDERICK W., editor. *Handbook of American Indians North of Mexico.* Washington, D.C.: Smithsonian Institution, Bureau of American Ethnology Bulletin 30, 1912.

INNIS, H. A. *The Fur Trade in Canada.* New Haven: Yale University Press, 1930.

IRVING, WASHINGTON. *Adventures of Captain Bonneville.* London and New York: G. P. Putnam, 1843.

KINIETZ, W. V. *John Mix Stanley and His Indian Paintings.* Ann Arbor: University of Michigan Press, 1942.

LARPENTEUR, CHARLES. *Forty Years a Fur Trader on the Upper Missouri.* New York: F. P. Harper and Company, 1898.

LEONARD, ZENAS. *Narrative of the Adventures of Zenas Leonard.* Clearfield, Pennsylvania: Printed and Published by D. W. Moore, 1839.

LOCKLEY, FRED. *Oregon Folks.* New York: Knickerbocker Press, 1927.

LOWIE, ROBERT H. *The Crow Indians.* New York: Farrar and Rinehart, 1935.

MANDELBAUM, DAVID G. *The Plains Cree.* Volume 37, Part 2, Anthropological Papers, American Museum of Natural History, New York, N.Y. 1940.

MERK, FREDERICK, editor. *Fur Trade and Empire.* (Harvard Historical Studies, volume 31.) Cambridge, Massachussetts: Harvard University Press, 1932.

NEVINS, ALLEN, editor. *Polk, the Diary of a President, 1845-1849.* New York: Longmans, Green and Company, 1929.

NEWELL, ROBERT. "Memorandum of Robert Newell's Travels in the Territory of Missouri, 1829-1841." (Copied from the manuscript, in possession of Kenneth Bannister, Roseburg, Oregon, by L. M. Lowell.) Transcribed manuscript, on file at Oregon Historical Society, Portland, Oregon.

PARKER, REV. SAMUEL. *Journal of an Exploring Tour Beyond the Rocky Mountains.* Auburn, N.Y.: J. C. Derby and Company, 1846.

"Portraits of North American Indians with Sketches of Scenery, etc. Painted by J. M. Stanley," *Smithsonian Miscellaneous Collections,* Volume II, Wash., 1852.

RUSSELL, OSBORNE. *Journal of a Trapper.* Boise, Idaho: Syms-York Company, 1921.

RUXTON, G. F. *Life in the Far West.* London: William Blackwood and Sons, 1849.

SABIN, E. L. *Kit Carson Days.* New York: Press of the Pioneers, 1935.

SULLIVAN, M. S. *Jedediah Smith, Trader and Trail Breaker.* New York: Press of the Pioneers, 1936.

THWAITES, R. G. *Original Journals of the Lewis and Clark Expedition, 1804-1806.* New York: Dodd, Mead and Company, 1905.

VESTAL, STANLEY. *Fandango: Ballads of the Old West.* Boston: Houghton Mifflin Company, 1927.

———. *Kit Carson.* Boston: Houghton Mifflin Company, 1932.

———, editor. *New Sources of Indian History, 1850-1891.* Norman: University of Oklahoma Press, 1934.

———. *Warpath.* Boston: Houghton Mifflin Company, 1939.

———. *Mountain Men.* Boston: Houghton Mifflin Company, 1939.

——. *The Missouri.* Rivers of America Series. New York: Farrar and Rinehart, 1945.

——. *Jim Bridger.* New York: William Morrow and Company, 1946.

VICTOR, MRS. FRANCES FULLER. *The River of the West.* Hartford, Connecticut: Columbian Book Company, 1870.

——. *Early Indian Wars of Oregon.* Salem: F. C. Baker, 1894.

WARREN, ELIZA SPALDING. *Memoirs of the West.* Portland: 1916.

WISLIZENUS, F. A. *A Journey to the Rocky Mountains in the Year 1839.* St. Louis: Missouri Historical Society, 1912.

YOUNG, F. G. editor, "Correspondence and Journals of Captain Nathaniel J. Wyeth, 1831-36." In *Sources of the History of Oregon,* Vol. I. Eugene: University [of Oregon] Press, 1899.

PERIODICAL LITERATURE

CHAPIN, JANE E., editor. "John McLoughlin Letters, 1827-29," *Oregon Historical Quarterly,* XXXVII (March, 1936).

"Diary of Rev. Jason Lee," *Oregon Historical Quarterly,* XVII (June, September, December, 1916).

DRURY, C. M. "Gray's Journal of 1838," *Pacific Northwest Quarterly,* XXIX (1938).

EBBERT, G. W. "Autobiographical Sketch of . . . ," *Oregon Historical Quarterly,* XIX (September, 1918).

ELLIOT, T. C. "Biography and Journals of Peter Skene Ogden," *Oregon Historical Quarterly,* X-XI (December, 1909—September and December, 1910).

"Funeral of Joseph L. Meek," *Morning Oregonian.* Vol. XV, No. 118 (June 23, 1875).

GRAY, W. H. "The Unpublished Journal of William H. Gray. From December, 1836, to October, 1837." *Whitman College Quarterly,* XVI, No. 2, (June, 1913).

HODGE, FREDERIC W., "A Proposed Indian Portfolio by John Mix Stanley," *Indian Notes,* VI, No. 4 (1929). Heye Foundation, New York.

MEANY, EDMOND S. "Diary of Wilkes in the Northwest," *Washington Historical Quarterly,* XVII (January, 1926).

MEEK, STEPHEN H. L. (Story of the Walker expedition to California; originally printed in the *Jonesborough* (Tennessee) *Sentinel*, March 8, 1837.) "Battle of the Fur Traders With the Indians Near the Rocky Mountains," *Niles Register*, March 25, 1837. Vol. 52, p. 50.

Nebraska State Historical Society, Vol. XX, Lincoln, 1922. Historical news items from *Missouri Republican and Missouri Intelligencer*.

QUAIFE, MILO MILTON, editor, *Kit Carson's Autobiography*. Chicago, 1935.

TOBIE, H. E. "Joseph L. Meek, A Conspicuous Personality," *Oregon Historical Quarterly*, XXXIX-XL (June, September, December, 1938—March, September, 1939).

A NOTE ABOUT THE AUTHOR

Writing under the name Stanley Vestal, the late Walter S. Campbell contributed a number of memorable books to the literature of the Great Plains region. Among the best known are *Kit Carson, Jim Bridger, Ballads of the Old West, Fandango, Warpath and Council Fire, Sitting Bull, Short Grass Country, The Old Santa Fe Trail,* and *The Missouri* (Rivers of America Series). While he was doing research for his book on Sitting Bull, the great chief's nephews adopted him into the family, giving him the name of their own father, Kiyukampi, which means Make-Room-for-Him.

Born in Kansas in 1887, Walter S. Campbell received his early education in that state and Oklahoma, graduating from Southwestern State Normal School in 1908. For the next three years he attended Merton College, Oxford, as a Rhodes Scholar, taking his A.B. and M.A. degrees with honors. During the first World War he served as a captain of Field Artillery with the A.E.F. Previously (1914) he had joined the faculty of the University of Oklahoma, and from 1919 until his death in 1958 Professor Campbell was a member of the Department of English. The School of Professional Writing which he established there has been called the most successful of its kind in this country. Among many other distinctions, Professor Campbell was a Guggenheim Fellow, a Fellow of the Rockefeller Foundation, and a member of the Oklahoma Hall of Fame.